THE EXPERIENCE

THE EXPERIENCE

DOUGLAS HARLAND

PRIMIX
PUBLISHING
THE WRITE CHOICE

Primix Publishing
11620 Wilshire Blvd
Suite 900, West Wilshire Center, Los Angeles, CA, 90025
www.primixpublishing.com
Phone: 1-800-538-5788

Published by Primix Publishing: 10/30/2023

ISBN: 979-8-89194-011-6(sc)
ISBN: 979-8-89194-012-3(e)

Library of Congress Control Number: 2023919091

In order to truly know God you have to be out of your mind.[1]

Honesty in vulnerability is the doorway to personal freedom.[2]

When you are green you grow, when you are ripe you rot.[3]

Science without religion is lame, religion without science is blind.[4]

[1]   ND Walsch, *Conversations with God Book 1*, Hodder Headline Group, Australia, 2000, p. 94.

[2]   Maryann Madden, Truth Seminar, Brisbane Australia, 13-16 February 1987.

[3]   Maryann Madden, Truth Seminar, Brisbane Australia, 13-16 February 1987.

[4]   Albert Einstein, Conference of Science, Philosophy and Religion in Their Relation to the Democratic Way of Life, Jewish Theological Seminary of America, New York City, 9-11 Sept, 1940.

FOREWORD

My name is Peter Long. I was first involved with Toowoomba Foundry in 1989 when I was undertaking Australia's first study into adult literacy in the workforce. It was instigated by the Australian Council for Adult Literacy in preparation for the first International Literacy Year. The study was a tripartite investigation involving government, employers and trade unions. One of the employer representatives, John Griffith, Chairman of Southern Cross Machinery, suggested I use Toowoomba Foundry as a case study because two-thirds of the employees were recipients of the twenty-five-year, long-service watch. He was concerned their literacy and numeracy standards may impair their ability to modernise the Foundry.

As a consequence of having this relationship, I was asked to tender for an executive leadership development program, which included a five-day live-in experience for the executives, plus ongoing development through a work-based learning project. Each executive then organised for their leadership team to undertake a similar experience in order to spread the learning and improve capability.

I first met Doug Harland in 1992. He'd attended a couple of workshops I'd facilitated and, when he was appointed general manager of the Foundry, he asked me to visit. He had some development ideas he wished to explore. I'd worked on and off for a few of the many general managers Doug describes in this book. I wasn't the traditional 'expert' consultant so the corporate high flyers were ambivalent about my ability to help. It was the time in Australian manufacturing when the 'accountant as manager' had failed to invest in either new technology or new socio-technologies. This was usually to keep costs down but the unintended consequences were obvious. They had an inability to compete. Globalisation policies and plastics had arrived and disrupted metalliferous industries across the world and most were unaware of the impact until too late. To add to the grief, corporate raiders were on the loose buying up undervalued businesses and 'selling the farm', or parts of it, unresponsive to both social and cultural implications. Doug was dropped into this environment.

In response to his phone call I drove up from Brisbane where I lived and walked into reception, past the product display and museum, a tribute to the diversity of past products (planes, trains, stationary engines, windmills, pumps and drains), to meet Doug in his office. The Foundry had occupied prime real estate barely a kilometre from the centre of the city. It was housed in pre-war buildings, surrounded by the emerging city. Doug was keen to work with his people to turn the business around. The Foundry's sales and marketing wing had been torn from it, and the Foundry was left with unfavourable terms of engagement – for example, having regularly to service products that were over a hundred years old at heavily discounted prices.

I listened to Doug, believed in his commitment and agreed to assist with developing a strategy. I suggested that we conclude our meeting with a walk and asked him what he saw as we moved about. Most of us can become blind to our surrounds and I suggested Doug pretend he was from Mars or another country. From the street the factory looked early industrial. There were old buildings with saw-tooth roofs, cluttered by the detritus of years of activity. Chemical pollution was a real possibility. The crib rooms and wash rooms were uninspiring. Ceiling ventilation, and lighting, had been covered by exudates. 'Steam' was obvious. Smoke poured forth. Neighbours lived cheek-to-jowl. Floors were caked with grease and coke. Machines were stacked upon each other in the shadow of a massive moulding plant. I'd visited new General Motors plants in Canada as part of my graduate studies. They were basically pods of robots in spotless tiled-floor buildings run by two or three humans. The contrast had always been stark to me.

'There's a lot to do,' Doug said.

'Yes, but a lot comes down to leadership and care at all levels,' I replied. 'That's your greatest asset, which you need to remind your team about. You all care.'

As Doug explains in this book he won the right to take his team to Noosa for a strategy meeting, which I facilitated. The group agreed on five 'Big Hits' to create a focus and avoid distractions; the group would also review each month – a process of which, upon their invitation, I was to be an ongoing part.

Doug was in the unenviable position of being a leader who had come through the ranks. Here wasn't a prophet from another land. It was like witnessing a family meeting. There was incredible energy, incredible honesty, much emotion. Doug wasn't allowed any free hits. Everyone knew his history, his technical failures, his strengths and weaknesses and argued until there was agreement. It was a totally different meeting from those I'd facilitated in the past.

While it was difficult it was also revelatory. In the past, outsiders had been appointed to run the business. This time one of 'theirs' had been anointed. In the past, the outsiders would walk past behaviour and not understand it, or swallow an excuse about why a machine wasn't running. An insider knows where the skeletons are hidden and can argue the toss. I still feel privileged to have been involved in that meeting and subsequent ones.

If the metals industry was to be run out of Australia, by a government asleep at the wheel while their lunch was being stolen, the new team's desire was to be, at least, the last foundry standing.

Doug speaks about using energy. It was obvious at the Foundry. He harnessed the energy of his people and over a short period of time they turned the place around. At a physical level, supervisors would organise voluntary clean-up working-bees on a weekend to rehabilitate areas of the site. Because there was no money for renovations from the corporate raiders, small projects were budgeted for and instigated, which contributed to a holistic plan. For example, sheets of transparent roofing throughout the old Super 10 asbestos roof were replaced one bay at a time over a number of years to improve lighting in the workshops. It all had to do with personal pride.

Again, this is where Doug comes in.

I often wondered if Doug was in the wrong job. I wondered if perhaps he shouldn't have been a psychologist or a pastor. But read Doug's book and you'll see that he was in the correct job. He loves his craft and the integrity of it.

I remember as a child on a Brigalow block in the Central Highlands driving past our starving cattle in the middle of a drought. We pulled cattle out of creek bogs, where the permanent waterhole had disappeared to a mud trap; we also had to perform the heinous task of shooting those animals whose eyes had been pecked out by crows. All this on the way to the site of one of the bores, miles from the house. I remember as if it was yesterday, how our spirits would lift if, from the top of the hill a mile away, we saw the arms of our pump jack moving, glinting in the sun, and smoke from the Southern Cross diesel engine drifting across the paddock in the chill mornings. The motor and plant chugging away twenty-four hours a day, day after day, represented the fine line between our family's tragedy and its survival. If the equipment survived, we survived. That type of integrity built the machines and the Foundry, and it would take that type of integrity to bring it back. Doug has integrity in spades and you'll see how it was put to the test in order to achieve what he did.

So, while he's an engineer first, he also loves human beings and contributes, where he can, in concrete human ways. He wanted the Foundry to survive and achieve excellence in engineering, but he also worked tirelessly to keep an industry alive in Toowoomba, and to put bread on his work family's table.

Later he volunteered his time at Sunrise Way, a start-up drug rehabilitation facility initially to assist with infrastructure, before circumstances drew him to assist with leadership and fund-raising. I thought it would make an amazing *Australian Story* for the ABC, of how someone uses what tools the universe has given them to create a unique healing centre for drug-ravaged rural youth. I brought it to the attention of the ABC but heard nothing back in response.

As Doug is at pains to explain in his book, he also has an important spiritual side to his life, which has been both a challenge and a comfort to him. He and Maryann Madden have a long and abiding professional relationship, how they bring their unique talents to the challenges Doug faced is a fascinating aspect of the book. Personally, he's endorsed and claimed his unique journey, and it's central to his life. However, I believe it's been difficult for him to explain to others and, as he writes in this book, this has at times frustrated him.

I remember first becoming aware of his spiritual side when I met with him, and another Toowoomba CEO, just before they headed off to their weekly meditation session (as I then understood it) in Brisbane, which was more than an hour away. I was very impressed at their New Age approach, in a conservative community. Although he's since shared his spiritual journey with me at different times, I certainly have a better understanding of it as a consequence of having read this book, and noted how he's defined terms, which sound familiar, but have a particular meaning to him. At times, his team would mutter, 'Doug's off on his "thing" at the moment.' They would try to understand and many couldn't, but his honesty, openness and generosity would draw a picture that words couldn't.

Doug has a questioning mind, and is a learner (my greatest compliment) who has influenced me and many others. He's been a dedicated partner and parent and I've been devastated to witness some of the recent events that have crossed his path, and have been inspired by the grace and resilience he and his family have demonstrated when dealing with them. The Foundry experience was important in my life and I went on, as a result of demonstrating what can be done in Toowoomba, to be involved in strategic turn arounds in numerous metals industry businesses, including: Whitco, Evan's Deacon Group, RWC, BHP Blast Furnace 6, and Walkers' Maryborough to mention a few. The Foundry was a gift to Australia that keeps giving. Finally, Doug is a great writer and has created a complex, well-structured work that's insightful, gripping, relatable and a pleasure to read. I've no hesitation in commending *The Truth Seminar* to you.

Dr Peter Long
In2it Consulting

CONTENTS

DEDICATION

I dedicate this book primarily to my son Sheldon, taken suddenly and unexpectedly in 2017 while I was writing my second draft. It was eleven months before I could sit and write once more.

He and my daughter Samantha are much loved and Sheldon is greatly missed. My sadness isn't for him, as I know he's in a beautiful place; my deep sadness is for me now that he's no longer a physical part of my life. I treasure his memory daily, I miss him. He was a beautiful and gentle soul, my only son.

I also dedicate it to my cherished daughter Samantha and my mentor Maryann Madden. I love Samantha dearly and I'm tremendously proud of her generosity of spirit and her unwavering honesty and integrity. Maryann has been a true friend, confidante and the trigger to my life-changing spiritual experience. She has facilitated personal and spiritual growth in my entire family, and taught me much about integrity.

Also to Carole for all the good times we shared and the many things she taught me.

Finally, I dedicate it to all the people in manufacturing. I've personally witnessed amazing hand skills and innovative thinking from so many in engineering departments and on the shop floor in Australia, Europe, the USA and Japan. To watch many of these talented people around the world who were totally committed and proud of what they designed and made – being made redundant as globalisation polices took hold was heart breaking. So many dedicated people were forced to move from jobs that provided interesting challenges and daily fulfilment, to positions they had to take only for mere financial survival. I strongly feel we urgently need a global governance and an economic system that prioritises community needs over the profit expectations of corporations.

The reader may feel the book places too much emphasis on engineering and technical issues regarding the Toowoomba Foundry, where I spent forty great years. I include them for a reason. It was a company with a process born at the start of the Industrial Revolution. It's an operation that has the most variables to control of any manufacturing process and was deemed irrelevant, belonging to the 'old economy' by the government of the day. The Foundry was loss making, derelict and offered for a fire sale because the National Consolidated (NCL) Board of Directors believed it was a hopeless case. Endless consultants wrote the employees off as too inbred and in need of new skills they wouldn't be able to acquire. They were proved wrong.

This book is dedicated to the determination of the employees to make the Toowoomba Foundry viable again. I hope my book demonstrates the practical nature of what I now know to be a higher power, sometimes called God, whom I will call spirit, and the joy it can bring to every one of us.

Finally, my huge thanks to my amazing editor, Maria Simms who taught me to change my first draft from a didactic lecture on engineering into a story that brought the book alive. Her practical coaching was inspiring. Some family members and other characters have pseudonyms for privacy reasons.

CHAPTER 1
THE TRIGGER

It was 1986 when the senior engineers sat around the table in the work director's office, above the factory floor of the Toowoomba Foundry. Despite attempts to soundproof the offices, the works director's voice rose above the hum of cupola furnaces converting scrap metal into molten iron, along with the squealing protests of the carbide cutting tools whisking off metal on the machine tools below. There was occasional rattle of the window as air from the George Fisher, Swiss-made, automatic- air-impact moulding line hit yet another green sand mould, adding to the cacophony of background noise.

'How could you not foresee this? Why wasn't it obvious?' the works director bellowed.

He was chiding the engineers who slouched silently, heads down like disobedient children. They were all seated around his large silver ash desk. They had seen this display so often they'd lost all resistance. They knew it was pointless. They didn't feel the need to justify themselves; none thought of himself as a victim. The issue was a fixable field problem on a new irrigator the company had recently launched in the market.

I wasn't enjoying the tirade. These were all capable men. I had my own thoughts about it.

I know and respect them. This is bullshit. Why don't we focus on fixing the fucking problem rather than this people bashing? Human beings aren't bloody machines, they miss things occasionally! Hindsight is a wonderful thing!

I'd made many mistakes in my designs earlier in my career. Luckily, they'd been noted and gently pointed out to me by my great mentor and boss Mick, the chief design engineer at the time, a self-taught man I respected greatly. I'd risen through the ranks and was now the chief tooling engineer. Although I wasn't a target of this particular tirade, I sat in silent rage at the opposite end of the table until I exploded internally. I'd had a powerful realisation that somehow changed me.

There's no right or wrong! The idea burst in my brain. *There just bloody well is!*

Things are the way they are so get over it!

This was September 1986. Driving home after work in my much loved rebuilt BMW 3.0 Si, I couldn't get rid of the feeling that my view of the world had shifted significantly. I was suddenly aware of a powerful realisation. There was no right or wrong. I wasn't concentrating on the evening traffic because that new thought had somehow changed my world in an instant. My old prejudices and beliefs were shattered. I booted the BM hard as I accelerated from the lights, venting my frustration,

I pulled into my garage still thinking, this doesn't make sense, yet I had the feeling it made perfect sense. I gave up trying to intellectualise it and went with the feeling, as I do today. This was a mind shift that started me on my journey towards a more spiritual way of viewing the world and living in it. That realisation was a factor that resulted in a revelational experience.

Some weeks later, the blaming scenario repeated itself on a production failing. I went home feeling discouraged and disillusioned – a rare state for me. I wasn't to know that in a few months I'd be changing a similar meeting from the heaviness of blame to a much lighter energy that overturned the whole group demeanour. I'd be able to switch the focus to solving the issue at hand, by the use of my energy. But that was yet to come.

Meanwhile, the heavy energy continued to impose itself on me when I arrived home. I ran a bath because I'd found a shower or bath often transformed my mood. It seemed to cleanse my energy and put me in a positive frame of mind. I've since learned that's exactly what a shower or bath does.

I was sitting in the elliptical tiled roman bath I'd so proudly made when the house was built, but I was weighed down by my sullen state. I was frustrated over the day's events when suddenly, from the very pit of my stomach came a very strong cry.

There must be a better way!

It seemed to scream from deep in my very essence. It was a cry of desperation from my very soul! I sat there in silence. Then I suddenly felt cold. I was spooked by the sensation that someone had actually heard me. I kept looking around the bathroom to see who it was. The sullen feeling was replaced by an odd feeling of wariness; I just knew someone had heard me. In early 1987 I would find this to be true.

Months passed, until in late 1986 another in a long line of consultants was hired by the Southern Cross Board, the holding company for Toowoomba Foundry.

'Sort out our loss-making company!' was the usual order barked at them.

Nothing productive had resulted from the previous consultants. Several questioned the ability of production employees. Some even suggested they were too inbred and that the company urgently needed an injection of new blood if it was to be successful. News of the new consultants hiring and his unusual requirements filtered through to all and sundry in the factory. It became obvious there was something very different about this appointment. I heard through the grapevine the board had asked the consultant to start on the factory floor to work out what needed to be done. This was apparently met with a quick reply from him.

'I start in the boardroom or not at all,' he said.

With this caveat to his contract accepted, the consultant added a second unorthodox condition. He'd spend two days with each director. During that time he'd sit with them while working, stay and sleep in their home, and eat with them at breakfast, lunch and dinner.

All employees were shocked to learn all board members agreed – and he was hired. There was a sense of fear growing in the workplace at his appointment because the consultant had a strong personality. He was extremely forthright with his comments. The feeling of change was in the wind. I first met him when he did the rounds of managers to introduce himself.

'Doug Pope's my name. I'm here to see if I can provide some direction for the company to improve its competitiveness.' He said it with great authority as he shook my hand.

'Doug Harland, pleased to meet you,' I replied.

We engaged in some small talk for about ten minutes. Then he said, 'Do you believe in miracles?'

'Yes,' was my quick response.

This guy is certainly different and a bit intimidating. What an odd question. He then questioned me about my management role and its purpose, before leaving. I was later told that the consultant addressed the board after his two-day interaction with all directors, and he apparently communicated many home truths.

'My observations have led me to believe no director is really committed to making Southern Cross a world-class manufacturer,' he said. 'One director is only interested in getting his pumps and farm machinery repaired, another is focused on building boats. The rest of the board has not displayed any active interest in the company.'

A senior manager confided to me later, 'The chairman became very emotional and upset, other directors appeared embarrassed but reluctantly acknowledged the truth in Mr Pope's briefing. The board soon spoke of restructuring itself.'

A short time later the board was disbanded.

The chairman was replaced with his nephew, and his son became managing director. The pair set about selling off assets to refocus on investing in a much-needed upgrade of the Toowoomba manufacturing facility everyone called the Foundry. Immediately after the changes at board level, formal interviewing started at the various levels of management to assess the appropriateness of functions and appointments. Staff were continually watching 'The Pope', as he was soon named, when he moved between offices interviewing managers. One questioned me, 'Do you think anyone is going to lose their job? I'm not sure what to make of this bloke.'

'I'm not sure either, just wait and see.'

The board restructure was seen as an unprecedented event and staff were concerned other 'restructures' may follow. Morning tea became a hotbed of theories as to what may transpire. Many were openly saying, 'The board reshuffle may be a good thing because things haven't been too good lately – we need new thinking, we need to modernise.'

Days passed while the interviews continued.

'He told me he's having trouble actually working out what's true,' A senior manager confided in me. 'He's getting confused because he's getting different versions of events from people.'

It was now early 1987 and The Pope had left the site. On his return, we learnt he had engaged the services of Maryann Madden. She was a very experienced crisis counsellor whom he had apparently contracted to assist him before. A day or so later he dropped in to my office.

'Maryann's a spiritual healer with the gift of heightened perception,' he said. 'She can see people's auras, allowing her to discern when people were being truthful, or protecting some hidden aspect of their lives.'

At the time I was at level three in the organisational structure, as departmental head of a tooling and process designs office with the title of Chief Tooling and Process Engineer, following a second promotion.

The Pope came in to my office a second time and asked, 'Would you be willing to undertake a personality test?'

I quickly agreed.

'Have you done many management or professional courses?' he asked.

'Quite a few,' I replied.

'Out of a score of ten, how would you rate the lasting effect after a few days?'

'A two or a three, if that,' I said.

'What would you say if I told you I know of a course that I call a ten-out-of-ten course? It brings definite long-term change. We'll be offering it to all directors and managers.'

'I'd like to do it.' My quick response surprised both him and me because I didn't have time to think about my answer before blurting it out.

'You just can't decide to do it; you may not be ready,' was his response. 'You'll need to consider it over the next few weeks.'

'No, I feel I need to do it.' I was insisting without understanding why.

'No, you need to think about it over time.' He left the office and I remember thinking, *Why wouldn't I be ready*? I went back to the task at hand while still pondering what had just transpired.

A few days later, Pope returned to begin the personality assessment. I sat in the training room with other managers while doing my personality profile. Pope reviewed all profiles before explaining the results. It was a Performax test that rated the individual by the DISC method, where 'D' was a measure of dominance, 'I' influence, 'S' steadiness and 'C' compliance. He turned to me in the training room.

'I can't understand your result.' He didn't elaborate.

The test showed I had zero dominance, high influence, medium steadiness and low compliance. I was mystified by his comment because it was the first time I'd taken this test. The next day he came to my office.

'I don't understand how you became a manager with zero dominance,' he said.

'Well I am.'

He had no response to my reply while rebuffing my repeated questioning of him about attending the course run by Maryann.

What's going on here? What's the barrier? I wondered.

'During interviews I'm getting conflicting information,' he said to me. 'Everyone I interview seems to have a different priority for what's needed to turn the business around. I cannot clearly work out who's responsible for what. Sales forecasts and reporting accuracy are questionable. Who are the key employees? The sales people blame the factory people for major customer complaints. The factory people blame the sales staff. It's very confusing.'

'What's new?' I said.

'That's why I needed the services of Maryann Madden.' Pope said. 'Her wisdom has helped me get clarity on a previous consultancy.'

Maryann was busy interviewing directors and managers above my level and I was becoming curious. I was looking forward to my interview. I'd never met a spiritual healer before and wondered what she'd be like, and see in me. I kept pestering The Pope to allow me to do the course. I'd heard that the directors were doing it and managers above me were also about to do it. I couldn't see any reason why I couldn't.

Alec, the contract manager, said on his return, 'It sure was unusual but great!

I've never been on a course like that before. It's so different.'

The hard-nosed works manager was obviously happy on his return. He wanted to paint the factory in bright colours and the other directors all came back enthusiastically telling staff how enjoyable it was. There was definitely a new and positive energy emerging in the executive and management staff. Things were changing.

The positive feedback increased my desire and impatience to do the seminar, so I felt frustrated at The Pope's continued rebuffs. I couldn't really explain my eagerness to do the seminar. I didn't understand why my soul was 'chafing at the bit'.

CHAPTER 2
MARYANN'S HEALING

A few weeks had passed since my first meeting with The Pope and nothing had happened. Then he walked into my office. He was a tall man with a dark complexion and shiny black hair. There was an aura of power about him. He wasn't afraid to use it. I had the feeling he enjoyed wielding his authority. I decided he had a pretty big ego. He sat down to give me more detail about the course.

'Okay,' he said. 'The course is called the Truth Seminar. It's conducted over three days. You live in the venue with other participants for the duration of the seminar. You're also required to do some preparation beforehand. Do you want to go ahead?'

I looked past The Pope through my open door and saw many of my staff watching us. They saw me look at them. Thirteen sets of eyes dropped back to their drawing boards, except one who gave me a cheeky wink first. I looked back at The Pope. *This bloke has really got everyone's curiosity aroused.*

The office was long, with stained timber parquetry on the floor. The scuffing was the result of workshop boots bringing in either foundry black sand, cutting oil from the machine shop or grease from the maintenance department. It was all embedded in the floor to give it the unique character common in many busy manufacturing offices. It also had a unique smell as a result. A row of large adjustable draughting desks were mounted on cast iron frames made by the Foundry's pattern makers. The desks had articulated precision drawing machines mounted on them and they lined each side of the office. It was an era when 3D computerised design technology was just being developed.

The slight odour of burnt coal dust from the automatic moulding line was drifting through the office, occasionally tinged with a stale urine smell emanating from the core room. It was obvious everyone was wondering what was going on. My curiosity was also aroused by this different approach.

'What sort of preparation?' I asked, returning to the task at hand.

'Are you religious?' he asked.

That's a strange question for a consultant to ask.

'Not really, I was brought up in a Protestant family. We went to St. Luke's Anglican Church. I changed to being Presbyterian when I married my wife, Carole, because that was her religion.'

There was a pause. The Pope seemed to want more.

'We both wanted our kids to have a spiritual foundation when they were young,' I continued. 'We enrolled them at the Sunday school and I started teaching there. I'd taught for a couple of years until I became uncomfortable with what I was seeing some church members and elders do outside the church. I also couldn't relate to some teaching material, so I resigned. Carole and I encourage the values of honesty and integrity in our children instead, and I think it's worked. While the teachings did nothing for me, I believe Jesus existed.'

The Pope leaned back in his chair, looking carefully at me. Then, seeming to have made a decision, he sat upright again.

'I've decided you can do the course. I think you're ready.' On hearing this I was pleased.

He still seems to have some reservation about it.

There was an air of caution in his manner as he spoke to me.

'You'll need to go to Mary's Inner Energy Centre in Brisbane three times a week for three weeks. This will be a healing session. It's necessary before you can do the seminar.' He always referred to Maryann as Mary.

I learnt much later it was Maryann who made the decision that I was ready.

This sounds a bit strange. Intrigued, I said, 'Okay, I'll do it.'

His wariness seemed to be of my enthusiasm to participate in the seminar. He was guarded while he spoke and had a questioning look on his face.

I wonder what the problem is?

I was still puzzling when Pope stood up and said.

'I know how you became a manager with zero dominance, it was your integrity that enabled it.' He turned and left my office.

With hindsight I understood that I hadn't realised something was missing in my life. As I wrote earlier, my soul was chafing at the bit to have this opportunity!

Although I wasn't a religious person, I'd had a Christian upbringing, which lingered with me in some way. While I felt very strongly that I must do this course, I started to feel a little uncomfortable about my decision to have the healings. I guess it was the fear of the unknown. I didn't know people were engaged in these practices in Australia. I'd heard of spiritual healers but knew nothing about them.

I turned back to the original tooling drawings spread all over my desk that I'd been checking and pondered my fear. Somewhat distracted, I pawed through the 14x20in sheets, then the 8x11in sheets, of smaller tracing paper. The sheets contained detailed hand-drawn HB and 2H pencil designs of patterns and core boxes for the moulding and casting of cast iron; aluminium and bronze components in the iron and non-ferrous foundries; drill jigs and milling fixtures; special lathe chuck jaws and lifting jigs. Among them also were designs of special go and no-go gauges for quality checks of part dimensional tolerances in the machine and fabrication shops.

I finally put my doubts aside. I stopped the drawing review and immediately dialled the manager of the Inner Energy Centre. I booked in for my first healing. Over the next few weeks I observed more board members, directors and managers who'd been through the process. They all came back with positive responses, which I found reassuring.

'That was a bloody great experience; my wife can't stop talking about it,' I overheard one board director say on his return.

Around this time I was sitting in my office working away when I heard an almighty commotion. Someone came storming down the stairs into the draughting office.

'Unless there's an apology put on all factory notice boards by 8am tomorrow I'll be starting defamation proceedings!'

The voice boomed down the office for everyone to hear. It was The Pope storming his way to my office with another manager behind.

Shit, what's all this about? He sure sounds worked up. The Pope then came barging in to my office.

'It's a bloody outrage! I won't tolerate it!' he exploded.

'What's going on?' I gasped. All draughtsmen had stopped work and were watching Pope and me intently. Everyone in the neighbouring offices could hear every word.

'You have a foreman spreading lies about Mary's course. If it's not stopped immediately and an apology posted by the foreman on all notice boards by eight o'clock tomorrow morning I'll be starting defamation proceedings.' He took a breath, looked around in an agitated state, then started again.

'There was an article in a Melbourne newspaper describing a Room 10 at the Top course run recently. It made the press because all the participants were apparently engaged in a sex orgy. Your bloody foreman is telling everyone that's what Mary's course involves!' He was red in the face, steaming with anger.

If this is true then the foreman needs a good kick in the arse. This thinking flooded my mind.

'Who's saying this?' I asked. The Pope gave me the foreman's name.

'I'll fix it. Leave it with me.' I stood up and left immediately to confront the foreman, with whom I'd had a long association.

'Eight o'clock tomorrow I want that notice posted,' The Pope yelled as I hurried toward the door to the factory.

I marched through the door of the shop concerned, walking straight up to the foreman to confront him.

'What's this bullshit that you're saying the ten-out-of-ten course The Pope is offering is a bloody sex orgy?'

'You know what these people are like.' The foreman gave me a smug smile.

He obviously hadn't heard about The Pope's defamation threat.

'I wouldn't be so fucking flippant about it if I was you. I'm telling you The Pope is going to launch defamation proceedings against you tomorrow. If you don't put up a typed apology on every factory notice-board by eight o'clock tomorrow morning you'll be in the shit.'

His demeanour changed. He went pale.

'Are you shitting me? I'm not goin' to do that.'

'Do you think for one minute that the directors, the works manager and managers you know and work with would participate in such a bullshit course?' His chin hit his chest as the seriousness of his flippant gossip finally hit him.

'I'd look a fool if I did that, surely I don't have to? Can't I just apologise to him?'

'You'll look more of a fool reading about it in the local papers after a defamation case is launched against you! I'll arrange to get it typed and help you with the wording, but I've no doubt you need to write the apology and post it on all notice- boards,' I retorted.

His knees seemed to buckle as the realisation weighed heavily. It was obvious he wasn't keen on writing a public apology.

'It was a silly bit of gossip. You should've known better.' I said.

I was a bit more supportive because I could see he was getting stressed about what he had to do.

'Do it and it'll all be behind you tomorrow. You'll have learnt a lesson to be far more careful about what comes out of your mouth.'

The apology was posted on every notice-board, The Pope was appeased, the foreman less talkative. And so my booking with the Inner Energy Centre was assured once more.

It was the end of January 1987. I drove the BM to Brisbane on the Monday for the first healing. I slowly turned into the rear entrance of the centre through an open gate with a well-kept white picket fence on either side and parked in a pebbled car park. My feet crunched on the pebbles as I walked to the brick-paved path. I admired a tidy and well-kept garden with a mass of healthy looking plants that belonged to a very well kept, two-story Queenslander house, converted for use as a healing centre. I took a breath and entered the Inner Energy Centre. The sign explained it as 'A Natural Healing and Meditation Centre'. Once inside, I was immediately struck by the calm and welcoming ambience.

This feels nice. I soaked in the calming energy.

Walking through the door into the centre for the first time felt really good – it felt safe. Any concerns I had melted away in an instant. I was also impressed by the down-to-earth and genuine warmth of an attractive young lady with dark hair sitting in the room waiting for a healing session. I stood at the unattended polished pine reception desk not sure what to do. The seated lady noticed my hesitancy.

'You need to ring the bell,' she said. She was obviously a professional woman.

She was immaculately dressed in a white-laced blouse and navy-blue skirt. She had a coloured scarf elegantly folded around her neck under her shoulder-length black hair. We'd become friends later, after she joined me in the seminar. When I rang the bell, the manager of the centre, Christine came to out to greet me and she also exuded genuine warmth. She wore a smart floral dress and had a welcoming smile, bright eyes and a gentle manner. After I'd filled out some paper work, I was introduced to a male healer who came out of a room down the hall. The centre was simply but tastefully decorated and was obviously loved. Similar to the outdoor garden, a variety of very healthy plants decorated indoor areas. Two large, very clean and tastefully landscaped fish tanks were placed opposite the seating area. The centre had a calming ambience; its energy felt good.

'Doug, this is Russell. He'll give you the healing today,' Christine said. Russell was a slim man wearing dress shorts, a check sports shirt, and long white socks in tan shoes, which was a common summer dress standard at the time. I observed he had kind eyes and a gentle manner. He led me to a private room.

'The process needs you to sit on the couch while I sit beside you and place my hand on your back to give you a healing. Is that okay? Do you feel comfortable with it?' he asked.

'Yes that's fine,' I said.

Both of us sat as he put his hand gently on my back, giving me a healing for a few minutes.

I can handle this, it feels pretty good.

It felt very relaxing. There was no conversation. After the healing he told me to lie down on the couch and let the healing integrate. He left the room and all I felt was a comfortable and relaxed feeling. I later learnt my healer had been a high school woodwork teacher in his previous career. This somehow increased my confidence because it gave me a sense of the practical nature of what I was undertaking.

At the end of the session, he knocked gently on the door then entered the small room. I was again impressed by the warmth of his manner.

'That's it, you're free to go,' he said with a smile.

'How much do I need to pay?' I asked.

His response boosted my confidence in the integrity of the process.

'Money isn't an issue here. We operate on a donation basis only. Whatever you feel is appropriate.'

It was the first time I'd struck a private organisation, other than charities, offering a quality service on a donation basis. It also boosted my confidence regarding the integrity of the service and its people. I haven't found any since. While driving home after the third healing I remember having a strong feeling that my calling, whatever it may be, was near. I didn't understand what this meant but it felt really good. The next week Maryann moved her interviewing to my level of management.

I was due to meet her at the Foundry on a Tuesday late in the day, but I arrived to find her having a long session with a troubled manager. It was the first time I met her. I was surprised to see she just looked like an ordinary person, not the fanciful image I had of a spiritual healer with long flowing hair and dresses.

'Douglas is it?' she queried while entering my office.

'Yes, I'm pleased to meet you.'

'I'm running late, Douglas, I still need more time,' she said. 'So, rather than sit here waiting, why don't you go home and I'll interview you first up in the morning?'

I was warmed by her smile and impressed by her practical manner. I felt very comfortable with her, without really understanding why.

'I won't be able to meet you here in the morning because I'll be in Brisbane,' I said. 'I've been booked in for one of my weekly healings at your centre in Brisbane.'

'Don't bother going. I'll do the healing in the morning during my interview. I'll cancel your appointment.'

I left for home thinking, *I'm really looking forward to this interview.*

The next morning, filled with anticipation, I met Maryann and The Pope in the carpeted area outside the company boardroom. We all entered the room and sat around a low silver ash coffee table at the entry end of the boardroom. A long black boardroom table with black, chrome-legged chairs filled the other end. A couple of tall pot plants completed the décor, apart from a large triptych photo of the molten metal being spectacularly poured in the foundry, and a row of photos of past chairman. After sitting down with Maryann and The Pope, I was immediately struck by how easy it was to talk to her. I had the feeling I could talk about anything. I hadn't experienced this sense of such total 'openness' with anyone I'd just met before. I was amazed by how quickly I became comfortable with her. I was really enjoying the engaging conversation.

'What's your role in the Foundry? Do you enjoy your job?' Maryann enquired. These were the only questions I remember during our chat across the small coffee table that lasted for about half an hour.

Not long after the introductory chat, Maryann came around the table to sit beside me. She placed her hand on my back while we talked. I felt some heat from her hand while the healing took place. When she'd finished the healing she stood up.

'Douglas is a very honest man,' she said to The Pope. She then turned back to me. 'Now lie down on the settee to let the healing integrate,' she said.

She smiled as she stood looking at me. There was much authenticity radiating from her because I could feel her calming energy. I just knew her smile was genuine as she gave me an encouraging wink. She and The Pope both left the board-room, closing the door while leaving me lying on the settee. The managing director's secretary was preparing for an executive meeting. She bowled into the boardroom.

'Oh, I'm sorry,' was all she said. She was obviously shocked at seeing me lying on the couch.

She looked embarrassed and left in a hurry, almost slamming the sliding door. I sensed her great confusion about the strange things going on. She was a well-dressed professional person and I doubt if she had witnessed anything like this in her career. I liked and respected her.

It had been on Wednesday that Maryann gave me the healing. I was at home the following Saturday morning when the strangest and most amazing experience occurred.

It was to change my life!

CHAPTER 3
THE EXPERIENCE

It was the Saturday morning following Maryann's healing, just before daybreak in February 1987. I was about to turn forty in March – and I now do believe that life does start at forty. I woke in our bed in Sardon Street, Toowoomba, right on daybreak. A shrill bird call woke me up. It was amazing to find I was feeling an extremely intense sense of well-being and joy. The feeling kept accelerating and building until I finally began to cry. It was as though I could actually feel every single molecule in my body moving into a state of pure love and joy.

'I'm not worthy,' I kept saying to myself. 'I'm not worthy.' Was a spiritual event unfolding here?

The sensation was outstanding. Beautiful, beyond intellectual understanding! The feeling intensified until I was surrounded by, and bathed in, pure white light. Then, a most extraordinary thing happened – I was levitating above the bed, still bathed in white light. It was indescribable. I felt like I'd been contained within an intense bubble of the most powerful tenderness and pure love.

Over the next few days the only conclusion I could come to about levitating was that my consciousness, or my soul, rather than my body, was above the bed, as I was probably not physically levitating. It was such an extraordinary moment that it seemed as if I was. Yet I was unaware of my body below me so I guess I'll never really know for sure. The beauty of the light and my feeling of being infused by the love in it were intensifying. I was still crying with joy. The purest love, wrapped around me. I was completely enveloped by it. I was immersed in what could only be described as the most sacred energy and love. In fact, I'm in no doubt that's what it was.

The energy of this entity encompassing me was so loving, yet, I was in awe of its power. This was despite being cradled so gently by this force I couldn't understand. The feeling intensified further, and I was sure something even more extraordinary was about to happen. The feeling, was so beautiful, it felt like ecstasy. I was euphoric and seemed to be moving to some other level. I was suddenly overwhelmed and fearful. It had all happened quickly. It was so unexpected, intense and powerful. It was beautiful beyond anything I considered possible. The moment I felt fear, the experience stopped. I lay in the bed beside my wife, Carole, who'd remained asleep, completely oblivious to what had been going on beside her.

The experience had stopped but the joy remained. I instantly understood a significant spiritual event had just taken place.

'I'm not worthy. I'm not worthy.' I repeated, still crying.

Carole slept on.

I realised there was something very different about me. I had a feeling of inner peace that I'd never had before in my life. My head felt crystal clear. It was like a huge vacuum cleaner had sucked all the 'crap' out of it. My hearing had become very sharp.

The early morning bird-song outside seemed extraordinarily loud. Everything was new and beautiful. I felt like I was looking at the world for the first time.

It was magical. I had a sense of 'oneness' with everything. I'd never felt so connected to my surroundings. I was really *feeling* my surroundings for the first time. It was gentle and beautiful. While I was in this divine state, my senses had been heightened. The knot I'd always had in my stomach disappeared and never returned. I had complete inner peace and joy – it felt fantastic! Miraculous!

I usually had cold extremities. My toes, fingers and ears were often cold. Now, warmth was infusing every part of my body, even in the early morning in Toowoomba's seven-hundred-metre mountain altitude. I felt my system had been totally reconditioned. I leapt out of bed alert, filled with great energy. The humdrum, the go-slowness of my mornings, the ordinariness of my existence, had disappeared. I couldn't wait for the day to begin.

I walked to the bedroom's large window to take in the world outside. I saw the backyard garden and surroundings as if for the first time. Again, everything felt so different. I looked with fresh eyes at the intricate detail, colour, and beauty of the plants in my back garden. I could now clearly see and *feel* the miracle of nature.

Carole was still sleeping.

I'd never before been so fully within the environment around me. It was a truly joyful experience. While I was at the window, I realised I could meditate, which, the day before, I'd have said was crazy and only for the hippies. It was just one of my many prejudices, I discovered now. There I was, standing at the window, feeling completely at peace in a world that had become intensely serene to me. The clarity in my head was fresh and clear.

I found I could draw a blind down in my mind against the world if I needed to. Literally within a second, I'd enter a state of serenity. My mind would be absolutely quiet and totally blank. I knew what true and total inner peace felt like for the first time in my life. I felt close to what I can only describe as my creator. I felt the presence of a loving entity beside me. I knew then that I was not alone and never would be. This loving higher power had always been and would always be with me. I could feel it. The reassurance gave me profound relief. When I looked in the mirror I believe I saw a light in my eyes that I hadn't seen before.

The next day, Sunday, I woke at daybreak and the experience repeated itself. I was once more levitating above my bed immersed in white light, crying tears of joy.

'I'm not worthy,' I found myself repeating. But once more the energy of this pure love enveloped me. The experience began to intensify a second time as it had done on the Saturday morning. Again, in spite of the ecstatic feeling and love I felt, fear surfaced once more, and the white light experience stopped abruptly.

Eckhart Tolle in his book, *A New Earth*, in the chapter titled, 'The Peace That Passes All Understanding'[5], describes the peace that I felt. The chapter 'Breaking Free' clarified for me the loss of much of my ego, so aptly described as the loss of my pain body. I lost my sense of being a victim of life.

My new life began that morning!

---

[5]   E Tolle, *A New Earth*, (10th Anniversary), Penguin, London, UK, 2016, p. 56

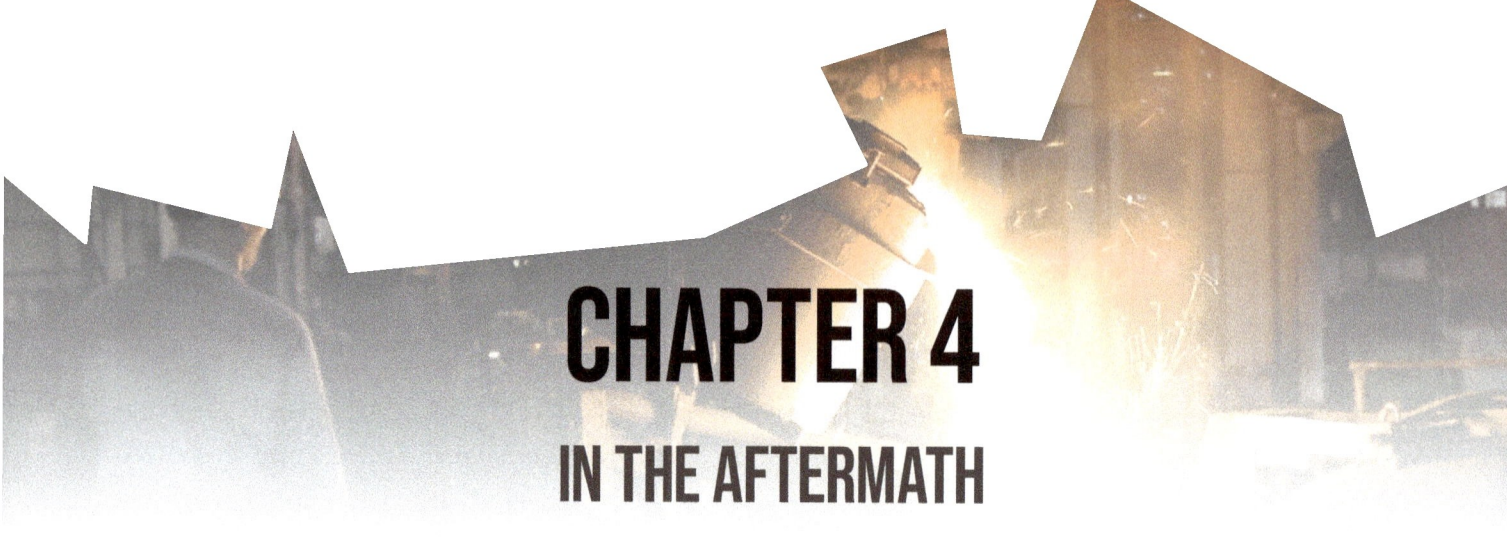

CHAPTER 4
IN THE AFTERMATH

'You obviously dreamt it,' was Carole's first reaction. She was struggling to understand my odd behaviour I'd described to her, with great excitement, what had just transpired.

'It really happened, it's awesome and there is a God.'

This was the gist of it, but my words were jumbled. 'My eyes are now different,' I kept saying. 'In the mirror … I can see a light in them that wasn't there before.'

This was really unsettling Carole. My seventeen year old daughter, Samantha, was watching, giving me funny looks while saying very little.

My son Sheldon didn't seem fazed until one morning when he arrived home at daybreak. He'd finished his night shift at a local flour mill where he was training as a flour milling technologist. I opened the front door before he could insert his key, welcoming him with a big hug, something I hadn't done before. I could see I was freaking him out. Normally his dad would have been in bed, sleeping. Dad wasn't a 'hugger'.

While in this state of high awareness I'd be out of bed with the first bird-call of the morning. The birds became my alarm clock. I'd hear them then I'd bounce out of bed, filled with boundless energy and enjoyment, ready for whatever the day offered.

I think it was Sheldon I overheard saying,

'Is Dad on drugs or something?'

There was often whispering among the family members when they were unsuccessful in trying to understand my change in demeanour and what was happening to me. I began to wonder, myself, if I'd been hallucinating. I now understand how confronting such a sudden behavioural change would have been. I didn't look any different so how could people know what was happening inside me? I was certainly behaving a lot differently!

I continued my healings.

When I entered the room after the next session Russell said, 'You've been crying is everything okay?'

I simply replied 'Yes, they're tears of joy.'

Surreal occurrences kept dropping into my life. Synchronicity and coincidences took on a new meaning. I came to the realisation that there was purpose in them. I started to look for what it might be. I was a technical manager at the time. I remember deciding I needed a meeting with four shop foreman who were spread over the ten-acre- plus site of the factory. I walked from my office to where Ros was working. Ros was my first secretary. She was always dressed nicely in colourful clothes, and had a pleasant personality. She always acted professionally and efficiently. I enjoyed working with her.

'Ros,' I began, 'would you arrange for the foreman from…' when I looked up all four walked into the area just outside my office.

Crikey, how good is this? This is so amazing.

'Don't bother, Ros, they're here,' I said, without telling her of the miracle that just transpired.

This meeting of daily practical needs continued through the high awareness period. It was great fun to be the recipient of it. It felt so magical. If I needed someone in my office, they'd just appear. The joy of experiencing such regular miracles was fantastic, while the precision of synchronicity was almost too much for the mind to accept.

Coincidences kept happening. One day, while driving home for lunch in the BM, I was listening to the car radio. I was pondering a question in my mind, when the announcer on air at the exact time answered it as part of the conversation he was having. The same experience happened while I was walking past two people who were conversing on the footpath. I overheard one answer the question that was in my head. Then I had a technical problem at work, when a magazine was dropped on my desk with an article on the same issue I was pondering over. The solution was in the article. The words 'coincidence' and 'synchronicity' now took on a very special meaning for me. I was beginning to understand that what I now know as spirit was present and with me when these synchronous events occurred. It was very comforting.

Sometime after my experience I purchased a book by Neale Donald Walsch called *Conversations with God, Book 1*. By the end of chapter one I could see my incredible synchronicity and coincidence experiences defined in writing. It had been written with far more eloquence and clarity than my attempt. Along with a strong feeling of truth while reading this book, my belief in the truth of it was really reinforced by the description of God communicating to us:

> So go ahead now. Ask me anything. I will contrive to bring you an answer. The whole universe will I use to do this. So be on the lookout. This book is far from My only tool. You may ask a question, then put this book down. But watch. Listen. The words to the next song you hear. The information in the next article you read. The story line of the next movie you watch. The chance utterance of the next person you meet. Or the whisper of the next river, the next ocean, the next breeze that caresses your ear – all these devices are Mine; all these avenues are open to Me. I will speak to you if you will listen. I will come to you if you will invite Me. I will show you then that I have always been there. All ways.[6]

I now believe the more we're able to keep our mind in the present moment, or just '*being*' rather than '*doing*' as Eckhart Tolle describes it[7], the greater the chance that the miracle of the precision and the gift of universal synchronicity will appear.

In addition to these amazingly synchronous events I found I could also consciously channel energy. I could clearly feel energy flowing out of my gut like a 'power beam'. I could direct it. When it first happened I was completely astounded. I had a feeling of great personal power. It often came out of my stomach area in great bursts. It was a truly wondrous feeling, and I could direct it. It was like a controllable beam of energy.

I remember a day when I was sitting with a group of senior managers. We'd been called together to

---

[6]   ND Walsch, *Conversations with God Book 1*, Hodder & Staughton, London, UK, 2000, p. 58.

[7]   E Tolle, *A New Earth*, (10th Anniversary), Penguin Random House, London, UK, 2016, p. 213.

discuss solutions for another potentially expensive product shortcoming that was generating problems in the field for users. Emotions and blame again started to arise. I simply 'beamed' love to the group. I could feel a strong surge of energy moving out of my stomach. Immediately the group became more relaxed while the focus moved to finding meaningful solutions. Humour and smiles actually started to appear as the intensity that existed before disappeared. How the energy could be changed amazed me, reinforcing my view about the primitive nature of our technologically advanced human race. It showed me how from a universal perspective we're probably still in an infant stage of our development. It would have been easy to go on a power trip while this gift was operating. I was saddened when it eventually faded.

Another unbelievable ability surfaced while I was in this heightened state. It was what I called 'windows of clarity'. When I was searching for a solution to an issue, often, but not always, I'd see a little window appear in my mind like a movie screen with the solution clearly shown. I really enjoyed it when it appeared. It hasn't happened since.

I realised and now believe that the Indigenous people of the world, so unkindly referred to as heathens and savages when they were first colonised, actually had in many cases a closer relationship with what I call spirit than the vast majority of Western-cultured 'religious' people. Probably a better relationship than the missionaries who often forced their religious beliefs on them.

After experiencing my temporary ability to feel things that I'd previously deemed impossible, I came to believe many Indigenous people, if not all, could actually feel their environment in a way educated people couldn't.

I'm sure this is why these people in many countries around the world worshipped their various Gods in most objects, simply because they could feel the presence of spirit in them. As a result of my experience, I feel they just didn't have the intellectual knowledge supported by science training to put it into context. I now believe that the simple truth is that God is in everything as everything is God, including us. To many Indigenous people spirit was real, practical and tangible. They were told that one had to read a book to have a relationship with God.

In spite of their so-called 'savage ways', many Indigenous people acted with great integrity toward their people, wildlife and the environment. It seems to me the well-being of the community was their major focus. They were in harmony with nature. My experience stimulated a belief that there must be a better way of governance for countries that focusses on the well-being of the community rather than the corporation.

Soon after the experience I attended Maryann's Truth Seminar on February 13th 1987. It provided more astonishing experiences. I and many other attendees were bussed late in the day to a resort in the mountains near Brisbane. After unpacking our bags I strolled around the lush garden surrounded by tall gumtrees. It had fallen quite dark as it was dusk. We waited excitedly for the start of the seminar. I was standing quietly by myself.

How privileged I am to be having such a joyous experience and to feel the way I do, so loved and connected to God. The incredible love this being exudes.

I was admiring the beautiful night sky full of stars unaffected by city lights. I immersed myself in the energy around me. The moment was exquisite. I was appreciating my recent revelational experience when my attention was caught by a bright star. I was stunned when its light suddenly started travelling down from the sky toward me at great speed. It actually touched me on the right hand, then returned to the night sky. It was an incredible experience. I was astonished. I shook my head in wonder. It was an experience way beyond what I considered possible. I felt so honoured. I told no one because people were bound to say I imagined it. With time my mind started to rationalise that this must surely be the explanation.

About twelve years after the Truth Seminar I was at another of Maryann's weekend personal growth seminars sitting beside a lady I'll call Tiffany. She told me she was having trouble with her cat and we seemed to hit it off. She was very quiet and shy but she exuded great empathy. I was taken by her extremely happy demeanour.

'You seem very pleased about something, what brought this about?' I asked.

She chose not to tell me. The weekend progressed and I kept asking her to explain why. I could see something was making her joyous. I pressured her again.

'I loved my mother very much. Just before she died she told me she'd give me a sign after she passed over to show me she was okay. Recently it happened,' she said, slightly embarrassed.

My curiosity immediately aroused, I pestered her to tell me during the weekend. 'No, you'll laugh at me and think I'm silly,' she repeated.

When the weekend seminar was almost over I said, 'You can't leave me to go home without telling me, you've made me very curious.'

She finally relented, 'I was standing on my back balcony one night looking at the night sky just contemplating how beautiful it was and how much I loved my mother. Suddenly a star I was looking at caught my attention. Its light came streaming down from the sky. It touched me on my hand, then it went back to where it was.'

Her voice was quiet. Her eyes were cast down in readiness for a critical reaction.

'You're not silly,' I immediately said. 'You're privileged, I had the same experience years ago also, it's really beautiful and amazing. You're the first person I've told.'

'It was beautiful,' she replied with a beaming smile, while adding, 'I don't feel so embarrassed to talk about it now that I know it happened to someone else.'

I mused on this.

The power of love and spirit is mind-boggling, we ended up sitting together for a reason.

It was another example of synchronicity.

The Truth Seminar started with music. While it played I felt every molecule moving in and out of my body like a stretched rubber band in unison with the music. The music was alive inside me, it was an incredible feeling.

How lucky am I? If only everyone could experience this feeling. What a different world it would be if everyone felt this.

During the seminar I had my first 'energy shower' where I felt a reassuring flow of energy pouring through my being from head to toe. It was a beautiful feeling that made me completely convinced that spirit was with me. These showers happened many times during later years in different countries. I've decide they're either spiritual healings or spirit letting one know it is present. It's most likely both.

I arrived home after the seminar totally 'out of my tree'. I was overflowing with joy. I was dropped off by a new friend who attended the seminar with me. Carole was shocked to see me skipping joyfully up the driveway to the back door where she was standing. This really unsettled her further and she expressed concern about my mental state. After the seminar I returned to the Foundry and Maryann walked into my office. 'Hello, how are you travelling after the weekend?' she asked.

'It was really great, it was life-changing. I need to talk to you about my spiritual experience. It was so overwhelming. I became fearful when it developed. I now regret the fear.' I explained.

'You're privileged to have had that experience. There is no need to ever fear spirit. No harm will come to you, it may happen again, so don't worry.'

I did regret my fear, rationalising at the time that fear and pure love cannot co- exist. I also came to believe just how narrow and closed-minded I was about many things. My blinkered view of life expanded to three hundred and sixty degrees. Most things were possible. As I became more accepting of the differences in people, many of my prejudices melted away.

I now related to what I had believed from my religious teachings, that God is love. For me, the form of God is energy; I believe it to be the purest kind, love. I had the distinct feeling that God is both male and female, but yet, neither, that God is gender but also beyond gender. I know this dichotomy doesn't make sense to many, but it feels okay and right to me.

I guess I came to the conclusion that God is all things, is in all things, and is beyond human intellectual understanding as everything is connected. Through this connectedness I also realised that as we destroy our natural environment, we're also destroying ourselves. My reading of Neale Donald Walsch's trilogy of *Conversations with God* [8] reconfirmed to me that this 'God energy' is within us all and in every living and inanimate object.

I also relate to the definition of God by Patrick Francis in his book *Grand Design –1: Reflections of a Soul/Oversoul* [9]:

> God is an infinity of spirit, who has existed and will continue to exist through infinity, who is the source of all creativity, who is the life force of all creation, whose inspirational creativity never ceases nor ever will cease, who cannot be contained or confined in any limited or finite idea such as a person, place or thing; all creation, and each bit of creation

---

[8] ND Walsch, *Conversations with God Book 3*, Hodder & Stoughton, London, UK, 2000, pp. 50, 79, 182.

[9] P Francis, The *Grand Design – 1: Reflections of a Soul/Oversoul*, 8th Impression, Colour Books Ltd, Dublin Ireland, 2004, p. 32.

individually, is a part of God, but it cannot be said that God is the sum of all creation because that would be putting a limit to God and there is no limit; each part of God has a share in God's infinite creativity, above all else, God is love, infinite love.

I also had the feeling of God's absolute power.

I've seen the raw power of nature at work many times, and as an engineer observed, and felt up close, the key power sources generated by humankind. I've stood beside large power stations with their turbines cranking out 1400 megawatts of energy; 1000-HP dragsters making the ground shake; sailed on 140,000-tonne ocean liners; experienced Formula 1 cars in Melbourne; and F111 fighter jet engines at a local air force base. But I've never had the comparable feeling of the presence of so much power as when I was in God's presence. Yet the paradox is that this all- powerful entity is totally gentle as it exudes only love. Again, words and intellect are poor and inadequate tools, incapable of describing this omnipotent being. It has to be felt.

The documented words of Jesus in the Bible – 'The only path to the Father is through me' – caused me some bother. Many had preached Christianity to me saying Jesus is the only way to God. Some misguided preachers proclaim that people of other religions or beliefs are destined to the realm of Satan. This is total nonsense. I'm of the view that while this statement by Jesus was very relevant to a gathering in the distant past somewhere in the Middle East, the globalisation of this statement has been a corruption and gross amplification of its intent. No religion has exclusive access to this higher power. It does not 'take sides'. This entity loves all and isn't punitive. The belief in an angry God destroyed many Indigenous cultures, in my view. Jesus could also have meant he was truth and the only way to the Father was through truth. So much of the Bible involves symbolism. Interpretation still remains another ongoing debate.

Carole's concern when I came skipping up the driveway after attending the Truth Seminar settled down after I had her meet some of the local business-men who were 'normal' and had also completed the healings and the seminar.

Over the following days after arriving home I was chuffed that animals and babies responded differently to me. My constant talking about what I saw in people's eyes and how babies and animals responded to me also unsettled the family. My sudden change in demeanour caused not only concern at home, but significantly at work with close workmates.

Initially, I assumed everyone could see the changes like I could. I wondered why they were not getting excited about what had happened, when it dawned on me that I looked just the same to everyone even though, on the inside, I'd had a huge shift. I soon stopped my 'born again' behaviour with my friends and workmates because I could see the strange looks. Like my family, they were starting to think I was on drugs or something.

I know many scholars and scientists are offended by the idea of a world beyond human understanding, and that they have a need for proof. It seems to me that intellectual belief is purely evidence-based and likely to be challenged by beliefs and ideas that have not been scientifically tested. During a dinner with a university professor, I decided to tell him about my many spiritual experiences. I was shocked by his reply.

'What you experienced were just tricks of the mind,' he asserted.

'It was no trick of the mind, it lasted over many weeks. The astonishing events I spoke of happened on a daily basis during that period – that would be one hell of a hallucination!' I retorted. He changed the subject.

An overseas friend who was a staunch atheist surprised me with an angry response. He accused me of lying when I confided in him. It changed our relationship. I found these conversations dismissive and somewhat arrogant. I couldn't help feeling saddened by the lack of open mindedness. I also understood that I may have dismissed such claims by others myself if I hadn't had that sense of awakening to something so real and very different.

I can now understand the logic of Wayne Dwyer's book, *You'll See It When You Believe It*. I've come to the conclusion that your belief becomes your reality. Now, I rarely disbelieve people when they confide strange experiences to me and it feels authentic. With the benefit of my subsequent studies into this field of spiritual awareness and development I've come to believe my soul was most likely out of my body during the experience, and that was what made me think I was levitating. But maybe not!

I remember a retired shop foreman from the Foundry and also a relative confiding in me that they once had the ability to move their soul out of their body at will.

Core shop foreman, Tom, was dying. I visited him each week in a Brisbane hospital; he was a man I respected.

'I know you meditate Doug. I wonder if you could help me?' he said during a visit.

'Sure Tom, if I can,' I responded.

'When I was promoted to foreman I was young, very nervous and stressed. After arriving home after work each day, I'd lie down to rest and move my soul out of my body and experience a beautiful and peaceful state. One day when I came back to my body I was paralysed for a long while. It scared me so much, I haven't done it since. I can't do it anymore. I'd like you to teach me how once again. When I'm getting my radium treatment lying on that bloody table it is horrible. If I could get out of my body, it'd make it okay.' He sighed.

'I'm sorry Tom, but I don't know how to do it either. I've a friend who knows people who can. I'll ask her and let you know next week. Okay?'

'Thanks Doug,' Tom replied.

The next week before I visited Tom I met with a friend, a school-teacher.

'I can't do it either,' she said, 'but a book by an Indian writer explains it. I've a copy you can borrow.'

I gave the book to Tom during my next visit but he was visibly disappointed that I wasn't able to give him a quick resolution.

The next week I visited him in hospital.

'I couldn't read the whole book as I'm so, so tired. I'm going home, I'm bloody sick of this,' he said.

'The reason you became paralysed was because you didn't mesh properly when you came back in. At least that's what I read in the book.' I said.

'Oh,' Tom said, dejectedly.

'It apparently was fear that caused the paralysis. You cannot hold fear indefinitely, so once you relaxed then you meshed properly. Again, that's in the book,' I explained.

A few days later I visited Tom at his Toowoomba home after work.

'I'm giving up, Doug,' he confided. 'This whole thing is giving me the shits, I just want peace. Here's a poem I wrote, I'd like you to have a copy.'

Tom passed away that night. The poem was featured in the company magazine; unfortunately I no longer have a copy.

The relative who had levitated told me she worked on a night shift. When sleeping each day her mother would insist on vacuuming around her bed. She'd float out of her body to be away from the noise to be at peace. She also told me she's lost the ability to do it. These two experiences told to me by people I knew and respected led me to think my soul was out of my body when I had the experience. But I could be mistaken, as I mentioned earlier!

I now believe that when the soul is out of the body we see things in the spiritual realm. This belief was reinforced years later when I was general manager. We had a fatality in the machine shop in our factory the day after the planes flew into the Twin Towers in New York on 11th September 2001. A first-aid attendant in the Foundry witnessed an accident on the floor of the factory involving a fellow employee named Leo. He saw Leo's soul leave his body and go up a shaft of white light. Leo's death was to have unexpected ramifications. I was to use my different way of viewing the world, and the people in it, to address the many confronting issues it raised.

This temporary period of my experience was magical, because I explored a world where all my needs were met. I had no fear or self-doubt. A couple of weeks after the initial weekend experience, I still didn't fully understand my new state of being. This changed a week after the Truth Seminar. My new friend Sandra gave me a copy of *A Course in Miracles* by Helen Schucman and William Thetford – it was published in 1976 by The Foundation for Inner Peace. Sandra was the lady I met when I first entered the Inner Energy Centre. She was also the only person at the time that seemed to believe me when I explained my spiritual experience.

When I read the following excerpt from the first chapter it all became clear.

Revelation induces complete but temporary suspension of doubt and fear. It reflects the original form of communication between God and His creations. Revelation unites you directly with God. Revelation is intensely personal and cannot be meaningfully translated. This is why any attempt to describe it in words is impossible. Revelation induces only experience. Revelation is literally unspeakable because it is an experience of unspeakable love. Awe should be reserved for revelation, to which it is perfectly and correctly applicable. You are a perfect creation, and should experience awe only in the presence of the Creator of perfection.[10]

I was uncomfortable with the male reference to God, but the rest really felt truthful to me. I accepted and felt privileged that this excerpt clearly explained what happened to me. I was on a hunt for information about what had happened to me so I also checked the Bible in the 'Book of Revelations'. I was disappointed to find I couldn't connect with anything that really explained it.

I became concerned after reading the above excerpt that this heightened state I was in would be temporary. I didn't want it to end, as it was so immensely joyful and empowering. The absence of fear and self-doubt was incredible. When it did end after about twelve weeks, I was barely aware of my return back to my 'normal' state. Spirit operates with love, not fear as many propound. It brought me back gently and seamlessly. One day I suddenly had the realisation it had gone and my first reaction was,

Oh no, it's passed, I don't want this state to end. Then I felt appreciation.

It's okay Douglas, you came to know it would be temporary, what a privilege it's been. My life is still very different and for the better after having it. I'll never view the world the same again. I can use this to contribute.

I lost my need to 'get'. It was replaced by a strong urge to contribute as a result. My material and financial 'want list' and ego reduced dramatically.

Prior to this life-changing event, I had no inclination to read the wide range of spiritually oriented, personal development books available. In fact I regarded them with great disinterest and cynicism. I was okay. I didn't need any help. I was very broad-minded, or so I thought in my arrogant and misplaced view. It usually was the 'other person's' problem – at least that was my misguided thinking.

For the first six months after the experience I couldn't read enough books on personal growth and spirituality. I had a real hunger to read books of this type. I read heaps of them. I found my need to read a book cover to cover disappeared; I was content to read a book until I had the feeling I found what I needed. Dan Millman, Richard Bach, Louise Hay, Wayne Dyer, Shirley MacLaine and Vernon Howard are just a few of the authors whose books I immersed myself in directly after the experience.

---

[10]   H Schucman and W Thetford, *A Course in Miracles*, Foundation For Inner Peace, Tiburon California, 1985,p.4.

Once this reading frenzy was over, it became a rarity for me to read a book on issues relating to personal growth or spirituality. The only exception is the series *Conversations with God* I mentioned earlier. I find these books describe, clearly and simply, many of the experiences I had. I certainly recommend them. They're an enlightening read. I often reread chapters of Eckhart Tolle's book *A New Earth*. I love his work. I felt his style would appeal to a person with a strong intellectual focus. I'm in admiration of the wisdom and clear descriptions of spiritual issues in this book. I regard Eckhart as a highly evolved person. His You Tube clips are enlightening.

While my openness about my experience often resulted in strange looks and rebuffs, as a result many people became comfortable in telling me about their unusual spiritual occurrences. These often heartfelt, practical stories helped to further shape my understanding of spirit. I was now on a committed journey of spiritual development. The Truth Seminar was my spiritual awakening.

I knew, intuitively, that what I'd found in *A Course in Miracles* was true and it was relevant to me. It described almost exactly what had happened to me. I agree with Helen Schucman as quoted earlier, that it's impossible to put the experience into words.[11] While my earlier description doesn't begin to give the reader a feeling for the awesome nature of the experience, it's the best I can do.

Having read only the first chapter of *A Course in Miracles*, one night I casually opened the book and happened on a page describing a process for committing to spirit. I knelt in our sunroom and committed myself to spirit. I waited and waited. Nothing but sore knees and a bit of embarrassment resulted. I went to bed. During the night I had a most vivid and memorable dream, which I still remember today. I never fully read the book because it seemed a bit too religious for me. I remember Sandra's similar words when she gave the book to me.

'It's a profound book, but it's too black and white and too religious for me.'

Sadly, I can no longer find that page, although I've searched for it. I've often wondered about it.

The dream was about Puggy. It made perfect sense when I became general manager of the derelict, loss-making and unloved Foundry.

---

[11]   H Schucman and W Thetford, *A Course in Miracles*, Foundation For Inner Peace, Tiburon California, 1985, p. 5.

CHAPTER 5
MY RETURN TO WORK

In the vivid dream I had a meeting with 'Puggy' Griffiths, the previous chairman of the Southern Cross Board who died while I was working at the Foundry. Southern Cross was the parent company for the manufacturing division Toowoomba Foundry. In its heyday, it had been the largest manufacturing facility in the Southern Hemisphere.

Puggy was wearing sunglasses, signifying to me in the dream that he was deceased. His two grandsons were with him. All three were chatting. The grandsons, in real life, had just acquired the positional responsibilities of the chairman and managing director – a reshuffle of the board, the result of Pope's visit.

The meeting was in a men's toilets that was very old, below the ground floor. It was adjacent to the tool drawing office where I worked, which was a converted World War II air raid shelter. It would have been the oldest part of the office block. I was engaged in a deep, and very friendly, conversation with Puggy and his two grandsons, although in reality I rarely spoke to them. Suddenly, Puggy grabbed me by the back of my collar and hurriedly led me up the stairs into a disused canteen area, designed to feed about a thousand people in the company's heyday. Still with his hold on me, he began running until I took off and was flying free – it felt fantastic. I remember it clearly to this day, flying high over beautiful green fields. I was confused by the message in the dream. I wondered if I needed to leave the Foundry. In the absence of any clear feeling on the matter, I kept working as normal, even though some of the employees were starting to wonder about me.

It was only after I was appointed general manager that I came to really understand the purpose of my Puggy dream. It was that I was to be the leader of a rapid turnaround and reinvention of the then-ailing and derelict company.

After the dream I cast my mind back to my early days in the Foundry and reflected on a meeting I had with Puggy when working in the designs office in the late 1960s. I remembered Puggy coming to my drafting table in the smoke-filled upstairs designs office a year or so prior to his death, with his pet dachshund running bedside him. I was designing a new metric range of fabricated squatter tanks for storing large volumes of water or other liquids. Australia had just changed from imperial to metric measuring systems. Steel sheet sizes had just been metricated. A new design was required to modernise the design to replace the now-obsolete imperial-based sheet sizes.

The dog was walking in front of Puggy. It strutted up to my articulated drafting table with a short erect tail. It immediately lifted its leg, peeing on the cast-iron legs while the pee ran all over the polished Australian hardwood floor. The wall beside my draughting station was made up of white shelves behind white timber-framed glass doors, containing a comprehensive technical library. Puggy observed but ignored the dog's indiscretion while leaning over my table. He was a relatively short man with a weathered and kind face with grey hair. In his heyday many regarded him as somewhat tyrannical, even though the internal grapevine said he did have the welfare of employees at heart. He wore a tweed jacket – and it was the first time I saw a jacket with leather stitched on the elbows to stop them wearing out.

'Good morning,' he said authoritatively and gruffly. 'I see, boy, you're designing a new range of squatter tanks. Did you know I designed the very first range?'

'No Mr Griffiths I didn't.' He called most young men 'boy'.

I'm goin' to have to clean up that bloody dog piss after he leaves. Thank goodness it didn't pee on my folder of drawings on the floor near the table leg.

'Son,' he continued, while I was still thinking about the pee. 'Would you like to see my original writings on the design specs? I still have them.'

'Most definitely,' I responded. But I was thinking. *The old bugger is ninety- three years old, still drives his car and still has a very sharp mind. I hope he doesn't bring the bloody dog when he gives his notes to me.*

Puggy then turned and left abruptly.

The pee dog strutted off behind him on its tiny legs with its tail in the air, obviously pleased it had marked my desk and looking like he owned the place.

I set about getting rags to mop up his unwanted contribution.

Sure enough, a few days later Puggy returned. He gave me about ten pages of notes, beautifully written with a fountain pen, and left. Thankfully the pee dog wasn't in tow.

The Monday following the Truth Seminar weekend experience must have been quite comical. The normally reserved Doug Harland was chatting with workmates about all the astounding things that were happening to him, totally unconcerned that they might think me nuts. I had no self-doubt or fear, so why should I care?

I parked the BMW in the carpark, put the car cover on and walked over to three work associates chatting together.

'You'll never guess what happened to me on the weekend,' I blurted out. 'I had a huge spiritual experience and I met God, it was awesome.'

Three sets of eyes enlarged as each looked at the others with a very strange look.

'I can actually feel things I couldn't before. I can control bursts of energy out of my gut. It's bloody unbelievable!'

'Are you okay?' the quality technician enquired.

'Never felt better.'

Two of the party walked away talking with each other and they were continually looking back at me. I could see they didn't believe me. The maintenance engineer, David, remained with me. I had a close relationship with David and he gave me a concerned look.

'Doug, are you sure you're alright?' he asked. You don't think you need to see a doctor do you? Have you been taking some sort of medication?'

'I'm really fine. I haven't taken medicine in years. Stop worrying, it was a privileged experience. I wish you could have one also,' I responded. I headed to my office and decided I'd be a bit more selective about the people I told.

After a few days, I bumped into the contract sales manager, Alec. We often worked together when quoting for new product. He'd also done the Truth Seminar.

'Alec, the Truth Seminar was fantastic! I met God and had a beautiful experience!' I said excitedly.

'Hello, we've got a live one here,' he responded with a wide grin. 'Yes I really enjoyed it, but obviously not as much as you. Everyone is talking about you. Are you sure you're okay?'

'I've never felt so good. I can channel energy and feel things.'

'David told me. Maybe it would be good if you did see a doctor. Doug, you really need to tone it down.'

'I'll be okay, the last person I need is a doctor. I've never felt better,' I replied as I walked back to my office.

Everyone thinks I'm bonkers – if only they could experience what happened to me.

The quality manager Jeff had his office near mine. He had just returned from a field trip. I followed him into his office.

'You really need to do that course of Maryann's,' I said. 'It's God's course – it really changes you!'

He looked at me strangely, gave me a smile, shook his head, and ignoring my apparently outrageous statement, he told me about his findings on the field trip.

I remember one night while working late I felt something pass. I couldn't see what it was until I looked at the clock.

Crikey, it's just passed midnight; I felt the day pass – how is that possible? This aura I'm in is mind-boggling. If only everyone could experience these happenings, the world would change for the better. This wish remains with me today as I sadly watch the many world events unfold.

The next morning, the factory's accountant picked me up to take me to a seminar in Brisbane. I excitedly climbed into his car when I blurted, 'I had an incredible experience last night, I felt a day pass at midnight, it was bloody mind-blowing!'

'Doug,' he replied kindly, 'you need to stop talking about this stuff. People are really starting to be concerned about you. Even I'm beginning to wonder. Just stop talking about it please.'

I had made new friends from some of the people who attended the seminar, and I started catching up with them. Sandra, a solicitor I met when I first walked into the healing centre, also did the same seminar and we became friends. She was, as mentioned earlier, the only person who seemed to believe me other than Maryann. Her friendship was something I cherished. I visited her in the solicitor's office where she worked after work one day.

On leaving, we said goodbye. When I gave her a hug, an extraordinary event occurred that left me in awe. I looked at her, and bright lights like pencil torch beams shone from each of her eyes. I felt enormous love radiating from her. It engulfed me. I left the building stunned.

That was so beautiful, she must have a beautiful heart. The lyrics of the songs 'Stars In Your Eyes' by Air Supply and Herbie Hancock are true. The songwriter must have seen the same thing. It's awesome, this world of spirit.

My sister Daphne, an extremely religious person, wanted me to visit a local minister of her church. She was convinced I had been taken by the devil.

My brother Graham had said to me following our visit to her, 'Daph pulled me aside when you were outside. She said you have the eyes of the devil and need to speak to her minister.'

'He's the last person I want to speak to.' We both laughed.

I did quite a few extraordinary things at work while in this 'love bubble'. I started insisting on any report I wrote that all the names of employees who'd assisted me, gathered facts or contributed to it in some way be named on the front with me as joint preparers of the report. This received strange looks from the works manager at the time, who requested I cease doing it. There was another fascinating incident when I did something completely out of character. I waltzed into the office of the newly appointed managing director. I'd had very little to do with him.

'Hi Richard, I need to talk to you about a loan,' I said, putting my hand on his shoulder. 'I need to take my wife, Carole, to Heron Island on the Great Barrier Reef for a week!' It was completely out of character for me.

Surprisingly, he said, giving me a huge smile, 'Sure thing Doug, not a problem.' He reached for the phone to call the accountant.

I left his office in a daze. I'd never have contemplated doing this in my wildest dreams before I'd had the extraordinary experience. The absence of fear and self-doubt drove these spontaneous events. The 'love bubble' around me seemed to bring warmth from everyone I came across. During this period, I also remember being chased for a monthly report by the works manager for submission to the general manager. Totally out of character, I walked into his office.

'I've more important things to do than the monthly report, so I'm going to visit an elderly relative in a nursing home to have morning tea with her,' I declared.

The usually very hardnosed works manager simply laughed while saying, 'Good on you, Doug, I couldn't agree more.' And off I went.

After I arrived at the nursing home, a small group of elderly ladies and I gathered around a piano, as one resident played it. We all had morning tea while the elderly lady kept playing the piano. Again the 'love feeling' was strong. I watched the superintendent of the home weep while we all sat there. It was a very special moment. Nothing was said as we listened to the music. I knew the superintendent was feeling the love 'bubble' energy that brought a feeling of reverence to the performance.

I felt sadness when this ability to feel and transmit energy so strongly and clearly, eventually abated, along with the sense of intense serenity surrounding me.

Incidentally, I never did the monthly report. It wasn't missed. Having been in the presence of energy of the purest love, during my state of elevated awareness it was like I was encased in love the whole time. I know people responded to the energy that enveloped me at that time. I find it sad that there is so little of it in our modern world, particularly in business and government and the day-to-day interactions of people. Love is our absolute reality yet we still follow a reality based on economics, self-interest, fear and increasingly, greed. People and nature are the only real things, everything else is man's misguided idea of what is needed.

Weeks later, I almost lost my best friend Bruce because I pestered him about my new state of being. I remember meeting him shortly after the experience purely by chance outside a local shopping centre, after many years in which we'd not seen or spoken to each other.

'Hi Bruce, it's great to see you,' I said. 'I've just done the most unusual course. You really need to do it.'

Bruce was obviously taken aback. He looked at me suspiciously. 'What are you talking about?'

Unbeknown to me, an old school friend, whom Bruce hadn't seen in many years, had recently and suddenly tried to befriend him again. Bruce found out the motive of this approach was for him to become a member of a pyramid selling scheme, so he assumed I was attempting to sell him a course.

'I'm not interested,' Bruce replied with a coldness that shocked me.

I explained in detail what had happened to me, then I realised he was withdrawing further.

'I'm sorry, I didn't mean to offend,' I said. 'But I got such life-changing growth from the course I'd have loved it if you could do the same.'

A long time passed before I was able to communicate to Bruce in detail what happened to me. We remain the closest of friends in spite of him living on the other side of Australia.

The reaction of my best friend Bruce shocked me and further helped trigger a realisation that it was difficult for people to understand what had transpired in my life. My inner changes were not visible to them. Many other friends were obviously put off by my strange outpourings, because like a born-again Christian I wanted them to have the same beautiful experience.

A few months later Carole decided to do the seminar and I was shocked when she returned home crying and unhappy. I couldn't understand her upset and wondered if the opportunity for change proved too daunting.

I came to understand I had no right to impose myself on others, because I now believe the soul finds its own way when the person is ready. We must respect the individuality of a person's spiritual journey and each person's free will. God gives us total free will, and I've come to understand we need to respect the free will of those we come in contact with and not force our beliefs on them. I now believe that when the soul is ready, the teacher will appear. I ultimately came to respect the free will that was lovingly provided to each of us by God and quickly learnt not to impose my will on anybody. I've also come to believe it's inappropriate to pray for someone without first gaining their permission. From my reading of spiritually-based books, I feel that what happens at the soul's level before entering the earth plane is that we predetermine what experiences we plan to have. Praying for a person without their permission may be interfering with those predetermined choices. Patrick Francis in his book *The Grand Design – 1: Reflections of a Soul/Oversoul* covers this eloquently in the chapters on prayer and free will.

CHAPTER 6

THE CONFIDENCE-BUILDING EUROPEAN TRIP

It's interesting that twice I planned to leave the Foundry due to the many management changes and the resultant turmoil in the business as it struggled to return to profitability, new opportunities arrived. Morale was very low, the result of constant redundancies combined with a continual focus on cost-cutting. The first time I was close to resigning, the works manager and the managing director, suddenly and unexpectedly, sent me on a six-week trip to Europe to benchmark industries of my choice and visit cast metal research organisations and trade shows.

I don't believe my name was plucked out of the air for this. I suspect I was sent on the trip because Maryann Madden recommended it to the new managing director. This would have been during her short consultancy just prior to the offer being made. But it was to enhance my life and boost my career. I was surprised by this directive but I relished the opportunity. Looking back, I feel spirit was preparing me for my leadership role.

I visited the European offices of key customers, cast iron institutional research authorities in the UK and Switzerland, a process licensor in Sweden, and benchmarked many foundries across many European countries. It was an exhausting six-week schedule involving late nights, early morning starts and a different hotel most nights. The trip gave my professional and personal confidence a great boost because I found I was able to meet and converse comfortably over a broad range of industry topics with senior executives of all organisations visited. I felt their respect for me.

I never imagined for a moment it would lead to my one and only marriage indiscretion.

I had an early flight out of Brisbane, so I stayed overnight at Sandra's house in Brisbane where she was living with her daughter. It was March 24th 1988. I left, saying goodbyes early in the morning while Sandra and her daughter were still in bed. I needn't have bothered. My Qantas flight from Australia to the UK was delayed by six hours, resulting in an eight-hour delay at a transit stop at Narita International Airport, Japan. The scheduled connection had departed and the next available flight was scheduled eight hours later. I had to check in at the Narita service counter many times to receive updates about ticket availability.

Each time I went to the counter, a nice-looking woman who appeared to be in her sixties chatted with me while we waited for flight updates. Eventually we went to have a coffee together and more synchronicity occurred. We were the only two passengers on the Qantas flight travelling on to the UK.

'I'm Doug. Where have you travelled from?' I asked while we walked to a nearby café.

'I'm Tricia. I've just had a long trip from Tasmania, I was there on holiday.'

I ordered the coffees. I returned and as I sat down Tricia said, 'I've been watching you. There is something in your eyes that says to me you're a very spiritual person.'

'We all are,' I replied. 'You're very observant because I recently had a major spiritual experience.' I explained what happened to me.

Tricia then talked excitedly.

'I've been touring around Australia. In Tasmania I stopped at a B&B where the lady who owned the house started me on a spiritual journey. I felt a serenity and love that I've never experienced before when I talked with her. It changed me in an instant. I'm so excited about the future. I want to know more. I want to learn about my spirituality. I want to keep growing.'

'I'm working on developing myself spiritually also,' I said. 'I understand the hunger for more self-understanding one has after a life-changing event. I now meditate daily and have a weekly healing in Brisbane.' I then described the helpful books I had read.

'I'm keen to start a meditation routine and explore my spiritual development further in the UK when I get home,' she said.

We arranged to sit together on the flight, talking spirituality all the way to Heathrow Airport. The pilot announced we were flying at a higher northern latitude than normal to get the benefit of the jet stream. It was daylight all the way with clear skies. I was amazed at the vastness and lack of signs of inhabitation across Siberia. I kept walking to the rear viewing window to stretch my legs to check out the scenery below. This proved helpful years later, in 2008, in my role as CEO of the Infrastructure Sustainability Council of Australia (ISCA) when industry professionals told me of the major issue developing with the melt of the permafrost in Russia, Alaska and Canada. While I was working with ISCA I was shown a video12, dated 2010, on climate change impacts. It featured two Australian scientists visiting Siberia. They had concerns regarding a major frozen river that had active methane gas bubbles moving visibly under the ice.

One scientist drilled a 100mm-diameter hole and methane gas gushed out. The slight temperature increase due to global warming was thawing plant matter on the bottom of the river and methane hydrates were being emitted. He then lit a match, placing it near the gas stream and was shocked when a one-metre-high flame jetted out of the ice.

Why wasn't this serious and significant event making mainstream news? I guess no reporters ever visited such remote and desolate areas. Methane bursts are now bubbling up in the Arctic Ocean, a result of global warming.

In 2016 my son, Sheldon, showed me another video of a scientist's presentation at a university in the USA. The scientist noted that since we began burning fossil fuels, an estimated 350 billion tonnes of CO_2 had been released into the Earth's atmosphere. He then said if the permafrost melts it will release one million billion tonnes of methane, which is at least twenty times more damaging than CO_2 in relation to global warming. He showed a video of scientists walking on the permafrost in Siberia, and the ground was springing up and down under their feet similar to walking on a trampoline. One scientist dug the heel of his shoe into the surface and methane gas hissed out.

I hadn't understood the magnitude of the frozen north until that flight. I now reflect that it stimulated my commitment to instigating programs at the Foundry and ISCA to mitigate climate change.

During the flight Tricia turned to me.

'Where are you going to spend your time in the UK? What'll you be doing?'

---

[12] 'Exploding methane gas bubbles', Earth: The Power of the Planet, Australian Academy of Science, BBC Explore/YouTube video; https://www.science.org.au/curious/video/exploding-methane-gas- bubbles

I pulled my UK itinerary out of my travel bag and passed it to her.

'You'll be spending four visits within twenty minutes of my home in Stratford-upon-Avon. Why don't you stay with me? I've the room. It'd be great to continue talking about spiritual things.'

'Okay,' I said. 'I'll call you when I'm scheduled to visit The British Cast Iron Research Association (BCIRA) and another couple of foundries. It'll probably take about two or three days. What do you do?'

'I work at an art shop in Stratford-upon-Avon, I love art,' she said.

We didn't sleep on the flight as we just enjoyed each other's company and the conversation.

When the flight landed we had become close friends.

I was exhausted when I arrived at Heathrow Airport, but we managed to hug as we parted company. We'd flown economy class and being tall I found the seating very cramped – I didn't get much sleep on any of the flights. The next day I hired a car and set off, visiting two organisations a day. I was grateful for an upgrade to a top-of-the- range, brand new, Ford Granada. I really enjoyed driving on Britain's windy and scenic roads. I had some quick trips on the motorways.

I'd put my road directory away. I'd drive to the next foundry by using my feelings and while I didn't always arrive at the front door, I'd end up stopping somewhere where I could see the building and its sign. I spoke to a truck driver about this ability and he said he did it all the time. I stopped doing this back in Australia, and when I tried it recently I was hopeless at it.

If you don't use it you must lose it, or I'm too much in my head to feel it.

The first visit was to a high-output foundry in southern England. My first impression wasn't good. All the employee cars in the carpark were spattered with black mud, the result of poor maintenance of a wet dust collector system. I remember thinking *I expected more than this from the Poms*. I parked the Ford a safe distance away and walked to reception in a drizzling rain. I was taken to the managing director and introduced myself,

'Hi, I'm Doug Harland from Australia, I sent the request for a visit. I appreciate the opportunity to tour your high-output foundry.'

'Welcome to the UK,' he replied. 'Your Toowoomba Foundry has a great reputation over here for the quality of the castings. We produce high-quality casting here also; we make the cheapest castings in the UK due to the high volumes on our many moulding lines.'

He took me on a tour of the plant and I was thinking, *You don't have very good housekeeping here, and, from what I've seen, maintenance isn't up to scratch.*

It was a cold day of drizzling rain. I was shocked to see the end of a moulding line sticking outside the building with an operator wearing a raincoat unloading castings off the line.

People aren't too important here by the looks of things.

I assumed incorrectly this was because it was just a new line and the building hadn't yet been extended. I revisited the plant about seven years later when I became general manager of the Foundry, and there he was – a man still standing out in the weather, unprotected. After both visits I left with the view the only important thing here were pounds sterling, but I could see there was so much costly waste! I had a strong intuitive empathy for the people on the shop floor and was often troubled by some of the treatment I'd seen in businesses. My experience had changed my thinking totally in relation to the treatment of employees.

Each day while driving to the next destination, I'd often think, *People don't seem to be valued or important in many businesses anymore. How much better it would be if CEOs and boards worked with practical spiritual values rather than the pure profit motive. When is enough, enough?*

I became tired of eating alone each night and missed having someone to converse with. One evening I walked to the reception of a classy restaurant in the Midlands. I was standing beside another businessman booking a table.

'Excuse me sir,' I began as he stepped back in surprise. 'I've been travelling all over the UK for weeks. I'm from Australia and wondered if I could join you for dinner to have some conversation?'

He looked a bit shocked as he eyed me off for some time before answering. Having decided I wasn't making a pass at him he said, 'Okay.'

I'm sure that I'd never have made such an approach if I didn't have my spiritual experience; it increased my confidence in various situations significantly.

It was a large restaurant. While walking to our table, I eyed off fourteen diners, male and female, each sitting alone down one side looking bored while trying to avoid eye contact. After some introductory small talk and exchanging our personal history, I learnt he was a shop fitter based in London.

'You know what? I dunno know why people don't do this more often,' he said in his strong cockney accent. 'It sure beats sitting by y'self, it's so bloody boring. I'm goin' to start doin' this in future. Trust a bloody Aussie to start me on a new routine.'

'Look at 'em,' he continued while nodding in the direction of the fourteen travellers sitting alone in a row. 'It's really quite bloody silly.'

We finished our meal, paid and shook hands while walking to our cars. I visited foundries and organisations in all parts of England, Wales and Scotland. I decided the universe was smiling on me, as at every single visit, the manager I spoke with said it was the best day weather-wise they'd had in a long time. Many said the previous day was miserable. I was appreciative. *What a nice bit of synchronicity by the universe.*

It was an exhausting schedule involving eighteen-hour days.

My scheduled visit to BCIRA was next so I drove to Stratford-upon-Avon in Warwickshire and rang Tricia. She was just finishing work so I dropped by, picked her up and we drove to her home. It was a small house attached to another dwelling and was obviously well maintained with a small and neat garden. Tricia showed me my bedroom. I unpacked all my things while she prepared dinner. I admired her various art items spread through the house. It was obvious she had excellent taste.

I showered and walked back to the living room.

'It's been a long day so I'm off to bed,' I said while hugging her. 'Thanks for the dinner and putting me up.'

Tricia tried to kiss me and said, 'Would you like join me?'

I was taken aback and replied, 'I'm sorry but I'm married.' We went to our separate bedrooms. I walked to mine thinking, *Tricia is attractive but don't make this complicated Douglas.*

The next morning I drove Tricia to work after breakfast and headed off to my BCIRA visit at Alvechurch. This was in Worcestershire, about twenty minutes from Tricia's house. It was great to stay in the one place for a few days. I had many technical questions answered by BCIRA personnel and two queries I had were met with negative responses. I note this because following my later visit to the Georg Fischer (GF) research centre in Switzerland, the question resulted in positive answers. It came to demonstrate how far ahead the Swiss were in new process and material development.

'Is there a way to weld SG iron?' was my first question to the technical director at BCIRA.

'No, its quality can't be controlled due to the carbon. It wouldn't be structurally reliable,' was the researcher's response.

I'll explain SG iron to the reader as follows. Traditional iron castings are made as grey iron, with its graphite dispersed through the iron matrix in the form of flakes (like corn flakes) which make them weak and limited in strength. The flakes represent flaws. Fireplace grates are an example of grey iron. These castings can't be bent either as they would break if bending was attempted. Spheroidal graphite (SG) iron has its graphite dispersed through it in small spheres (like rice bubbles). This increases the tensile strength significantly and makes it ductile (bendable).

'Are UK and European foundries making components out of austempered iron yet?' I asked my second question. We had made an irrigator gear out of austempered iron and I was keen to get a better understanding of the process controls needed.

'No, some foundries are talking about it but they've yet to find a practical application,' the director answered.

An explanation for the reader is as follows. Austempered ductile iron (ADI) is SG iron that has undergone a very controlled heat treatment process that changes its microstructure to a needle-like matrix, making it extremely strong and wear-resistant. It's as strong as high-tensile steel. (Steel is simply iron with the carbon burnt out of it. Because steel doesn't have the 'cornflakes or rice bubble' graphite inclusions that weaken the microstructure, it's generally stronger than iron.) ADI was invented in the 1940s, and heat treatment processes were only now advanced sufficiently to ensure consistent quality.

I had dinner with a BCIRA researcher and returned to Tricia's house. When I arrived she met me and led me into the kitchen where she introduced me to her younger neighbour Sue. We chatted over tea and biscuits. About ten minutes into our discussion I realised Tricia was trying to play matchmaker for Sue and I.

Tricia's sixty-two. She obviously feels I find her too old and thinks I may prefer a younger woman. I had to give her marks for her initiative.

'It's been a big day,' I said, 'I've got an early start in the morning so I'll leave you both to chat on.'

I was off to bed, pondering.

I'm sure Sue wasn't too keen either.

I had to laugh the next night. I was writing up my visit notes and overheard Tricia talking on the phone, 'It's like I'm married again, I cook his meals and do his washing but I'm really enjoying his company.'

I had come to like and appreciate her warm friendship and happy demeanour.

It was the last night. I wanted to thank Tricia, so I decided I'd treat her to a nice dinner at a good restaurant. We had a great dinner and a bottle of red wine in a beautiful restaurant, and when we returned to Tricia's house I gave her a nice bunch of flowers.

I gave her a hug goodnight and thanked her for her great support. When she kissed me I didn't resist. We stood, arm in arm for some time, before going off to bed together. We made love and the next morning I woke and sat on the edge of the bed looking at the floor. I was contemplating what I'd done when Tricia saw me.

'I'm sorry, I shouldn't . . .' Tricia started.

'Please don't ever think that, it was nice. Don't hold any regrets about it, Thank you.' I said.

I showered and dressed. We had breakfast and said our goodbyes.

'Thanks for your guidance and all the book titles you suggested, I'll read them.

I'll learn to meditate. I want to grow spiritually,' Tricia said.

'Be wary of those who want a lot of money or want to control you,' I cautioned.

I waved goodbye and drove off to my next visit in Wales. It was to be my first and only marriage indiscretion in my forty-nine years of marriage. When the Granada reached the end of Tricia's street, I reflected back on Carole's two affairs.

It happens so easily and it seemed so special. Maybe it was the wine, no, probably just the circumstance. There was definitely an air of synchronicity about it that's for sure.

I told no one.

I completed my foundry visits in Scotland and returned to Heathrow. I flew to GF in Schaffhausen in Switzerland. I was impressed by the drive to the facility. The scenery was breathtaking, the quaint village houses with red geranium blooming in the many window boxes. Snow-capped mountains framed many of the small towns I passed through. Unlike the USA, I loved the roads in both Germany and Switzerland. They were free of in-your-face advertising billboards with minimum traffic signage so nature featured instead. Everything was clean, well maintained and had the appearance of being 'loved and respected.' I had the feeling these people were more driven by their spirit rather than their head.

I was given tours of GF's multi-storey research building by a senior development engineer. It was home to many brilliant minds operating impressive research facilities, where automotive product for BMW, destined for production in five to seven years, was under testing for durability and fatigue. I saw many castings being load stressed, vibrated and the cycles counted, while GF proved the long-term fatigue life and durability of new designs of safety-critical components.

As we walked back to his office, I reflected on how my spiritual event changed the way I viewed people and business practices. I felt a real connection and respect for the Swiss engineers, and many of the other people I had met. This realisation came when it became obvious to me that integrity and quality were the motivations driving their professional responsibilities. I had a feeling of sadness when I dealt with CEOs during my trip and in Australia who were only driven by the profit motive. I have the view this thinking is spiritually corrupt.

I should point out that there is nothing inappropriate about making a profit, in fact it's essential in business. My issue is how that profit is made, the size of it and how employees are treated.

On arriving at the office I raised the many questions I had and the researcher answered authoritatively. He improved my knowledge in my area of expertise considerably. I then asked the researcher the same questions I'd asked BCIRA.

'Is there a way to weld SG iron?'

'But of course,' was his prompt reply. 'We produce the rear trailing arm for the current model BMW 735i in SG iron and we weld the axle flange on it.'

I was shocked to learn GF was so far advanced that they were already doing it on high-volume production runs for a prestige vehicle.

'How do you do it?' I questioned.

'The suspension arm is selectively heated on the end in a 120-hour heat treatment process which decarburises the casting on the end. It's then safe to weld.'

Wow. I was impressed. *This is incredible. No wonder GF is held in such high regard internationally.*

'Are you making components out of austempered iron yet?' was my second question to BCIRA.

'For sure, the same model BMW has its differential crown wheel made in austempered iron; it's in production. ADI dampens vibration better and is as durable if not better than the steel gear it replaced.'

I was in awe of the many significant achievements I witnessed during the tour and technical discussions. The fact that GF produced equipment for the cast metals industry while operating foundries that produced automotive componentry was, in my view, where they had a great advantage over pure research organisations like BCIRA. GF had the resources to push the envelope as a result of its corporate structure. BCIRA was a great and respected organisation. It was one that Toowoomba Foundry relied on heavily for technical and metallurgical advice. But I could see how it did not have the resources to innovate the way GF did. It had to rely on research funding.

An engineer took me to dinner that evening. I found it amusing that on the way to the restaurant I had to show my passport at two border points when the road to the restaurant cut across the edge of Germany.

I was curious when he ordered the meal and said, 'We only want one serving.'

'Why did you say that?' I asked.

'In early times, restaurants were not heated like they are now. As the meal would go cold quickly, it would be brought out in two portions. Now, unless a new visitor asks specifically for one, you'll get two meals and pay twice as much.'

'Really?' I said with a degree of scepticism.

'It's a tourist trap. If you don't ask, you pay double. It often causes arguments.' I really enjoyed the hospitality of my host, Jo. I was saddened to learn he had multiple sclerosis.

The following day Jo drove me through the very long Gotthard Road Tunnel (joining Switzerland to Italy) to a foundry in Italy near Lugano. The owner apparently ran the business purely to pay for his love of Lamborghinis.

I was astounded by the differences between the British and Swiss research organisations. We drove at 180km an hour to the airport where I was to fly to Germany, but I was still able to give it thought.

The Swiss are so innovative and produce such quality, this visit has been a real eye opener – they're truly world leaders.

Years later, soon after the Berlin Wall fell, the foundries closed and the multi- story building was virtually empty. Car manufacturers were buying castings from Russia and East German foundries originally developed to supply the munitions factories. The quality was poor but the product was much cheaper. I guess it meant a lot of bonuses for purchasing managers. Globalisation is about bloody price, not quality. The loss of these companies that operate with integrity and innovation and care for their people must eventually result in lesser quality product and services. If only true spiritual values could be the driving force in business and government. I believe we need a new economic model.

Following my experience, as mentioned earlier, I developed the view that the world's indigenous people were in many ways much wiser than those in business in the Western world. They seemed to have the security and well-being of the community as their priority whereas my view is that impersonal economic theory used globally favours corporations over community. How does a highly skilled researcher or tradesman, proud of their technical achievements, deal with being suddenly unwanted and unemployed? I've seen too many quality organisations, with very talented people, close because of corporate greed.

I then flew to Cologne, where I was picked up by a driver from the large organisation, Bergische Patentachsenfabrik GmbH in Wiehl (BPW). This was the largest trailer-axle manufacturer and distributer in Europe. These were the Rolls Royce of axles. BPW was also a customer of the Toowoomba Foundry. The Foundry supplied its Australian distributer. Having this German-backed customer enhanced the Foundry's reputation for quality.

The driver with his black gloves revved the black Mercedes sedan out in each gear while he swiftly and smoothly changed gears while accelerating to 160km per hour on the motorway. I was enjoying the fast ride and conversation and feeling the g-forces when he cornered at high speed. I had the feeling the driver enjoyed driving fast also. In your face billboards are banned in Germany and the 'golden arches' were confined to a small sign above the door of the McDonalds. It was refreshing to see only forests and minimal road signage while we travelled. The factories I visited were also well hidden behind avenues of trees.

I left BPW with the feeling they were a company that based its operation on integrity. I had come to know this was spirit-based. Their commitment to training was also excellent.

I flew back to Heathrow and then on to Stockholm, Sweden. I was reviewing a process, patented by Sandvik, of bonding carbide in cast iron wear parts for power stations to increase durability. It was under licence to the Foundry. A communication problem meant no one met me on arrival at Stockholm airport. I arrived just after midnight and it was soon obvious my flight was the last that night. I waited for someone to approach me and became concerned when I was the sole person in the airport except for an old lady cleaner mopping the floors.

I approached her, and she greeted me with a nice smile.

'How do I get to Stockholm?' I asked.

She looked questioningly at me and I realised she had no English.

'Last bus! Last bus!' she shouted, pointing in the direction of an exit door.

I ran outside dragging my large suitcase and laptop just as a bus was pulling away.

A cold blast of wind stung my face. It was freezing outside!

I rapidly waved my hand and thankfully it stopped.

'Does this bus go to Stockholm?' I asked the driver, who was seated in virtual darkness. My question did not seem to register.

'Does this bus go to Stockholm?' I repeated. He just shook his head and said something in Swedish that I didn't understand. I studied his tired and haggard face, illuminated by the reflected light on the instrument panel. I tried different ways to communicate but he seemed disinterested and eventually dismissed me by waving his hands outward showing he didn't understand. He gestured and pointed me to the back of the bus. I had the feeling he just wanted to get home to bed. I retreated to a seat at the rear.

Where in the hell is this bus going? We're way out in the sticks, it's bloody freezing. It could be going anywhere. Hopefully there is a hotel, wherever it goes.

Had this happened before my experience, I'd have been stressed while I grappled with the fear of the unknown. Now, I was unperturbed but anxious to get a bed for the night. The bus drove on for about a kilometre, and I was pondering why he was driving so bloody slowly when a female voice from the front of the bus spoke quietly.

'I speak English, can I help you?'

'That would be greatly appreciated. Thank you. I was supposed to be picked up, but obviously something has changed. Is this bus going to Stockholm?'

'Yes,' she replied. 'I gave a sigh of relief. It was almost 2am in the morning.

'Would you ask the bus driver to drop me off at a hotel?' I asked.

My saviour spoke to the driver who nodded in agreement. Everyone nodded off. It was quite a distance to Stockholm and the bus was still travelling slowly. It was snowing lightly. Several times I felt the bus slide sideways when we rounded bends. *There's ice on the bloody road, no wonder he's going so slowly.* We came to the outskirts of what I presumed to be Stockholm. The bus came to a halt on a divided road with all the buildings in darkness. The driver turned, stood up like he was in pain, and pointed at me. He then pointed across the road.

'Hotel.'

The lady confirmed it was a door across the other side of the four-lane roadway.

'Thanks, your help is really appreciated,' I said while unloading my bag and the bus left. There were no signs for a hotel just a single door on the footpath that the lady on the bus pointed to. The street was deserted and quite dark. There was very little street lighting. It didn't feel or look like a friendly place, the buildings were very old and showed signs of wear. *It's just dark and I'm bloody tired.*

I crossed the grassy median strip between two bare scraggly trees and walked to the doorway in the dark shadows. I opened it hesitantly, and was greeted by a long dimly lit narrow hallway that went to what looked like a dead end. There was still no signage to indicate it was a hotel. I walked up to the end where a worn vertically-sliding timber shutter caught my eye at bench height. I noted a door on my right. I slid up the shutter to find a well-worn buzzer, which I pressed. After about five minutes a window at the other end of the opening, revealed by the open shutter, slid upward, just when I was about to give up. A person appeared. She'd obviously just got out of bed. Her grey hair was sticking up and she wore an old faded light blue night gown with tattered sleeves that looked like it had been put on in a hurry. She said something in Swedish in a tired and laboured voice. I shook my head and said, 'I don't speak Swedish.'

'Want room?' she said in broken English.

'Yes,' I said with relief. She closed the window and I heard heavy footsteps on floorboards as the door suddenly opened beside me. She led me up a narrow flight of dark natural timber stairs that creaked to a small, old, but neat and tidy room with dark unpainted timber walls. Turning to me she said, 'Fix up in morning,' and presumably retreated to her bed.

I looked around at the small room. *Surely Stockholm has better hotels than this. At least it's nice and clean.*

The next morning I rang my contact and he called around and took me to a modern hotel in the heart of Stockholm. A fax had missed me by one day and my mobile wasn't connected when I was at the Cologne airport, so I didn't know I was to arrive a day later.

My Swedish host didn't get many visitors so he was keen to make use of his authority to spend money on visitors. I was being offered so much alcohol that I was glad when I left his company to visit the Saab foundry. It was one of the cleanest foundries I've ever been in. After Sweden I flew back to Munich to connect with my flight home. I had two days before the flight left and had planned to do a lot of sightseeing. I was totally exhausted, so I only went on short walks but did visit the BMW Museum, which I found inspiring.

The night I arrived home in Toowoomba I jumped out of the bed in the early morning to go to the toilet totally confused, saying, 'Where am I? Where am I?'

'You're home, you're home,' Carole said.

I returned to work. Walking through the office I met the works manager, expecting him to enquire how the six weeks went.

Instead he said, 'When will the helical rotor tooling be ready?' Feeling saddened at this snide remark, I mused, *Fuck you too. Yes I learnt a lot and thanks for asking.*

Instead I answered, 'I haven't had a chance to find out.' I walked away pissed off at his rudeness. I had the feeling he resented that I was sent and not him.

I dropped in my trip expenses to the general manager's secretary. After reading the $12,000 total she said, 'You've obviously made a mistake.'

'No, I took my time and I'm certain it's all correct. I checked it twice.'

'It can't be,' she protested. 'The GM has just returned from five days in Japan.

His bill was $16,000. Your bill for six weeks can't be right.'

'He must have bloody lived it up then,' was all I could say.

I developed a feeling of synchronicity about the timing of this 1987 trip to Europe because much later, in early 1993, the year I became general manager of the Foundry, I planned to resign once more. I was 'the meat in the sandwich' between two general managers that I'd come to disrespect. This was just before Southern Cross and Toowoomba Foundry were split up and Southern Cross was sold. The two general managers were pitted against each other and I favoured neither. Each was trying to get me to side with them. Although I must say one was at least 'human'. As mentioned earlier, synchronicity had taken on a whole new meaning for me.

I applied for a job of lesser responsibility at a company in a picturesque country setting in a valley below Toowoomba. It included a much better remuneration package with a vehicle and I was the successful applicant. Driving through the green fields and tree-lined roads to the acceptance interview I was admiring the great scenery. Yet every molecule in my body was resisting the visit. I had a very bad feeling about it. I wondered, *What a peaceful place this is after the Foundry, why am I feeling like this? It would be great to work here.*

I parked the BMW and walked to the low-set administration building, admiring the gardens and the tranquillity of the setting. The receptionist led me to the manager's office and I was studying the basic but homely furnishings while we walked. The building had an air of quality about it. The manager stood up when I entered his office, reached across the table and shook my hand while exclaiming enthusiastically, 'Congratulations, you're the successful candidate; we all look forward to working with you.'

'I'm embarrassed to say this. I'm very sorry, but something just doesn't feel right.' I said it before he could say another word. 'I can't accept the position, I'm really grateful for the offer and embarrassed that I've put you to so much trouble. It would be great to work here, I could do the work competently but is just doesn't feel right. I'm finding it difficult to understand why.'

'That's a shame, but I understand completely. Don't feel bad about it. It's really okay. We can always find someone else.'

I was reassured by his calm and gracious response. Nevertheless, I left the building very confused at what had transpired.

Is fear stopping me? If it is, it doesn't feel like it. That was unsettling, telling him I didn't want the job.

I went back to the Foundry wondering what I'd done and why.

A month later I was appointed general manager of the shambolic, derelict and financially loss-making Foundry. An onerous sale contract had just been negotiated. I'd turned down a promising job with a pleasant and prosperous company to become the general manager of a mess!

What was the meaning of it all, I wondered. But I had a strange sense of purpose when I embarked on the job of reviving the Foundry.

How did a frightened, shy kid get this far?

CHAPTER 7

MY CHILDHOOD

I can now see how my childhood experiences shaped me. They laid the foundation for my life-changing episode when I was forty. My mother, Lily, was forty-three years old when I was born. I was unplanned, a post-World War II 'accident'. Although I was loved, physical touching, showing your true feelings and hugging weren't done in our family. I wasn't one for showing physical affection until I had my transformation at forty.

I was told mum worked as a housekeeper for a doctor in Roma. Roma was a rural town in outback Queensland. It had a dry climate and a great supply of red coloured hot artesian bore water. It was the curse of women at the time when washing clothes that were often stained. It was here she met my father Charles, who worked as a carpenter. He came from Bungeworgorai, a small town situated twenty kilometres from Roma. Even today I understand it is almost deserted with dry dusty roads lined with scrub leading into it. It was originally a small settlement of sheep and cattle farmers who didn't respect the original Aboriginal landowners, resulting in the settlers living with great hostility directed at them.

Dad and Mum married in Roma and moved to Toowoomba, as it had a better climate, was green all year round, and had tree-lined streets. It was viewed as a better place to live, raise and educate children. I was told by a relative, a long time after her death, that Mum was a trendy dresser for the times, and outgoing with a zest for life – a follower of fashion. She loved teaching her friends the Charleston and other dances when she came to Toowoomba from Roma. I was told she created great excitement when she arrived and a crowd would flock to the railway station to meet her. She was obviously well-off as she apparently travelled interstate regularly. This was a mother I never knew. My only memories were of a sad mother, introspective, with health issues.

I now jump forward in my story, the result of a surprise event in April 2019. My brother Graham and I were both shocked and greatly moved when our sister Daphne was clearing her house in readiness to move to aged care. She produced a box of high- quality studio photos of Mum as a young woman that neither of us had seen over all the years. We had only seen one faded photo previously. I was almost brought to tears and greatly moved as I looked at each photo. I'd just 'discovered' my mother.

Mum had lost two children. A boy, apparently unnamed, died from a 'cot death' within a couple of weeks of birth. I was told a baby girl, Dulcie, died from pneumonia a month and a half after birth. A hospital nurse had washed her in cold water in the middle of a cold winter. Mum also had numerous miscarriages. She had a weak heart, severe arthritis and had become somewhat bitter, tending to see the negative in the world, yet she certainly was very caring. She provided well for us all. She had a strong influence on me in ensuring I acted honestly. She was quite deaf. In spite of an old- technology hearing aid she still had difficulty hearing conversations. I'm sure this also proved an isolating factor in her life. Mum had a phenomenal sense of smell. When a car pulled up in front of the house, she instantly knew.

'Someone's here, I can smell the petrol,' she'd say. She'd be right.

My elder brother, Graham, and sister, Daphne, make up the rest of our family.

We're all six years apart with Daphne being the eldest.

I remember bringing my best friend home after school one day and introducing him to Mum. She gave us some milk with home-cooked biscuits and we went outside to play.

'Gee your mother's old, how come she's much older than my mum?' Bruce said.

I didn't have an answer, I had never considered it. She was Mum and that was that. This comment prompted my first awareness that Mum gave birth to me at a much older age. It explained to me why the majority of my neighbourhood friends were all older than me. I became more conscious of it over time. I'm not proud to admit it but, at times this became an embarrassment to me. It was also when I realised I'd never had the opportunity to meet my grandparents because they'd all passed away. Friends talking excitedly about their grandparents prompted a sense of something missing.

I was always the young kid on the block. My opinion usually counted for naught; I certainly wasn't a leader. I learned to go along with the older kids – the big guys – who convinced me that they knew it all and had all the answers. If there was any doubt, they'd physically reinforce this from time to time. I was inclined to be a loner as a result. When I grew older I was sometimes regarded as a deep thinker. I feel this prevented me from getting a big ego, or showing sensitivity.

I was a very fearful child. I remember on my first school day I hid under the house to avoid going to school. My mother enlisted the help of Bev, the daughter of my next door neighbour, to drag me out.

'Come out Dougie, I've got some lollies. I'm not going to hurt you, you know that.' Bev kept enticing me.

I liked Bev. Her gentle coaxing won me over so I crawled out from under the house to get my lolly. Grabbing my hand, Bev led me over to Mum who firmly took my other hand. We all started the one-mile march to school. I was fighting them most of the way.

'If you don't stop this rot I'll give you a belting,' Mum said.

I had never had Mum speak so strongly to me before, so I stopped protesting and walked with them, begrudgingly. Walking through the school gate filled me with fear. Mum and Bev relaxed their grip as we entered the school grounds, so I seized the opportunity to break free. Both Mum and Bev turned in surprise when I took off running as fast as I could towards home.

'Come back here at once!' Mum yelled while Bev gave chase.

'You little bugger,' I heard Bev say. I could also hear her footsteps gaining on me so I increased the pace. I made it all the way back home. Bev gave up the chase about half way. I hid under the house again. My godmother Millie was a teacher at the school. She, along with Bev and Mum, arrived sometime later in Millie's car to fetch me back. I was scared. I knew I was in serious trouble so I just went quietly.

'Don't you ever do that again you silly little boy, there is nothing to be afraid of. You'll love it here,' Millie chided me while walking me to the headmistress, Miss Wadley.

She also admonished me. I was marched into a classroom full of kids I didn't know. It was terrifying. I sat down up the back with all eyes on me. It felt like everyone knew I did something wrong.

I continued to be fearful in my first-grade class. On one occasion we were given a white square of a mesh-type fabric and had to sew on it a simple house shape using a needle with coloured woollen thread. I sewed the first line and ran out of woollen thread. I was too frightened to go out front to get more thread from the teacher as all the other kids were doing. During this craft period, over a week I unpicked the thread and sewed the first line over and over, feeling increasingly miserable each time. I was sure I was going to get into trouble when the teacher saw how little it had progressed compared to what the other kids were doing.

When all the kids had completed their stitched house, the teacher walked around the class inspecting the results.

'What have you been doing, Harland?' she asked while looking me in the eye. She held up my one-line effort to the class. Many simply laughed. I was so scared and embarrassed, I said nothing. She just walked on to the next desk, much to my relief.

Some months later during a winter's day I was busting to go to the toilet. I was too scared to ask the teacher so I held on until it got so bad that I finally put up my hand and made the request.

'Yes, but don't be too long,' she said.

Greatly relieved, I walked down the stairs. As I started along the long passage to the toilet at the other end of the building, I couldn't hang on any longer and shit my pants. A groundsman was walking toward me and turned up his nose when he walked past.

'I think you better get up to the toilet,' he said as he kept walking.

I was thinking I was going to be in trouble again. I didn't know what to do. I walked home crying most of the way. Mum was shocked to see me walk into the kitchen, she cleaned me up. She walked me back to school where we were met by a very concerned teacher. Millie appeared and I was taken to Miss Wadley again – I had to wait outside her office on an old wooden chair. Her door was open. I could see a little boy dressed in an overcoat with thick clothing in her office. He must have done something bad because while I was watching she laid him over her knee and struggled to pull his pants down under his thick coat until I saw part of his bare bum which she hit with her open hand. He stood up crying, running out of the room while pulling up his pants.

She then threatened to put me over her knee and spank me but Millie appeared again in the nick of time. I was scolded by Miss Wadley and sent back to class thinking *I'm glad she didn't smack my bum*. I wasn't enjoying my first months at school because I didn't seem to fit in. However, I liked a nice blonde girl called Alison who had lunch with me sometimes. She was very kind to me.

I've no idea why I was such a scared child. I can't think of anything that consciously scared me in my pre-school years. After my experience I came to learn through reading that we can carry fears from past lives into our current life. I often wonder if a past-life event was the cause of my fearfulness.

Much later in my life, while I was leading the development of a drug rehabilitation facility, I attended a dinner and lecture night put on by the local Buddhist Pure Land Learning College to thank them for a generous and unsolicited $200,000 donation. The guest speaker was a Buddhist woman from Hong Kong, I think. She spoke of the movement's efforts to scientifically prove and document the reality of reincarnation and gave a few examples. The one I particularly remember was about a young American man who had a strong and debilitating fear of water. Even a running tap sent him into a distressed state.

There was no explanation for this unusual behaviour until he underwent hypnotherapy. While in the hypnotic state he revealed he was a submariner and proceeded to give his name, rank, service number and the vessel on which he served. A search of records confirmed the submarine concerned. It was sunk during the war. The seaman's details provided by the fearful man corresponded with those of a sailor who was a lost soul on that submarine. His age made it obvious the event didn't occur in his current life cycle. This history was later communicated to the man and he apparently lost his fear of water.

My childhood passed in very simple times. I remember we only had electricity to power the lights in the house. An ice chest was our refrigerator. My job was to fetch an ice block from the iceman using a fine woven hessian bag during his daily rounds in a horse and cart. He was a friendly bloke. He let me pick up ice chips from the floor of his cart. I'd suck on them while I carried the ice inside. I regarded it as a real treat.

A wood stove was used for cooking, so my brother Graham and I often had to chop wood and chips to fill the wood box each day. It was a big solid pine box, with a red top and shadow blue sides that Dad had made. It sat beside the stove. It was where the many visitors usually sat and chatted when they came.

Mum had a large deep copper pot over a wood fire outside that she boiled the clothes in while stirring them with an old broom handle. I used to help her transfer them to the concrete laundry tubs for a scrubbing and turn the wringer handle to squeeze the water out. I used to love the smell of the copper when the clothes boiled over the wood fire, the pine scraps Dad brought home from his building jobs crackling underneath.

We called the toilet the 'dunny'. It was a hardwood, weatherboard-clad, tiny building in the backyard that Dad built. It had a door and a wooden seat with a hinged wooden lid. A metal shit pan was mounted underneath, accessed for removal by a small door at the back of the dunny.

Every few days a man with a leather cover on his shoulder would come running into the yard with a fresh pan to change it for the full one. Our next door neighbour, Mrs Hooper, had two dunny-man indiscretions. Once she was sitting on the wooden seat when the dunny man opened the rear door to change the pan.

'He changed the pan while I was sitting on it, it was so embarrassing,' she said to Mum over the fence.

They both laughed about it.

The second event was one Christmas morning. Each Christmas morning people used to leave beer bottles for the dunny man to collect. The dunny man tripped at the bottom of the Hoopers' back stairs, spilling a full can everywhere.

'I think he's been drinking too many of his bloody Christmas presents,' Mr Hooper said to Dad over the fence.

Christmas Day was eagerly awaited, not only for the presents but also because we'd have a roast chook for dinner, and it was a real treat. Chicken was only eaten on special occasions and the local shop would open for a while in the morning. I'd run to buy ice cream in small cardboard 'buckets', which was also a rarity on a dinner table.

Dad used to kill one of our chooks at these special times. I'd watch how far it ran after its head was chopped off. I was allowed to do the chopping on one occasion. Boiling water would then be poured over the dead chook and the feathers plucked. My sister Daphne would turn up her nose at the smell but it never bothered me. Then I'd remove the 'gizzards' as we called them. The chook would be ready for cooking after Mum put in her homemade stuffing.

When I was nine, a new house was built in the back street. I met my first neighbour Dale, who was the same age as me. We had much fun together. We used to hide high up in a large camphor laurel tree beside the city's main street at the end of our back street. From our hideout in the tree we'd drop a ladies handbag, attached to a dark string, onto the road and watch motorists' reactions. When a passing motorist screeched to a halt we'd quickly pull the bag up into the tree leaving many mystified. Many saw the humour in it when they realised they had been tricked and what had happened. One guy tried to skid his car on it the second afternoon he drove by. Then he screeched to a halt and ran back to the base of the tree yelling.

'Okay you little buggers I'm coming up the tree after you little shits! I'm sick of this crap.'

Climbing up the trunk, he was giving us such a mean look that we scurried higher up into the tree.

He struggled to get up the trunk. Finally he gave up, muttering something under his breath while he walked back to his car. He scared us enough that we stopped doing it.

I became adept at entertaining myself alone, and I spent many hours by myself reading and drawing. Then at about ten years of age, I discovered motor cars. I couldn't read enough about them and how they worked. The interest in cars, coupled with a fetish for restoring things, were most likely the foundation for my engineering career. I restored anything, like old lanterns, mowers and various machinery items available on my brother-in-law's farm while on school holiday there. I also learnt a lot about mechanical things as I gained confidence in fixing things with the generous help of my very affable next door neighbour, Mr Hooper. No matter how busy he was, he'd always drop what he was doing to help me mend a pushbike, toy, mower or whatever it was I was tinkering with. I often reflect how I took this great encouragement and support for granted. I'm amazed at how I'd suddenly be his priority no matter what he was doing.

'What's your problem today young fella?' he'd say. After checking out my problem for the day he'd have an encouraging, 'We'll have this fixed in no time.'

Visitors to our home would often get a free car wash and detail. I simply enjoyed making a dirty car look new again. I was a 'Mister Fix It', something I continued to be called during my engineering career.

During this isolated childhood, I tried a number of sports, but felt inadequate because all the other kids used sporting terms I hadn't heard of. They knew rules of the game that were foreign to me. I found out much later that their dads had taught them about sport from a young age, whereas my father never played sport with me. Around this time, Uncle and Aunty Bob moved into a rented house in Parkinson Street a few houses down from us. My seventeen-year-old-cousin Glen 'adopted me'. He became my hero when he started work as an auto electrician at Grundon Motors in the city.

I ran down the street each afternoon to meet him when he came home from work. He'd ruffle my hair saying, 'What've you been up to today young Dougie?'

I liked Glen a lot but only a few months later he was diagnosed with a cancerous melanoma. Glen was tall with a solid build, yet he was a gentle and caring person with a great personality. He was in and out of hospital as he had many operations. His family eventually bought a house on the other side of the city. They relocated before Glen turned eighteen.

Late one night about a year after they moved, in 1957, Mum and Dad took me over to Aunty Bob's in

Dad's blue Dodge ute. The mood on arrival was sombre. Many relatives were gathered. All took turns in visiting Glen in his bed. I went in to find Glen lying down in his bed. He grabbed my arm and smiled.

'It's good to see you Dougie, you be a good boy now,' he said softly.

I turned and left the room without really understanding what was going on. I sat in a chair in the busy lounge room. *Glen looks really pale and skinny.* Within half an hour, Aunty Bob came out of the room in tears followed by Uncle Bob. She was holding a white handkerchief to her face.

'He's gone, he's at peace at last,' she said.

The area outside the bedroom was quite large, with an open lounge and dining room, so the news quickly became the subject of conversation amongst the many relatives gathered. An undertaker was called. Aunty Bob was going around the people asking them to pay their last respects to Glen before he was taken away.

'Dougie, do you want to go in to say goodbye to Glen?' Aunty Bob asked gently. It was then I knew Glen was dead. I was terrified of seeing a dead body. The fear was stronger than my love for Glen. It was a time when I was in a 'spiritual vacuum', with little understanding of what was happening.

'No Aunty Bob,' I replied shaking my head.

'That's okay,' Aunty Bob said softly. She left the room only to return in a few minutes with a drink and homemade biscuit. She was a very kind and soft lady. I found it difficult to understand that Glen would no longer be around. I missed his great company, and friendship, before I finally accepted it and moved on. I think I felt loneliness for the first time after Glen died, but in time it faded away, as did my fear of death. The fears of my early childhood were still present much later in life, along with a lack of confidence and self-esteem.

It was around this age of ten that I really started connecting with my intuition, although I didn't realise it at the time. When faced with a decision I'd often ask myself what I'd do if I wasn't educated and didn't follow my parent's view, but did what came naturally. I'd then take that course of action. I've come to understand that this approach may have partly prepared me for everything later. It seems I'd made an unconscious decision to question things presented to me as truth. My feelings and responses about things in life were based on what I actually observed, experienced and felt. I had unconsciously started making decisions based on my feelings, which I came to know much later as the communication vehicle of spirit.

I was often the target of teasing at family gatherings by the many male relatives who were all about six years or more older than me. It would be Glen who would often come to my aid. I was the young kid mixing it with my older teenage relatives and my teasing simply became the entertainment. Glen had a very kind nature and was fun to be with. I remember on one weekend afternoon at a family gathering, about five male cousins were goading me for a long while. They started chasing and pushing me. 'Who's the good little schoolboy? Who's going to run to mummy? Who's the little sookie?' The taunts went on and on. I was being passed from one to the other while they continually tried to pull down my pants.

I was getting really pissed off. In a fit of anger, which they all seemed to recognise, I broke free and raced into the garage to grab a tomahawk and I immediately turned the tables. Now it was me chasing all of them.

'You're not so smart now are ya?' I screamed while running after them feeling good that the tables were turned. I had no intention of using the tomahawk. They didn't know that! I was enjoying having them on the run for a change. There was a lot of loud yelling when I pursued the now-scared bunch around the yard, so much so, that Dad came out to see what the ruckus was about and shut it down. I never was teased much after that. Years passed. I finished primary school and enrolled at Harristown High School. I now believe this was where I started my journey of truth seeking that led to my experience.

I was pretty confused at this time about religious matters. I didn't separate them from spiritual awareness and self-understanding. I wanted to believe there was a higher power that was love, but most things I witnessed in the 'religious' people around me showed no demonstration of this. I couldn't relate to the idea of a fearsome God, when at the same time I was taught God was love. It never seemed or felt logical to me, even at a young age.

How can one fear that which is love? My parents loved me and I don't fear them so why should I fear God if he loves me?

In my Sunday school days, one teacher would explain verses from the Bible. The next teacher would have a totally different view of the meaning of the same verses, so I concluded, probably unkindly, that neither of them really knew what they were talking about. During religious instruction at school I occasionally attended the classes for different faiths, to see what 'the other side' believed. However, it was more of the same only the rituals were different, often to my embarrassment when I was unable to repeat verses or motion with my hands appropriately.

I was raised in a Protestant family, and was never welcomed into any Catholic homes. I remember the mother of a neighbourhood friend who lived at the end of our front street. I always had to wait at the back steps of their home and was never allowed inside. I had decided his mother was a fussy housekeeper until one day some other friends hurried past me while I was waiting at the back door and ran inside.

'Hey! You can't go in there,' I yelled when all four ran past me into the house.

'Why not?' One stopped and asked while the rest disappeared into the house.

'His mum told me I couldn't go into the house, so why should you?'

'It's fine, we're Catholic.' He took off inside.

My sister Daphne used to walk to school with a friend who was Catholic. She did so for some time until one day a nun from the Catholic school approached her friend while they walked together. The nun told her friend she wasn't to walk to school with a Protestant and they had to walk to school by themselves. I cannot begin to understand, even today, how misguided and prejudiced those people were. Where was the love?

I also remember parents disowning their sons or daughters if they married someone of another religious faith. As a young boy I found it difficult to understand how a parent could do that to a son or daughter and why it was necessary. My sister told Mum that she was going out with a Catholic boy. After she left for her date my aunty and mum were angry.

'She shouldn't be going out with that boy, he's a bloody Catholic,' Mum said.

'It's disgraceful,' my aunt chimed in.

I sat there thinking. *This is crazy, if they love each other why can't they be together?* I remained silent, I knew better than to contradict my elders on such an emotive issue.

Dad's other sister was a converted Catholic and she and her husband disowned their daughter when she married a Protestant. It had a huge impact on the daughter. It made me think religion was about power and control. These prejudices were totally devoid of love. I remember one day at home the daughter, Vada, was visiting and we were having a great time because she was always fun to be around. Her father was a train driver. He did a daily run in a train called the rail motor, between Warwick and Toowoomba. While waiting for the train to be loaded at Toowoomba railway station for the afternoon return journey, he'd often visit Mum and Dad.

'Your dad's coming up the back street,' someone told Vada.

'Shit, I've gotta go.' She took off and disappeared running down the front street.

I was shocked. *This is silly, fancy having to run away from your dad.*

During these times, while a young boy, I lost respect for many parents because I witnessed their religious prejudices, even though I didn't know that was what it was called at the time. I rationalised that if I had been born to their family I'd have been a Catholic also, so religion became an issue of which family you came down the 'chute of life' to. This also made me cynical about religion.

I later came to know a few Catholics who, in middle age, confided in me that they were struggling with their self-esteem because they had been constantly told they were sinners and worthless by church hierarchy.

Faiths so often preach that their way is the only true path to God. This saddens me. I believe every human being has access to God. I've come to know we find God through our hearts, not our heads. I love the quote in the book *Conversations with God*, 'In order to truly know God you have to be out of your mind.'[13]

I believe it was Rotary that really kick-started me on my journey toward the experience. I'm not a Rotarian. I was in grade ten (junior) at Harristown High School in a chemistry lesson. It was close to Anzac Day and a Rotarian was speaking about his experiences in World War II as a soldier. He handed out small stickers of the Rotary creed to each student. The first two questions it asked – 'Is it the truth?' and 'Is it fair to all concerned?' – struck a real chord with me. I found myself really committing to this truth. I remember saying to myself excitedly, *I can really work with this.* I stuck the sticker on the cover of my physics book. I always enjoyed reading the first two statements. I could never remember the other two.

I never spoke of this commitment to the Rotary creed to anyone for fear of being branded silly. I often struggled to genuinely work with it because I found it hard to always be honest. I had a simplistic view of honesty. Basically, I was sure it was about not telling lies or stealing. Saying what you really feel without verbally or physically attacking a person, simply telling the truth and working with integrity, wasn't part of my understanding of honesty at that young age. I found a stronger urge to commit to this simple guide for living when I grew older.

Close to the end of my high school career, Dad was keen to help me find a job. One day, a visiting

---

13   ND Walsch, *Conversations with God Book 1*, Hodder & Staughton, London, UK, 2000, p. 94.

relative who held an executive position in a major bank approached me with Dad while I was riding my bike around the backyard.

'Dougie, Ken can get you a job as a teller at the local bank, what would you think of that?' Dad asked.

Before I could reply, Ken said, 'It's a great place to work. Overtime, if you do well you can be promoted and the pay is good. You could have a job for life. You could one day be a manager like me.'

Not wishing to be impolite, I replied, 'I'll think about it,' while thinking, *Yuk, I don't think so.*

I soon convinced Dad, after Ken left, about my lack of interest. With hindsight it was a great decision. I know three people from honest families who worked for two of Australia's major banks. Each was asked to do things they regarded as dishonest, and they resigned soon after. I've no respect for the practices of Australia's big four banks.

I wanted to be a racing car driver or an architect. I didn't have the required grades to do architecture and my parents couldn't afford to send me to university, so I was at a bit of a loose end. Sometime later, Dad was obviously concerned as he asked me to go with him to Brisbane to talk with a guidance counsellor. To this day I don't know who I met or what organisation it was. I went into a large building in the heart of Brisbane and a man interviewed me at length. He then took me to a very large empty room with many desks and told me to wait there. I sat at my desk alone in the large room thinking, *What's all this about? What's Dad got me into?* About ten minutes later the counsellor returned and placed a test paper in front of me. He gave me a set time to do it. I did a couple of different tests. He then gave me a test about mechanisms and said, 'Answer as many questions as you can in half an hour.'

I started to really enjoy the challenge of the many questions with levers, complex gear and pulley drives. I handed my results to him after half an hour.

Shortly afterwards he and Dad came back. The test man decided I had a great mechanical aptitude.

'No one has ever answered as many questions as you have, and not with such high accuracy,' he said.

I feel it was this test that ultimately motivated my father to see if he could arrange for me to be employed at Toowoomba Foundry. It was a major manufacturing operation in the heart of the city.

Linked to my mechanical ability was my love of cars. At seventeen, I passed my driver's licence test in my final high school year. Cars became my passion and my identity. I could drive for hours each night and day, never tiring of it. The faster the better!

When I turned seventeen I bought my first car with some financial help from Dad. It was an old Morris Z utility which I had saved for and paid $95. I believe it was this car that started Dad's concern about my driving, because my brother-in-law, Lyle, waved me down one Saturday night in town. He gave me a severe reprimand after his observation of me driving around corners on two wheels. The reprimand went straight over my head but I was really chuffed that I had the 'Z' up on two wheels. Dad was briefed. I didn't enjoy his admonishment but it changed nothing in relation to my driving habits. I think I was addicted to speed.

I purchased an old Rover 79 car and stripped it for hill climbing. My friend and I made six exhausts that stuck out of the bonnet up in the air directly from the cylinder head. It really bellowed. This was to be my first foray into racing cars. I put it in the local hill climb competition and it created great laughter from the crowd. I was the young fellow who could hardly see over the windscreen, in an old car making lots of noise, finally slowed to a halt half way up the hill due to the gear lever mount breaking off, preventing me from changing gears. My first attempt was a DNF – 'did not finish'. 'It's the noisiest car here today but it's going nowhere. Looks like young Harland has some work to do – can we get a tow truck?' the event controller blurted out over the loud speakers, much to my embarrassment. I'm sure my Dad who was a spectator was embarrassed also. I ended up scrapping it.

I decided I was going to become a racing car driver. Brisbane was where one of the only two full-time Australian racing teams I knew of was based. The sport was mostly amateurish at the time.

After my life-changing event, I looked back on this desire for speed and concluded it was about my need for an identity. After the experience, I realised my identity resided within me, not in external things, and the addiction to speed vanished. But my love of speed and well-engineered cars remained. I came to realise later this was a way of feeling my personal power before I discovered it through a spiritual pathway.

I completed high school in 1964 and quickly arranged an appointment with the BMC Racing Team's manager. I drove the 'Z' to Brisbane full of expectation. His office was filled with car magazines. Papers were strewed all over his desk. Photos of the Mini race car featured on all walls. John French was the driver.

He was a kind but forceful man. He shook my hand as I entered.

'I'm Doug Harland. I rang you last week about an appointment.'

'You've come from Toowoomba have ya?' he asked with a smile.

'I'd like to start an apprenticeship here and work on your race car.'

'Listen young fella, I admire your initiative and obvious enthusiasm, but a kid of your age, even if you stay with rellies or friends, you'd never be able to afford to keep yourself here in Brisbane.'

'Oh,' I said.

'A mechanic's wage ain't much. It's just not on, I'm sorry,' he said. 'I think you'd better look for another job in Toowoomba.'

My interview ended abruptly.

Being used to complying with directives from people senior to me, I begrudgingly returned home. The disappointment didn't last long. With the assistance of another relative, Dad guided me to Toowoomba Foundry. I passed my interview and question sheet. I then started my job as a cadet engineer at the Foundry in 1965 with great enthusiasm, as was my nature. It was the manufacturing arm of the privately owned iconic Australian Southern Cross Corporation. I hoped I'd be able to get on the engine design team that designed the Southern Cross range of stationary engines. Stationary diesel engines are a long way different from race car engines, however, the opportunity to be involved in their design still held great interest and appeal.

Now I was earning a wage, I could afford the payments on a car, which enabled me to buy my Mark 2A Austin Healy Sprite on hire purchase. It was to be my first and last hire purchase experience when I realised how much the car ultimately cost me. It was a carefree time in my life. It centred on work, study, driving the Sprite and going to dances on Saturday nights. During our technical drawing night classes, lasting three hours, the lecturer would give the class an assignment at the beginning and return at the end of the three hours to wrap up. A number of his class were Foundry cadets. We'd developed competency at draughting at work so we'd polish off the exercise quickly and then go car racing, making sure we returned before the end of the session. This ploy came unstuck one night when the lecturer returned midway through the session to find half his class missing.

Little did I realise that the Foundry was going to be instrumental in shaping my life and leading me to revelational spiritual experiences.

CHAPTER 8
EARLY DAYS AT THE FOUNDRY

I had achieved the necessary eighty percent pass mark on the Foundry questionnaire that had to be answered when applying for a cadetship in engineering, and was told I could start.

I remember my first day at work, I was sitting in the employment office. I was summoned to a meeting of all fourteen cadets starting that day. We were in an old canteen and the manager responsible for overseeing our training gave an orientation speech. He then spoke of the performance expected from each of us. I felt overwhelmed.

I wonder if I can really do this?

Another manager then took us all on a tour of the ten-acre facility. As I saw all the processes operating in this sprawling noisy factory a combination of excitement and apprehension took over, particularly when I saw the engines on the production testbed. Engines from the previous day's production had been running all night and the chequer plate floor vibrated under my feet while they were progressively shut down by Supervisor Cec.

I hope I can be selected to the designs office. I'd like to be part of the engine design team. Some of these other cadets seem much smarter and more confident than me.

I was then escorted to the moulding shop where I was to begin my training. It was a huge, dimly-lit shed engulfed in hot fumes and smoke. Poured moulds glowed white, then red, at the pouring basin where the molten cast-iron metal was poured. Black sand was everywhere.

'That metal is over 1300 degrees centigrade,' my supportive supervisor said.

I stared around dumbfounded.

This is a fantastic place. It's surreal.

My first job was wheeling rickshaws of black sand from a hopper full of newly mixed sand on one side of the shop to an elevator bucket on the opposite side. It transferred my sand via an elevator up to a man on a mezzanine walkway. He had another rickshaw on an elevated walkway and distributed it to the sand bin on a roll- over moulding machine at ground level. I became confused when everyone started to call the black sand green sand.

'It's called green sand because it's just been mixed ready to make the moulds. It's fresh sand so it's called green. It's nothing to do with the colour,' my kindly supervisor said.

A week or so later I was put on the moulding line. My first job was to drag red hot castings off the shakeout with a long hook end bar. The shakeout was where the moulding sand was shaken from the castings so it was aptly named. It was the worst job in the Foundry. The product was heavy railway wagon axle boxes. They required considerable force to drag them off the shakeout. Casting temperatures were still glowing red at around 800 degrees centigrade and the shop air temperature in this area was in excess of 60 degrees centigrade (140 degrees Fahrenheit).

I was dehydrating quickly so I drank copious amounts of water. I was totally exhausted and covered in black dust when I went home that evening. Mum and Dad were away so I was home alone and feeling unwell from severe dehydration. I blew my nose still full of black foundry dust and it started bleeding. It was gushing and no matter what I did it wouldn't stop. I ended up with a heap of blood-soaked towels. I got cleaned up and changed while holding a hand towel to my nose. I was worried.

A bloke could bleed to death here if I can't stop the bleeding.

I went next door to Mrs Hooper and knocked on the door.

'I can't stop my nose bleeding, what can I do?' I said when she opened the door.

'Come into the kitchen. We'll have a look at it,' she said while she sat me down with my head back. She put on her glasses to inspect the wound. Mr Hooper put an ice pack around my neck and after a while both decided I needed to go to hospital to get it stitched.

I drove myself to the emergency department, under protest from the Hoopers. It was a burnt artery so the doctor cauterised it and let me go home. It took over a year before my nose returned to normal. This was indicative of the poor working conditions in 1965.

In spite of this mishap I was enjoying the many new experiences and challenges. Every Friday afternoon there would be lectures on issues relevant to the factory or engineering, and a study period. It was a time when many industry suppliers would spend an afternoon training company personnel in the correct application of their products. They'd pass out quality literature with guidelines on how to correctly specify and use their product. I learnt about oils, fuels, bearing selection, belt drives, fasteners, plastic, rubber, machine tools and many other engineered products relevant to the Foundry operation and product design during these very practical and worthwhile sessions.

I witnessed the decline of these training sessions during the late 1970s and 1980s, when cost cutting became the daily emphasis in manufacturing; training became a cost rather than an investment in the future. It was during this time I also observed an increasing focus on accounting and budgets rather than a well-developed business strategy. This practical, hands-on training also formed relationships and respect between many of the people on the shop floor. It provided a solid grounding and real understanding of the processes and issues employees face on a daily basis, as well as insights into their many tricks.

This experience and the resultant empathy I felt for shop floor people proved invaluable when I was made general manager of the factory. These character-building training programs no longer exist in most companies. Now, university graduates are expected to perform immediately. They are often too proud to want to work at a lower level to gain practical experience. I see many bright young graduates dropped straight into positions of great responsibility. While they have a whole new theoretical toolkit of supporting technologies, they have no practical experience. I see their hunger for advice from 'old mentors'. In some cases they suffer unnecessarily high levels of stress, and fear making decisions, which, in many cases, leads to procrastination. Big egos often disguise a lack of experience.

Knowing about something and experiencing it, are two different things

I have come to believe this intellectual focus only leads to poorer decisions because it misses the benefit of intuitive decisions based on real experience.

At the completion of my indenture period I was told to report to the employment manager. I was taken to his office, and sat down opposite him. He gave me an abrupt acknowledgement and continued reading papers on his desk. I was nervous because I knew this was about being sent to the department where I was to work.

When I first began at the Foundry, he'd told me to lift my game when I was in the machine shop. For some reason I found some of the machine shop technology difficult to grasp. In his office I pondered.

I hope I don't get put in work study or estimating. Mick (the chief design engineer) seemed to think I was okay but some of these other cadets are brighter than me.

It was now late 1967.

'We're pleased with your progress. All supervisors were satisfied with your work ethic and your willing application to tasks. Well done Doug, but two supervisors noted areas for improvement so we're basing you in the designs office. If you prove satisfactory in the first three months this will be your permanent position. You'll start as a detail draughtsman.'

These were words that made my heart sing.

'Thanks, it's really appreciated. That's where I really wanted to end up. I'll give the job my best.' I replied.

I headed up to Mick's office. Mick Zerk was the chief design engineer who ran the design department. He was well respected by everyone. He took me to a draughting desk. 'Let's see what you can do young fella. Go to Ian's layout and design the rocker cover for the 5HP engine.'

'Okay.' With that my engineering career really started.

It was extremely satisfying to be involved in designing and drawing components for the engines. I loved watching the necessary tooling and parts being made, assembling them in the research laboratory and hand cranking them on engine dynamometers for the first time to bring them to life. I used to love checking progress in the pattern shop. Extremely skilled tradesmen hand-carved wooden patterns for each of the cast components. Many of the complex shapes had the appearance of real works of art. I issued my rocker cover drawing to the pattern shop and was called down by the shop foreman.

'You can't make this because the section does not work when it transitions to the side of the cover; you needed to have drawn another view,' he said.

Embarrassed that my first design couldn't be made, I quickly modified the shape so it could be. Imagining everything in 3D in one's head and drawing in 2D, I learnt, was a skill I needed to develop. Engine design was a great 'mind challenge'. When I became general manager and the engineers were designing cylinder heads on 3D modelling computers, I reflected on the mistakes that could have been avoided if that technology was available when I was a designer. A new generation range of 3000rpm, stationary diesel engines were in development and my involvement was with the 5HP single cylinder and 10HP vee twin lightweight engines. It was sad to see this era brought to a close in 1970 and the manufacturing and research equipment dismantled. The result of high-volume global competition.

I was uncertain if I'd stay at the Foundry with the demise of the engine program, but soon found enjoyment in designing centrifugal pumps, a gearbox and irrigation componentry. I decided I still liked working at the Foundry because every day had a new challenge. It proved to be a life-changing decision, and a journey into the world of the qualitative.

CHAPTER 9
DAD AND MEETING CAROLE

Dad was pleased about my new career. He wasn't strongly mechanically minded. As a carpenter he taught me a lot in my childhood about materials and tools. He always explained and demonstrated the need to look after equipment. During rainy days I used to love being with him after school because he'd be sharpening his tools. He would often go to a pub in Toowoomba's main street on these days for a social drink with workmates. I'd tag along and he'd buy me a raspberry. His friends were always nice to me. Dad would always wear his khaki King Gee overalls with no sleeves and straps over his shoulders and a long-sleeved light khaki-coloured shirt.

'Give the lad a raspberry,' Dad would tell the barman, who called him Chas because his name was Charles.

I'd sit on a stool sipping my drink while taking in the surroundings. The walls were dark, hung with old faded-looking pictures, mostly of race horses. The bar area often had the stale smell of burnt cigarettes. There were usually ashtrays on the bar with many 'dumpers' in them, as the butts were called. While most of the patrons were sober and chatty, there was occasionally a lonely drunk sitting in the corner mumbling to himself. I'd watch him cautiously out of the corner of my eye. I was mostly ignored by Dad and his mates while they chatted. I'd pass the time swinging backwards and forwards on the bar stool. A couple of times when we arrived at the pub he'd tell me to stay in the Dodge while he went in for a drink.

I used to think, *What's different that I can't go in?* I never figured out why and never asked him. Once he brought a drink out to the Dodge.

He also removed my curiosity about alcohol, and would often give me a 'shandy' of beer with lemonade in it. This helped me resist strong peer pressure to drink, I suppose as an expression of manhood. I was amused that schoolmates who were not allowed to drink at home would get themselves extremely drunk, often on their first unaccompanied night out, when they eagerly tried the forbidden brew.

Dad used to take me to his building projects during school holidays, where I did odd jobs to earn some money. My brother Graham was just completing his apprenticeship with Dad at the time. He told me that Dad thought I was far too slow at my tasks. Dad never spoke of this, however, his non-verbal appraisals of my poor handiwork usually left me with the clear impression I had to improve my performance. I used to punch nails in the floor and install finishing strips. My occasional misses with the hammer left bruise marks on the finished floor and timber mouldings. This caught Dad's attention and reprimands followed.

An extremely strong and very honest man, Dad was often highly stressed. I remember at the annual tax return time he'd be sitting at his small silky oak writing desk in a lather of sweat. It often dripped off him while he did his calculations surrounded by paper everywhere, even spread out on the lino floor. The first year I walked up to him.

'What's all that for?' I asked.

'Not now Douglas, I'm busy.' It was delivered with such intensity I learnt not to bother him at taxation time. Calling me Douglas instead of Doug or Dougie made it clear he wasn't to be bothered.

Graham used to say, 'Why don't you have an accountant do your return?'

'I don't want people knowing my bloody business,' was his curt reply.

When I was older Graham told me Dad paid far too much tax. He was in the Royal Australian Air Force's 4W Works Unit during World War II and was posted to New Guinea, where he used his carpentry skills to build infrastructure such as aircraft hangers for the war effort. He never spoke much of the war except to lavish praise on the Indigenous people he called the 'Fuzzy Wuzzies', whom he'd obviously befriended. He had the greatest respect and admiration for them. Mum told me he had a hernia operation while in New Guinea. I enjoy reading his war diary where the daily routines and the many Japanese bombing attacks are described. I often wonder in hindsight if Dad had PTSD.

He also talked about his return to Australia by sea, and how he witnessed the wasteful disposal of a large number of trucks, planes and supplies by dropping them off wharves or ships into the ocean. I overheard him tell an uncle that one day the Japanese soldiers raided a village and raped all the women. That night the Fuzzy Wuzzies left camp and came back days later with many Japanese heads. He had a verse written in his war diary which only surfaced after his death that read, *All I have seen teaches one to trust the creator for all I have not seen.*

I was only shown his diary by my sister after his death and was unsure if Dad was the author. I learnt much later that this line was written by the 19th century American author Ralph Waldo Emerson. Dad contracted malaria in New Guinea and, occasionally, he'd be laid up in bed at home for a week or so with a bout of its reoccurrence. I'd visit him in the main bedroom and he'd be sweating profusely in his long pyjamas.

'Are you feeling better, Dad?' I'd ask.

On one occasion there was no answer. It was like I wasn't present, as his eyes seemed to be in a different place.

I found the intensity of some of his feverish bouts scary at a young age. He seemed to go to a 'foreign' place and was a different person when he moved in and out of delirium. I remember on one occasion he sat up in bed and saluted, obviously reliving a war experience. I never really came to know the impact the war had on Dad, but I knew that he greatly disliked aggression in other countries reported on the radio in the time before television.

'When will we ever learn? Will there ever be peace?' he'd say with a sigh when he heard of conflict raging somewhere.

Dad built and renovated many houses in the country. He always built strong trusting relationships with his customers and neighbours. He regularly came home with generous amounts of farm produce including meat, homemade sausages, fruit and vegetables. Typical of his honesty was the day he was renovating a very old homestead in the country in a remote area. He was apparently tearing up old floorboards when he found a large syrup tin under the rotting floor full of very valuable gold sovereign coins. My brother told me when they returned home that evening, 'Dad didn't even think about it, he drove straightaway to the owner's house and gave 'em all to him. I thought they might've given Dad at least one as a souvenir.'

Dad had a huge influence in teaching me the value of honesty, particularly on two occasions. One, when I was swapping his stock of new carpenter pencils with a young man in our street for model 'dinky toy' cars; and the other, when I was taking my brother's loose change from his wardrobe to buy lollies and ice creams for me and my neighbourhood mates. The talking to I received after both these events cured me of stealing. No physical punishment was handed out; however, the words used and the energy behind them sure made the necessary impact.

He was a very tolerant father. When I decided to start a stamp collection after a primary school mate showed me his father's huge and professionally presented collection, I saw some great stamps advertised in a comic book on approval. Not really knowing what on approval meant, I posted the form requesting them. I proudly glued them all in my new stamp album when they arrived. Dad later received a bill in the mail for around $100. After realising they couldn't be returned because I had glued most of them in my album, he begrudgingly paid for them . . . after a few strong words came my way.

In the age before television, Dad regularly stood at the external door to our lush fernery, or bush house as we called it, and watched the night sky. He'd call me in if he saw the very first satellite. He always seemed far away when observing the sky. I often wondered what he was thinking. I reflected he may have been thinking about his war memories. He always seemed calm when he watched the night sky. Now I wonder if he was thinking about God. If a huge storm was raging in the valley below the Toowoomba Range, we'd drive to the Picnic Point lookout and sit to watch the lightning display and listen to the thunderclaps. I came to love the power of nature through storm watching. I remain in awe of the energies involved when nature's full fury is unleashed. I still love watching storms.

On some Thursday nights he'd take me to the local drive-in theatre for Western Night and we'd enjoy the cowboys and Indians movies. Randolph Scott, Audie Murphy, Rory Calhoun, Henry Fonda and Clint Eastwood were a few of my favourite heroes. I'd relish eating fries at interval.

In spite of his occasional bouts of malaria, he maintained general good health until he was fifty-five years old, when he contracted cancer. If I had been a bit more mature, I'd have realised Dad was on his cancer journey at the time. While travelling to Brisbane to buy the Sprite I mentioned earlier, he stopped halfway and stood by the side of the road for a while, which he had never done on the many trips to Brisbane before.

'I just feel like a break,' he said.

I was so focussed on getting my new car I didn't pay much attention to it. I hurried him up to get on the road again. It was only much later, after his death, that I reflected on the fact that he had been in pain. His sickness coincided with the time he was doing a major renovation to convert a large house into a number of rented units for a Dutchman in Toowoomba.

The progress payments were promised but never paid. It turned out the man was totally dishonest. It was, most likely, the first case of blatant dishonesty that Dad was exposed to. Graham worked with Dad and told me he normally did credit checks and met with lending institutions in relation to people who contracted him to do large jobs. Apparently the man concerned had tricked him in this area somehow. He had some small jobs done and paid quickly, which tricked Dad into the major house extension he undertook next.

The financial impact was significant. Each time Dad approached the Dutchman for payment, the man became progressively more aggressive. I was told he placed a curse on Dad verbally and in writing. He had no intention of paying Dad. It was Dad's first dishonest client on a major job. He was having a lot of difficulty understanding the lack of integrity in the man. I wasn't shown the letters because my mother said they were too distressing, but I saw the impact it was having on him. He seemed withdrawn and was struggling to pay the other tradesmen involved out of his savings. He had just bought a new car, which had reduced his savings before this incident. The shock of my father finding himself faced with dishonesty highlights the integrity that was characteristic of our family.

It came to a head when he and Mum decided to take a long drive to Sydney for a holiday with a relative. By chance they stopped at a restaurant in the Blue Mountains west of Sydney, hundreds of miles from home and interstate. Dad was shocked to coincidentally find the Dutchman seated directly opposite and glaring intensely at him the whole time. I don't know what exchanges were made, if any, but my mother told me it was an extremely unsettling and most unpleasant event. He had to cancel the holiday soon after due to severe pain, and returned to Toowoomba only to find he had terminal cancer. After my experience I came to believe that there are no 'coincidences', and that these events have a spiritual purpose. I'm still not sure what the purpose of that coincidence was.

It was a Saturday night and I was driving past the end of the back street to get fuel and go parking with my first girlfriend, Sue, and saw the house lit up. I turned around and drove up the back street. I went inside to find Mum unpacking in the kitchen and said, 'How come you're back already? What happened?'

'Dad's really sick. He's in bed.'

I raced around to the bedroom, Dad was looking pale and haggard sitting up in bed with the light on. I asked, 'What's happened Dad?'

'I've got terrible pain inside. I think it'll be a knife job,' was his laboured response. His pale face grimaced.

I went back to Sue waiting in the Sprite to tell her what happened. Dad had an operation to remove part of his bowel and stayed at home while he recovered. Shortly afterwards Sue ended the relationship. She was my first girlfriend.

I was shattered at our breakup. Unlike many of my schoolmates who were mainly focussed on the area between the navel and the knee, and new sexual conquests, I was only interested in girls I really felt attracted to. The Sprite was my priority. I went swimming with two friends just after the breakup. I decided I was so hurt at being dropped by Sue that I was going to kill myself. I started to repeatedly swim into deep water hoping I'd become so tired I'd drown. Eventually I experienced real difficulty in deep water.

Bugger this, nothing is worth it, I'm just gunna go and try to date the girl I like best even though I probably won't have a chance.

That Saturday night, filled with a new positive attitude and brimming with new found confidence, I walked up to Carole at a disco.

'Would you like a dance?'

'I'd love to.' I was amazed.

After the dance I invited her for a drink upstairs. I was gobsmacked when she agreed. There was no alcohol served during this period so we talked over an ice cream soda.

We danced together and on closing I took her home where we had our first kiss. I decided I had found the love of my life. Each day I'd excitedly drive the Sprite to where Carole worked in a United Cooperative Store (UCS) that tailored to the needs of farmers. I would park outside while I waited for her to finish work. Carole worked in the administration area. I'd drive her home and park outside her parents' house and talk, sometimes for a couple of hours. I was attending night school at the local technical college at the time so Friday and Saturday would be our fun nights. Often on Sunday I'd take her for a drive and occasionally I'd compete in the local auto club gymkhana while Carole watched. I was chuffed at my first gymkhana in a bitumen city carpark when I beat all seasoned competitors and introduced Toowoomba to the handbrake turn. I also broke the class record in a local hill climb. We'd attend dances on those nights and then leave early to go parking in one of the many 'parking' spots often visited by like- minded couples.

Dad's condition worsened when the cancer became active once more. He was bed-ridden for many months while the cancer ate at him. Even at the age of nineteen, I had no real understanding that he was dying. I naively thought he was just sick. I don't think I was particularly mature at the time. He was a seventeen-stone, solidly-built man, reduced to less than seven stone. During this time I also lost respect for our local Anglican minister, who on one visit to our home, tore strips off me for not attending his weekly prayer sessions with Dad. He left me extremely upset with his outburst and criticisms. I certainly didn't feel the love of God through him! I wasn't comfortable with his rote weekly ritual.

Dad's three sisters were staying with Mum and me to support him during his illness. One would also berate me for not attending the bedside services. Dad called me in to his sick bed one day when he was near death, while I was home on a lunch break from work. I was still working in my indentured time.

He said, 'I need to talk to you about something important.' It was the only time he really upset me.

'Doug, I'd really like you to give up any notion of racing cars. It's really too dangerous. I don't want to see you hurt,' he said.

'Okay Dad,' was all that I could say. I left the room with tears in my eyes.

He knew I was always speeding in the Sprite and that at times I was driving dangerously. These days I'd be called a 'hoon'. I was probably called that at the time, by many people. Driving was my greatest love at the time. The faster the better. I was single and carefree and I would spin the Sprite nearly every night on deserted back roads. Because I pushed it to the limit I'd only get 7000 miles of life out of my tyres and was at my happiest with the rev counter locked in the red. I never drove dangerously when Carole was in the car.

I returned to work after Dad's request feeling depressed and almost teary. At the time I was still getting factory experience in the Foundry's product assembly area. That afternoon I vented my disappointment through my work. I assembled so many windmills that at the end of the shift the shop foreman, a very kindly assembly foreman named Ted Muller, came to me.

'I don't know what's troubling you boy but somethin' is. I've never seen so many windmills assembled in one afternoon. I think you've set a record.'

It took me days to recover myself. I was just hurt by Dad's request, which I regarded as being unreasonable. I had a smile at Ted's remarks. He was a man I greatly respected. He was one of the best mentors I had worked with.

The doctor gave Dad three months to live. However, his condition deteriorated over six-months as the cancer ravaged his body. It was only a month before he died that he spoke to me about giving up the idea of racing cars. The month passed and one Friday afternoon after I finished work an ambulance arrived at home to take Dad to hospital following advice from his doctor. I was perplexed when two ambos entered the house with a large collapsible stainless steel trolley.

'What's happening? Where's Dad going?' I asked my mother.

'He's being put into hospital. I can't look after him anymore,' was Mum's strained reply. She looked very tired and worn.

Dad was wheeled out on the trolley in the sunlight by the ambulance attendants, through his flowering, but now neglected, garden. In the bright sunlight, I saw sadness in his eyes. I was struck by his greatly deteriorated condition, as he left his home for the last time. The reality that he was dying and wasn't coming back, and the finality of it, hit me totally. My love for him was such that there was absolutely no fear of seeing a dead body. I couldn't leave his side until he drew his last breath. Graham and I sat beside Dad that day in hospital. Graham left at about 10pm.

'Let me know if he gets any worse.'

I couldn't leave him, so I sat all night at his bedside holding his hand. Morning came, and his condition worsened. I became concerned that I was the only person with Dad while he moved closer to death. Mum and my aunty were staying at home, which I didn't understand. My sister was out on the farm. I ran to the Sprite and drove stupidly fast to Graham to get him to come to Dad's bedside. It was the morning of Toowoomba's Carnival of Flowers and the city was full of visitors touring the display gardens before the annual parade started. I sped through congested streets.

'You have to come quick, Dad's starting to go,' I pleaded with Graham.

'There is nothing I can do. We're getting ready for the carnival.'

I quickly returned to the hospital, unable to understand why I was the only person with Dad when he drew his last breaths. I sat beside the bed.

What is this cancer thing? He's skin and bone. What a cruel and sad way for Dad to go.

I was holding his hand while he lay in the hospital bed, counting the seconds while the time between his breaths increased, watching them slowly fade. When they stopped, I knew a life force had left him.

I knew somehow that the life energy was my real dad. I immediately lost interest in the physical body that remained. To me it was no longer Dad. I've no real interest in visiting his grave. I now understand this was the first time that I came to the belief that a soul really exists and it has or is energy. The soul is who we really are. I cannot understand people having their bodies cryogenically frozen after death in the hope one day they can be 'restarted'. The idea of a soul must not compute for them.

He passed away on September 17th 1966 at the age of 57, on the morning of the city's Carnival of Flowers. It was a beautiful sunny day. The city was in full bloom with masses of flowers everywhere. It was timely for Dad because his garden was always a fest of colour with many varieties of flowers in every area of our yard. He always had a large vegetable garden also. I'm sure his garden was his beloved sanctuary.

Dad's sister wanted to view him before the funeral to say a last goodbye but the doctor spoke strongly against it.

'The cancer will still grow until nothing is left, his body will not be pleasant to view, I strongly discourage it. Remember him as you last saw him.' He said.

I was repulsed. *How horrible is this thing that invades peoples bodies?*

The funeral was arranged. I've very little memory of the actual event but many people attended it. I think I was in shock. Dad was interred in the local Garden of Remembrance. When I walked along this extensive piece of real estate I contemplated, *I'll just be burnt.* Two of Dad's sisters who lived out of town had said their goodbyes and left for home the day after the funeral. A couple of days after Dad's funeral I casually said to the remaining aunty who lived locally, 'I suppose you'll be leaving soon as well?'

This triggered a huge and unexpected tirade toward me.

'That's right. Just kick me out – I'm not needed anymore, I'm just the worker.

You inconsiderate little bugger!' A few words I remember!

I was so upset by this verbal abuse and the anger behind it while still in grief, that I ran out of the house. I jumped into the Sprite with tears flowing from my eyes. I headed out to a country road at high speed taking silly risks. Common sense finally took over and I slowed down and sought solace from my cousin Keith, my pretend grandfather. My brother told me later that when he thanked her for her support he also received a tirade. We decided there must have been a lot of resentment built up for whatever reason.

The admonishment from the minister and my religious aunty was probably another event that further disconnected me from religion, but not from a shaky belief in a loving God.

The words 'God is love' still struck a strong chord with me. It always felt right and felt 'warm'.

The author Doug Harland.

My first car, the Morris Z utility. My school friend Peter sitting on the mudguard and I'm on the left.

No 7 Parkinson Street Toowoomba. The home where I spent my childhood. Sister Daphne is sitting on the front steps and brother Graham is leaning on the fence.

The rebuilt sprite racing at Toowoomba's Echo Valley dirt circuit.

Competing in a local Auto Club Gymkhana.

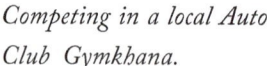

Sheldon and I waiting for the new owner of the sprite on the day of its sale.

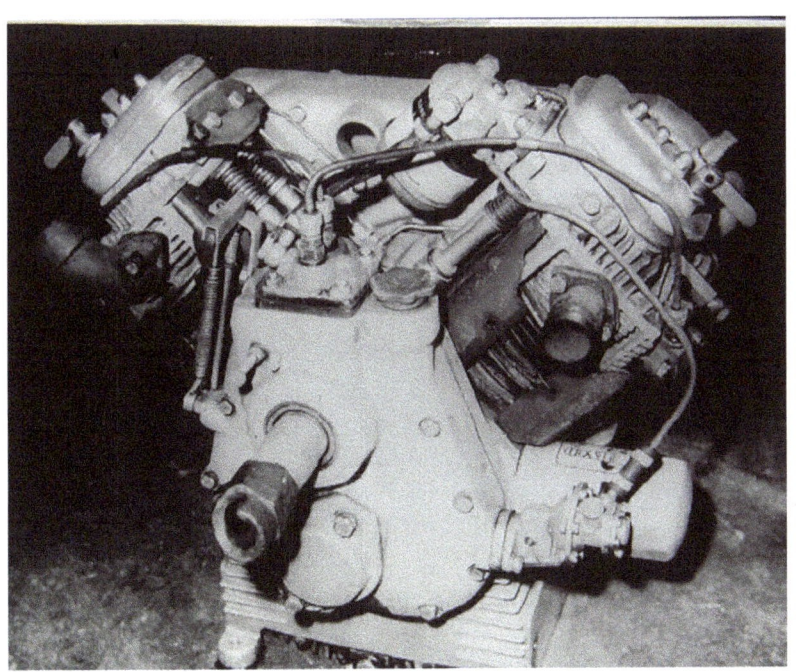

The 10HP 3000 rpm vee twin diesel engine Mick, Ian and I designed.

The board of NCL inspects Toowoomba Wheel Product during a site visit. Doug Curlewis MD is on my right.

The 5HP 3000 rpm single cylinder diesel engine–my first design experience.

Early days in the marriage. Doug, Carole, Sheldon and Samantha in joyous times.

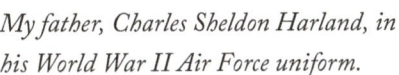

My father, Charles Sheldon Harland, in his World War II Air Force uniform.

The beautiful and vibrant mother I never knew.

This photo illustrates the derelict state of the Foundry. Prior to its rebirth.

Housekeeping on site was a low priority at the Foundry after many years of financial losses and constant management changes.

The same rear-yard area photographed after the transformation. A heritage Southern Cross windmill is on display in the background.

An operator pours molten iron on the Foundry's GF air impact automatic moulding line.

The upgraded front entrance to the factory, rebadged with the new corporate name and logo. It became a prize-wining garden in the Industrial Division of the Toowoomba Carnival of Flowers.

A photograph of the front entrance's sad return to a derelict state after its untimely closure in July 2012, after 141 years of quality manufacture.

Robotic technology installed for machining and assembly was introduced in the year 2000. It was introduced to machine Toowoomba Wheel Products

The machine shop was transformed from a dark and dirty workplace to a naturally lit and clean factory.

The author committing to the Australian Government Voluntary Greenhouse Challenge in 1997 at a ceremony at Parliament House, Canberra.

Foundry employees collecting their Christmas hampers.

Peter Long's monkeys that taught me to delegate.

Employees in their TMT uniform attend a GM briefing.

CHAPTER 10
MUM AND MY MARRIED LIFE

After Dad died in 1966, when I was nineteen, I became someone Mum relied on to do the daily chores around the house, such as shopping and ensuring her wood stove always had chopped wood. My brother managed the major tasks such as house repairs, painting and so on. My sister was married and lived on a farm in the country so she wasn't in a position to assist on a regular basis, apart from occasional weekly visits. While a young boy, my activities with my mother predominantly involved helping her with cooking, shopping and chopping and fetching wood and chips.

Sometime after Dad's death, I decided to break off my relationship with Carole. I really loved her but I decided I was too young. I reasoned that if I stayed in the relationship I'd end up getting married and my dream of racing cars would be finished. A week or so passed after the breakup and I was working in the works study department during my indenture period when a workmate sitting at the desk behind me said, 'Hey Doug, you're looking pretty miserable lately, why don't you go back to Carole, you obviously still love her.'

'If I do I'll end up getting married.'

'So? What's wrong with that?' was his curt reply.

That afternoon I drove to Carole's parents' house. After a tearful start we made up. We restarted our dance and parking routine. On one of those nights Sheldon was conceived. Carole became pregnant so we were married in January 1967.

Initially we stayed with Carole's parents. Then after Sheldon's birth we moved into a flat of our own. My workmates told me that many managers were not giving our marriage any hope of longevity. Carole's parent's Jack and Dulcie were not too pleased either. We stayed together for forty-nine years before we separated so I guess that prediction had no substance.

We had little money so it was a bit of a struggle financially, but we were happy. I imagined that one day I'd be able to race cars again.

Sheldon was born in July 1967 when we were still living with Carole's parents. I was with Carole in the local mother's hospital when her labour pains started to intensify. She grabbed my tie and pulled it so hard I nearly choked. Just then the head nurse appeared.

'You can't stay here any longer; you must go while we attend to her, the baby will be here soon,' she said.

Carole was in heavy labour for over ten hours. I spent the time waiting with Carole's parents.

When the hospital rang at 10pm to let me know I had a new son, my mother-in- law's reaction shocked me.

'No point in going to the hospital now, it's late. We'll all go over in the morning.'

At the time I was obedient to my elders irrespective of what I was feeling and left it to the morning before I saw Carole and Sheldon. Carole was extremely disappointed, I was sad and angry but said nothing. We stayed at Carole's parents' house for a few months while we searched for affordable accommodation. Then we moved into an old flat in the city.

Our first flat was extremely rundown and in need of many repairs, so in exchange for a couple of months' rent I tidied the yard, planted gardens and did up the inside. I completed much-needed repairs and closed in an open veranda, while Carole used her creativity to dye old carpets, sew and fit curtains and home furnishings. It became a pleasant place to live. The landlord, a retired headmaster, came around after I had completed the upgrade.

'You've transformed the place, it looks great. I'll make a list of jobs I need done so you can start on them,' he said, with a surprised look on his face.

I was shocked and politely said words to the effect of, 'I'll not be doing any more work; I was just making the place presentable. I'm now going to focus on my family and engineering studies.'

He mumbled something as he left disappointed. *Greedy prick* shot through my mind.

Samantha's birth in July 1970 was a surprise; I rang Carole from work at about 11.40am, just before lunch.

'Is anything happening?'

'Not a thing, come up and have lunch with me,' she replied.

I arrived at about 12.15pm to find Carole sitting up in her hospital bed with a beaming smile.

'We have a beautiful daughter,' she said.

'Oh yeah,' was my cynical reply.

'No, really, she just popped out.'

That was Samantha. To this day she still does everything fast and efficiently.

During winter I'd drop in to Mum's house each day and light her fire on my way to work at the Foundry. I remember one winter morning after I had fulfilled the ritual; I received an urgent phone call from her at work that the house was full of smoke. My fire had gone out because I had failed to open the draft slide in the wood stove. The wood continued to smoulder and filled the house with smoke. She took it in good humour. Most days I'd also drop in on the way home from work. One evening, when she was in bed, I dropped in on my way home from night school to deliver something. I soon realised how frightened she was. I heard her in bed, praying aloud and intensely. I could almost feel her fear.

I wish I could help her . . . she's so scared and lonely.

Mum never wore her hearing aid to bed, so she didn't know I visited until the next morning after finding the package I'd left. I wanted to comfort her, but I didn't know how. The lack of permission to express feelings was so well entrenched in our family. I often left her house feeling sad and impotent.

One day, a year or so before she died, I visited her after work. I walked in to find her weeping quietly at the kitchen table with her head in her folded hands, swollen and deformed from rheumatoid arthritis. With her grey hair falling over her face she looked so frail. She used to wear a woollen cardigan open at the front over a floral dress. I now regret that all I could do was sit opposite her and look empathetic. I felt helpless.

I don't know what you want me to do.

She calmed herself, looked at me with sad eyes, stood up and made a cup of tea while talking about incidental things. Again, I always felt impotent at these times. The only way I could show my love for her was by visiting her every morning and afternoon and doing her jobs – a hug wasn't in my thinking.

It was about this time a local university was built in Toowoomba, the Darling Downs Institute of Advanced Education (DDIAE). Part-time engineering courses were being offered so I stopped my diploma studies at a local technical college and enrolled in a part-time degree course in mechanical engineering. While many of the subjects I did were accredited to the first year of degree studies, I had to repeat my maths and electrical subjects, which didn't please me. It was a period I regard as character building. Over three nights each week I was attending three-hour lectures. To earn extra money to build our house, I was drawing house plans each night for local builders, often to the early hours of the morning. Finding time to study was difficult.

We purchased a block of land. I drew up plans for the house and, with funding from a local bank, my brother Graham was contracted to build it. We sold the Sprite to assist funding and I bought a cheap old second-hand Ford Anglia from a workmate. It had a larger motor and Cortina front disc brakes fitted. It was christened 'The Green Bean' because of its hand-painted green paint job. It was the most demanding period of my life.

I dug trenches and built retaining walls. Carole and I moved piles of dirt and planted couch lawn runners taken from a patch in her parents' yard. The house had no floor or window coverings, was unpainted and a few areas remained unfinished when the money ran out. Each weekend I worked from daylight to dusk, getting blistered hands on Saturday. On Sunday the blisters often burst when I dug trenches, moved dirt and completed the never-ending list of tasks. Carole focussed on tidying up inside and painted concrete floors, dyed old second-hand rugs, hung temporary curtains and used her creativity to make the interior a welcoming home. Sheldon rode his bike over the mounds of dirt with a group of neighbourhood kids, and Samantha tagged along with him. The house was often full of kids having fun. I cherish those times. I was very happy but close to exhaustion.

I was completely unaware that Carole was having an affair with a close friend and neighbour.

Once we'd settled into the house we decided the children needed a spiritual foundation to guide their lives. We enrolled them in a local Presbyterian Sunday school. I volunteered and as I mentioned earlier, started teaching each Sunday. I did this for two years.

Sheldon and Samantha completed their primary school studies in the new, controversial, open-plan Gabbinbar Primary School that opened in 1972. Sheldon enrolled in 1973 when the school was still embroiled in controversy, and Samantha in 1976, one year before I was awarded a one year industrial scholarship in the UK by the Confederation of British Industry (CBI). Students were taught to think rather than learn parrot fashion and had the freedom to sit where they chose and leave the classroom to go to the toilet without asking permission. Some community religious leaders saw it as an undisciplined place where kids could do what they like.

Carole and I were welcomed and attended many classes to ensure the rumours weren't true. We only found happy children working in a very responsible manner, enjoying this new method of teaching. One Toowoomba minister actually preached to his congregation about the decadence of the school, which he had never visited. He was shocked when Gabbinbar's headmaster, a lay preacher himself, stood up in the middle of his tirade sermon and brought him to account. He had heard of the minister's criticisms to his congregation through a church member.

This gave both Sheldon and Samantha a great ability to tackle issues from first principles. I'm often in awe of how they work out solutions very logically, innovatively and comprehensively, a trait that allowed both to advance well in their careers. Gabbinbar certainly played a role in this. Sheldon was more casual and relaxed at his studies while Samantha was very committed to study and always had better results. In 1981, Sheldon started at Centenary Heights High School and worked part-time at a supermarket to earn spending money. Just before he turned seventeen, when he was eligible for his car licence, he came to me one day.

'Dad, would you drive me to look at an HR Holden car I want to buy, and see if it's okay? I've saved up enough money. It's really cool, it's got mag wheels. It's really hotted up.'

I drove him to the address and we walked up the driveway to see the new car of his dreams.

'Looks good Sheldon, but it's a bit rough. It's really good value with a lot of great mods on it. With a bit of work I'm sure we could make it a great car.'

I gave it my tick of approval. While it was heavily modified, the workmanship was poor.

Sheldon and I then spent each weekend and some nights over a couple of months stripping the car and rebuilding the many performance modifications to a high standard and giving it a new paint job. He drove it to school after getting his licence and all the students were so impressed that the teacher had him do a show and tell on the car and its rebuild. He was proud of that.

During his childhood, Sheldon always had a fetish for rocks. No matter where we visited he'd have a sample rock in his hand and had a small collection at home. When he started a Bachelor in Applied Science (Geology) at the local university in 1985, Carole and I were pleased Sheldon had found his passion. It wasn't to be. He had only completed one semester when he came home one afternoon and told Carole he was no longer interested in geology and would do engineering instead. He said to me in the garage one afternoon, 'Picking up rocks is as boring as shit Dad, I rather do engineering.'

Six months passed and Carole and I became alarmed when he told us he'd drop out because he wasn't enjoying his studies. He was still packing shelves at a local Kmart. As the weeks went by I was getting concerned about his future until one day he came home and said to Carole and me, 'I've got a job at Defiance Flour Mill. I'm going to be a flour milling technologist.'

We were relieved and he went on to be highly regarded in the industry. He had an open nature and I saw that he had zero judgement of people in him. He was able to offer an appraisal of a person's unusual behaviours, but there was never a sense of judgement. I'm sure it was a reason why he attracted a diverse range of friends during his life. He also had the support of people working under him.

Samantha went through high school pretty seamlessly and always came home with glowing reports. She also worked as a 'checkout chick', as Sheldon used to call her, at a local supermarket and later started coaching kids in mathematics. Her interests were ballet and, for a while, swimming. Carole taught her how to sew, but she practiced ballet tirelessly to prepare herself for Royal Academy of Dance (RAD) exams. Carole became heavily involved with the ballet group because she'd design all the costumes for the annual breakup recital at a local theatre.

Her activity would start in January, deciding materials for outfits. Then she would do research and sketch costumes to the various themes set for the concert by the principal and her staff. The house took on the appearance of a clothing shop over a period of nine months. Her designs were always popular and her comprehensively documented sewing instructions were a labour of love. Her mother, Dulcie, never complemented Carole on her unique and beautiful designs. She just looked for a tiny flaw to comment on. It saddened me. Dulcie also had an issue with her brother when they were young and didn't speak to him for forty years.

Samantha advanced through her ballet exams and was ready to undertake her RAD intermediate examination. I'd drive her to Brisbane each week for additional high- level classes in preparation for her upcoming exam. I came to understand she'd have liked to dance professionally because she loved ballet. She was shattered when she didn't pass due to a short Achilles tendon limiting her style. She recovered from the disappointment and went into more intensive practice to have a second try at the exam. Again she failed due to the short Achilles tendon. But this time I was very proud of her when she said philosophically, 'It's obviously not meant to be, I gave it my best shot but I can't do much about my short Achilles tendon. It's disappointing but that's as far as I can go.'

Samantha decided she wanted to be a civil engineer and started engineering studies at a local university in 1998. She graduated with good marks, and spent twelve months applying for jobs with no success. She continued working at the supermarket while doing tutorials for students but I could see she was losing optimism about her future employment prospects. So one day I went to her and said, 'Samantha, if you like, I'll drive you to Brisbane and spend the day dropping you off at the door of various civil engineering companies. Dress nicely and you can cold call on them with your resume. I won't attend. You present well and it'll be up to you.'

'That'd be good Dad.'

The next week I dropped her off at several companies and was saddened to see her reappear in minutes. I then parked outside Sinclair Knight Mertz's (SKM) building and wished her luck once more. An hour passed with no sign of Samantha. About fifteen minutes later a smiling Samantha came out.

'I didn't get a job because they want someone with more experience, but they said I had potential. They're going to keep me on their records if a future opportunity comes up. They seemed like very nice people.'

She returned to her part-time jobs and refused to consider applying for a government allowance, for which she was eligible. I was regional chair of the local branch of Engineers Australia at the time, and the secretary, Lex, was a friend. He was the manager of SKM Toowoomba. A month or two passed and one day the phone rang in my office.

'Hi Doug, it's Lex, you wouldn't know of any young talented girls looking for a civil engineering job in town would you?'

'Why yes, in a matter of fact I do,' I said. We both laughed.

'When could she start? Get her to pop in and see me,' was Lex's response.

Samantha performed really well. At the SKM Christmas function that Lex invited me to, Samantha was engaged in conversation with the Brisbane manager of SKM. I was talking to Lex over a beer.

'Samantha is the only one who brings all her projects in on time and within budget, I'm concerned the Brisbane office will try and poach her from me.'

'No, don't worry about that Lex, she loves working with you,' were my erroneous words. At the very same moment Samantha was being offered a pay rise and a job in Brisbane by the Brisbane manager.

On several nights Samantha didn't come home because she worked an 'all- nighter' to bring her projects in on schedule. I was proud of her professional commitment and her passion for excellence. She moved to Brisbane a short time later and bought a two- bedroom unit, christened 'the hobbit house' by Sheldon, where she still lives today. Samantha resigned from SKM to get broader experience in spite of their efforts to retain her. She worked for Brisbane Water Corporation as the environmental engineer on a major new sewerage tunnel three metres in diameter and six kilometres long under the Brisbane CBD.

It was during this time she again filled my heart with pride. A close friend of Samantha's was very sick and hospitalised and concerned the mortgage payments on a house couldn't be met. Samantha simply paid them. It was a gift lasting many months until her friend was able to work once more.

Samantha was skilled at sizing sewerage mains and taught many clients how to use the software so they didn't depend on her. So many software items were sold that the company offered her an agency to sell the software.

'How can I recommend software impartially to a client if I'm making a commission on the sale?' Her generosity of spirit and her integrity make me very proud. Around this time Samantha also started her weekly healings and meditation at Maryann's Inner Energy Centre.

This all happened at a point in my career when I was to be promoted to chief tooling engineer. I was then progressively promoted to chief tooling and process engineer, and then manufacturing systems development manager in 1987 following The Pope and Maryann's visit. It was during this time at the Foundry that I was backing out the BMW down our long narrow driveway, heading to a professional dinner, when I heard a sickening crunch.

'What was that?' Carole asked with alarm.

'Oh no! I think I've run over Yassie,' I yelled with dread in my voice. Yassie was my favourite, and much loved, light grey Persian cat.

I jumped out the car to see her struggling to run to the front garden. I raced after her. 'Yassie,' I called when she slowed and collapsed on the path. I picked her up gently in my arms as she gave a soft meow, looked at me and passed away. I was holding her front and rear parts and cradling her, but when her soul left her body it went to jelly. I was struggling to stop her falling to the ground as she just kept sliding away from my hands because the 'beam' strength was no longer present. Sometime later, Yassie's male kitten Sasha contracted a mouth cancer and had to be put down. I took him to the vet and lay him on the stainless steel table, while holding him as I'd held Yassie. After the vet gave the injection and Sasha passed away I went to pick him up the same way I had placed him on the table to take him home. I couldn't support him, because again, the beam strength wasn't there once the soul had gone and he was a floppy bundle difficult to hold. I learnt from these experiences that the soul provides structural strength to the body when present.

On May 24th 1975 I graduated with a degree in Mechanical Engineering. I remember the disbelief at finally completing the eight-year-long part-time journey. It felt as though a huge load had been lifted from my shoulders. My studies were drawn out because I started with a diploma course, then when I changed to the degree studies I had to repeat subjects. I almost threw my studies in when I failed my repeated electrical engineering subjects. One lecturer had such a foreign accent we couldn't understand him, and the other was obviously brilliant but we couldn't rise to his level of thinking. The only reason I stayed with the studies was that nearly the whole class failed, even smart students working in the electrical profession. I was deeply saddened to learn one of those lecturers took his own life, obviously frustrated that he wasn't cutting through to students. The next year a technician taught us. I passed both subjects with a credit.

While I was building the house, I reduced my subjects to two a week. When the house was liveable,

I increased my subjects to four a week. The last two years were very demanding. Studying four subjects a week, some at night classes, drawing house plans at night for builders to earn extra money kept me busy. In addition, completing house projects, building a garage and rebuilding a damaged new car I bought cheaply from a finance company took quite a toll. I was exhausted at the end of my last year of study in 1975. I graduated in early 1976. Samantha was five and Sheldon eight years old. We arranged a holiday at the Gold Coast with our neighbours, sharing a beachside unit.

On our arrival, we unpacked and I needed to lie down. I was feeling exhausted in a way that I had never felt before. I mostly ended up lying in bed as though in a stupor for the first week of our three-week holiday, except when we took Sheldon and Samantha to the beach for a swim. Carole expected me to be relieved and happy. She couldn't understand the physical impact made by the previous year's effort.

This experience taught me never to give up, because digging trenches for retaining walls, moving dirt piles with modest equipment and laying bricks from daylight to dark, with seemingly little progress, was a great lesson in humility and perseverance. It also made me appreciate the material gains I made. This helped to contain my ego.

Fatigue had built up. All the long hours I worked, all the effort, were now impacting. The inertia suddenly washed over me and physically bowled me over. Carole started jibing me.

'You should be happy and full of energy; you don't have to study anymore.

Come on get out of bed and let's do something.'

The second week she persuaded me, and the wife of my neighbour, to tour the rainforest with her sister who was staying close by and was planning such a day trip.

'It will do you good to be around nature, you like it and will enjoy it.'

I agreed and said, 'Are you coming?'

'No I want to finish my book,' replied Carole.

She wasn't reading her book. She was alone with my neighbour who also had a 'book to read'.

We returned home and a couple of times a week Carole said she needed the car – so my neighbour drove me to work. He worked at the Foundry also. I remained blissfully unaware that he was 'going home for lunch'. I started to feel uncomfortable with Carole and my neighbour's relationship, most likely because it was increasing in intensity. One night the reality of what was going on finally struck me and I confronted

Carole about it. She admitted it and my life was shattered in an instant. I was numb; I didn't go to work. I was struggling to comprehend and absorb what I had just learnt. Carole moved to her sister's place for a while. The day after Carole moved out, while at home, I heard a scream and a distraught cry from the neighbour's house. I ran over to see what was happening.

I found the neighbour's wife on her hands and knees on the hallway floor vomiting violently and sobbing. Beside her was an empty bottle of sleeping pills so I put her in the car and drove her to the emergency department at the local hospital. I rang her husband at work.

'You better get your arse to the base hospital because your wife has just tried to commit suicide. I'll meet you at the carpark and take you to her.'

He arrived, ashen faced. He was most likely scared of seeing me. Grabbing him, I pushed him against a wall and pinned him by his collar ready to punch the daylights out of him. Looking him in the eye, I saw his fear spread across his face and I knew violence served no purpose; I loosened my grip on his collar.

'Go to your wife you fucked up little boy. She needs you. She's in the emergency department.' I walked off to go back to the Foundry, close to tears. I decided I need to get back to work.

'Don't you have a phone?' My boss Mick cheerfully greeted me with this when I walked into the office. I rarely had a day off and Carole or I always rang in with the reason why I'd be away from work. I had an enormous respect for Mick, as mentioned earlier.

'Hello, what's up with you? Hey, come into my office Dougie boy.' He could see the distress on my face.

We sat down and Mick said, 'What's going on, you look like shit.'

I told him what had happened and about my scuffle with my neighbour at the hospital.

'Shit, I'm sorry to hear that. You're a very civilised man. I'd have really worked the prick over. Take as much time off as you need,' he said with a caring voice.

'Thanks, but I need to work to take my mind off it. Hopefully we can sort it out,' I replied and walked to my desk.

I'm hazy on the timeframe, but weeks passed and Carole returned home. A semblance of order returned to our household. But I felt quite raw inside. I decided I'd have to come to trust Carole again but this took some time. I still loved her. Sheldon and Samantha, eight and five at the time, seemed very confused about what was going on. Neither said much while their mother was away. I just told them she was taking a short break. I know now they'd have felt the tension and my anguish even though I tried to hide it from them.

In May 1976, I was awarded a twelve-month industrial scholarship in the UK by the Confederation of British Industry (CBI). This was a positive boost after Carole's affair. It helped me to overcome any negative and distrustful feelings I had toward her. I needed to tell Mum. I was nervous when I entered her kitchen to tell her of my plans. After some small talk I mustered the courage to say, 'Mum, I've won a scholarship to Britain and will be working overseas. I'm taking Carole and the kids with me for twelve months, I leave January next year.' This would be in 1977.

'You've done really well, but who'll do my jobs while you're away?' Mum replied with some alarm. She looked down at the red-patterned Laminex kitchen table top.

'Graham will have to. It's only for twelve months.'

'He's always so busy at work,' she said. I could see her growing concern when she looked me in the eye.

Shit this is hard, but I'm determined to take this great opportunity.

'I'm definitely going. I leave in eight months' time,' I said to ensure it was really clear.

The scholarship only paid about three hundred pounds sterling a month and was totally inadequate to support the family in Britain so I planned to get a bank loan. I was determined to make this opportunity happen. Before visiting the bank I wrote a letter to the works director, Phil Chote, requesting twelve months leave of absence. He called me to his office the next day. As I entered he leant across his desk, shook my hand and with his warm smile said, 'Congratulations, that's a great achievement. There is no problem with the leave, but how are you going to afford to live? You said you're taking your family with you.'

'I'm going to get a bank loan.'

'Don't go to the bank, that's not a good option. Leave it with me. I'll get back to you.' His response filled me with anticipation.

Phil was much respected by all employees due to his warm personality, his authenticity and fairness.

About a week later he called me to his office again.

'I've spoken to the board. If you give me a commitment to stay with us for three years we'll continue to pay your salary for the twelve months,' he said with a beaming smile.

I agreed enthusiastically. It was sealed with a handshake. I could see there would be no financial pressure during the year.

Mum became ill before we left and passed away in August 1976. My sister Daphne said she was just making it easy for me. Mum died alone in hospital one night after I had visited her. I often felt this was reflective of her life in many ways. I never felt guilt about my decision to go abroad.

A year working in Britain was going to be a once-in-a-lifetime experience and a great boost to my career. It was also an opportunity for Carole and the children to broaden their horizons. But I'll have to go back in time to describe our year in the UK because it happened ten years before my spiritual experience in 1987. While the trip came long before my spiritual experience, it boosted my professional confidence and self-esteem and laid the groundwork for my future leadership roles. It also showed me the Foundry could be world-leading. Later in life I reflected it was another major step spirit was leading me through in preparation for my future leadership role at the Foundry.

CHAPTER 11
UK SCHOLARSHIP YEAR

Having made his daughter pregnant in late 1966, I was initially not that popular with my father-in-law, Jack Prentice. Yet, over time he gave me great mechanical guidance, particularly when I rebuilt my Austin Healy Sprite and a near-new, but damaged, Morris 1500 to a high standard. A bond of mutual respect developed, which I appreciated greatly. He was a self-taught mechanic and could repair or build anything. He helped me lay and tie the reinforcing rods in the foundation of our house and made toys and items for our kids. The kids remembered him as a bit grumpy. He eventually died of cancer so he was only available to me for eight years. I remember during a bedside vigil with him in hospital when he was close to death in March 1975, my mother-in-law, Dulcie, was sitting on a lounge chair down the hallway continually wailing. She wouldn't visit his bedside.

'I can't see him like this! I don't want to remember him like this,' she repeated as she sobbed.

'Who the bloody hell is dying here?' the night nurse exclaimed in anger when she entered the room and saw me holding Jack's hand while his wife wailed down the hall. I just shook my head. I said nothing.

I was holding his hand because he was unconscious. I'll never forget the look on his face when he momentarily regained consciousness and was shocked to see his son- in-law at his bedside holding his hand. He quickly pulled his hand away. I felt sad that his wife wasn't beside him and also that the social conditioning in his time frowned on men holding hands.

Jack passed away on Easter Sunday, in 1975, a year before my mother's death. It was the following year that I received the letter informing me I'd been awarded the CBI Industrial Scholarship, so I agreed that Carole's mother Dulcie could accompany us. She was still dealing with Jack's passing. I was excited by the prospect of spending twelve months with the family in the UK without any financial concerns.

On February 2nd 1977, at age thirty, ten years before my life change at forty, I landed at Heathrow alone and set off to find my accommodation at the Apollo Hotel arranged by CBI and get settled before the family and Dulcie arrived. It was my first overseas flight. It took an exhausting thirty-one hours to reach Heathrow after four long stopovers.

As this was long before the spiritual experience I had in 1987, I wasn't applying spiritual knowledge to my observations of the foundries I visited and my work experiences. But I already had an interest in and recognised intuitive knowledge when I saw it being used during the trip.

The family was travelling by sea on the Russian ship, *Turkmenia*, to Singapore then flying to London via Karachi and Istanbul. Their Istanbul stopover was unplanned but necessary for refuelling after the plane flew in strong headwinds.

During my own flight, at Kuala Lumpur, the next stop after Singapore, I changed planes from a 707 to a jumbo. It was the first time I'd seen a jumbo jet. I was thrilled at the prospect of flying in it to London via Frankfurt. I was amazed at its size and height. I counted twenty-five steps as I climbed the runway staircase to board it. I arrived at Heathrow in the morning and was excited to have the jumbo pull into the terminal beside a Concorde jet. The Concorde had only been flying commercially for a year and seeing it was a real treat. It had its maiden flight to New York in October of my scholarship year. I was like a sponge soaking up all these new experiences. I caught a train to my hotel in London. It was a wet and miserable day

'It sure is a bleak day out there,' I said to a nearby passenger as I stood on the crowded train.

I was surprised when fellow commuters gave me funny looks. Some even moved away slightly and no-one said anything.

Bloody hell, things are certainly different in big cities, and not very friendly.

Talking on public transport is a no no apparently.

I checked into the Apollo Hotel on Queensborough Terrace and immediately went sightseeing. It was my first overseas trip and I found it really exciting to be in London. The next day I attended a lunch after a briefing and orientation session with representatives of the Confederation of British Industry in a very quaint restaurant close to Westminster Abbey. I was very nervous. When I started my meal I had an embarrassing moment. My right hand was shaking uncontrollably when I spooned my soup. It also shook when I ate breakfast at the hotel that morning. It had never happened before.

'It must be the jetlag from my long flight,' I explained. I'm sure the CBI people had the same view because they nodded silently in agreement. However, it has repeatedly returned over the years and still remains part of me. It's been diagnosed as a hereditary benign tremor usually set off by nervous tension.

After lunch I went through an afternoon of briefings and at the end of the day a couple of staff members involved in the discussions took me to The Feathers pub for dinner.

I enjoyed my first English lager with a steak and kidney pie. I loved the extensive use of English oak throughout the pub because it gave it a very homely ambience. On the fourth day in London, after much sightseeing I took an English cab to Paddington Station where I caught the InterCity 125 (125mph) train to Bridgend, Wales and was met by Maynard, who was from North Wales. Maynard took me straight to the Borg Warner Kenfig plant. I was having great difficulty understanding his heavy accent.

I momentarily panicked.

Shit, I'm not going to be able to understand these people. I became alarmed at the prospect.

Thankfully, all the people I was introduced to in the plant were from South Wales and were easily understood. I fell in love with the singing accent of the southern Welsh people as the family also did when they arrived. After a long induction session and comprehensive plant tour I was sent to the head of HR. My reserved nature resulted in me feeling a bit overwhelmed. I answered his many questions when he exclaimed quite aggressively, 'You'd better liven up lad if you want to stay here. You need to shape up and show a bit more initiative. You'll be wasting my time and yours otherwise. You don't seem very motivated.'

I was shocked by this confrontation on my first day.

'I'll do my best,' I said quietly when I left the room.

I walked to the training department feeling confused and thinking, *I'm not sure I'm up to this.* I told Cyril the training manager what had transpired and he reassured me when he said, 'He's an arsehole, take no notice of him, he's always like that. You'll be fine. You're going through a big adjustment.'

I sometimes look back on my many fears that materialised as I coped with the adjustment to my new surroundings, people and culture. I reflect how much easier it would have been if it happened after my spiritual experience. I was still quite a fearful person at the time and repeatedly pushed myself through the fear. This often resulted in constant feelings of anxiety.

I initially worked as a supplier quality assurance engineer (SQA), then as the troubleshooting engineer on the assembly line, and as a road test engineer; I enjoyed the latter responsibility the most. The factory was relatively new, and very modern. It was Borg Warner's Automatic Transmission Plant at Kenfig, South Wales, where I worked for five months. A total of 250 Volvo, Saab and Hillman automatic transmissions were produced daily. Everyone in the plant was very friendly and supportive, and very different to the HR manager who admonished me. This eventually allowed me to relax and find more enjoyment in the many new responsibilities I experienced.

I settled in quickly and Maynard was put at my disposal to drive me to help me sort out accommodation, set up banking and register with a local doctor. The exchange rate was extremely favourable at the time. With the small contribution provided by the scholarship, it meant we were in a strong financial position during our stay in Britain.

I came to like Maynard very much. He was a gentle man with a kind, weathered face and he usually wore a tweed jacket. He was always willing to help, whatever the task he was given. He drove the Volvo station wagon extremely competently. We ended up doing many miles together.

I was driven to the Letchworth Research and Development Centre in Hertfordshire and toured the Jaguar and Rover transmission production facilities. I was introduced to American executives on site, the chief design engineer Mike, and immediately decided I'd ask if I could be transferred to the R&D centre later in the year. The initial scholarship award was for me to work at Kenfig for the twelve months. Walking through the designs office and hearing the engines growling and revving in the glass-walled dynamometer rooms while they cycled through simulated road conditions on the dyno made my hair stand on end. I was stoked.

This isn't work, it's fun. I need to spend time here.

An employee and his wife put me up in Porthcawl until I could find family accommodation. It was two and a half weeks later, on Friday 25th February, that the family arrived by plane. On Thursday 24th February I was given the keys to a very comfortable holiday house, owned by a doctor, in Porthcawl in Rest Bay Close on the common overlooking the Bristol Channel and Rest Bay Beach.

It had taken some time and documentation to convince the real estate agent that we were intending to return to Australia and not planning to become squatters in this luxury house, in a street sporting a Rolls Royce, Jaguars and Ferraris.

I went grocery shopping, stocked up the house and fridge, and bought a large bunch of colourful tulips and daffodils for the kitchen table. I wrapped gifts for everyone and my excitement grew at the prospect of the family arriving.

How good this is! What a life, just waiting for my chauffeur-driven Volvo in this great warm home on the Bristol Channel to take me to the family!

I sat there waiting, full of anticipation. At 11.10pm Maynard arrived in the Volvo wagon to drive me to London's Gatwick Airport.

'Are you ready to meet your family?' He greeted me with a warm smile.

'I sure am, let's get this show on the road.'

We arrived at Gatwick at 3am on Friday February 25th, an hour before the scheduled arrival time, to find the flight was delayed and rescheduled to land at 6.40am. We sat in the Volvo and generally froze. We had the occasional coffee from a thermos Maynard had thoughtfully provided. When it was too cold for even Maynard he ran the engine for a while. Maynard drove into the airport close to landing time. We learnt Heathrow and Gatwick were both closed due to fog. The plane had just tried to land at Stansted but the pilot aborted it close to ground. He apparently missed the runway due to heavy fog and was rerouted to Paisley. We raced over to Stansted only to learn of the aborted landing and its redirection to Scotland. We were told some passengers would be bussed to London but no further details were available. At 9.30am we received new advice that passengers were on a British Airways Trident flight that would now land at Heathrow, so off we went again.

At 10.40am Saturday I finally met a very tired but smiling family.

'Welcome to England!'

There were hugs, smiles and laughing all round. It was great to see Carole and the children again. At

Maynard's suggestion, he and I had decided to trick the family. He drove up to the smallest and oldest house he could find when we arrived in Porthcawl. As he slowed almost to a stop beside it, everyone looked at the old house sitting alone in an overgrown area with great curiosity.

'This is where we're going to live for the twelve months, we just have to go to the owner's place and get the key. It's a bit run down and small but it'll be fine,' I said.

All chattering stopped and complete silence filled the Volvo when we drove to the doctor's house. Maynard gave me a wink and a smile as he saw our treachery working. Carole and her mother were obviously not impressed but knew they could do little about it, as the total lack of conversation confirmed.

'This is a nice house,' Carole said, breaking the sombre mood when we pulled into the driveway of the doctor's house.

'We tricked you! This is really where we're going to live. Isn't it great!'

Everyone roared with laughter and Maynard regarded it a triumph. He couldn't believe how lucky we were to get the house on the coast and couldn't stop talking about our masterful treachery.

'You little buggers! You'd totally tricked us. This is wonderful,' Carole chimed in happily.

'I was thinking how in the hell were we all goin' to fit in that bloody tiny and dirty place!' Dulcie proclaimed while laughing loudly.

Sheldon and Samantha both came alive with excitement. I had the boiler on low heat and the family had a warm and welcoming home greet them on arrival. Everyone unpacked, settled in, had lunch and went to bed early in the evening after a bowl of hot soup feeling great. The family, as I did, fell in love with Wales and its people shortly after their arrival.

The Welsh people in the neighbourhood and in the village were all so helpful and supportive. The time spent in Wales was extremely enjoyable as we toured virtually every weekend in a second-hand Ford Cortina we purchased. I used a Volvo company car on one trip and the garage people couldn't believe the mileage on its return.

One lab technician said, 'I dunno what you bloody Australians get up to, I've never seen so many miles put on a car during a weekend!'

The children loved the open-plan West Park Primary School at Porthcawl and made lots of new friends. Sheldon was called 'kangaroo boy' and 'blue' regularly, a reference to his Aussie origins. Samantha and Sheldon won the hearts of their teachers and I think their Aussie accent played a major role. Carole and I were a little apprehensive and wondering how Sheldon and Samantha would adapt to a new school in a foreign country. Both made friends quickly and were doing well at school and seemed to be really enjoying the experience. We all adored the wild daffodils, foxglove plants, and the gorse that were in full yellow bloom all over Wales in March, the countryside was a picture. We were six weeks in Porthcawl before it stopped drizzling rain!

The Borg Warner factory was surrounded by blooming daffodils and that too was an impressive sight. I was immersed in my time in the factory and I was learning heaps. One day I passed by an experienced assembly employee charged with checking Volvo transmissions just before they went into the shipping box bound for Sweden. He'd turn the Volvo 'tranny' over by hand and if it didn't feel right he'd reject it. He didn't reject many but each one he did proved to have a fault. Later in life, after the experience, I came to understand the power of our feelings. The test dyno had monitors and data printouts on many parameters. It represented the quantitative and intellect- based decisions. This final check represented the elusive qualitative and intuitive decision, the gift of one's experienced soul, I'd come to learn.

One day I was learning to operate a computerised coordinate measuring machine checking a transmission main case as an audit. I browsed through the metallurgy files in the room while it was performing the lengthy check. I was amazed to see a folder headed 'Toowoomba Foundry' and quickly pulled it out and started reading it. I was chuffed to find the Foundry's castings were being used as benchmarks for their British suppliers. One letter to a supplier said, 'This is the casting quality we need you to aim for.' The metallurgist then pulled out casting samples from Toowoomba to show me.

That night I posted a letter to the works director at the Foundry and word quickly spread amongst all employees. I was told later it was a real morale boost.

Shortly after, I was working as an SQA engineer and visited a foundry in the heart of Birmingham about a porosity problem in a casting they supplied. I was with the senior SQA engineer and on arrival we met the site manager at the entrance and introductions started.

'This is Doug Harland, he's from Australia and is gaining experience at BW,' the SQA engineer offered. 'What part?' the manager asked me.

'Queensland,' I replied while thinking, *He wouldn't have a bloody clue about Queensland*. But he said, 'I don't suppose you know Toowoomba Foundry?'

I gave a huge grin. 'No way,' I said. 'That's where I'm from.'

'No kidding! You guys make the best castings in the world!'

I was gobsmacked; I was standing in a suburb with about fifteen foundries within walking distance. They all knew and had high regard for Toowoomba's product.

Here I am where the Industrial Revolution started and our small foundry in Toowoomba is the industry's quality benchmark. How good is that?

It was a great boost to my confidence. I was then treated like royalty and with much respect, much to the amazement of the SQA engineer.

We were able to tour extensively while in South Wales: Wales, England, Ireland, Scotland and Europe. Europe was the only tour where we left the children behind in Dulcie's care. They loved all the new sights in the UK and I really relished driving on the very scenic windy and narrow roads. I remember our first summer day when we woke to bright sunshine outdoors. Thinking it would be like Australia I said to Sheldon and Samantha, who were both dressed in t-shirts and shorts in the heated house, 'It's finally summer! Let's go for a walk along the common and then go down to the beach.'

Full of excitement we all ran out into the backyard only to do a quick U-turn and come back inside out of the freezing cold.

'It's bloody freezing,' I yelled while the children ran ahead of me laughing.

We all rugged up in winter clothing and went for our walk. The kids loved playing on the rocks lining the beach. They often played outside in the twilight until 10pm at night.

When I was posted, at my request, to Borg Warner's R&D centre in Letchworth, north of London, it was with some sadness we left Wales and the friends we'd made. The Plant Manager of the Kenfig Plant called me to his office on my final day.

'Congratulations on what you've achieved,' he said when I entered. 'I'm impressed by your ability to competently adapt to the many tasks that were allocated to you. It's a credit to the great training you obviously had at the Foundry. All the best for the future and I'm sure you'll enjoy your time at the Letchworth plant.'

'Thanks. The people have been great. I've thoroughly enjoyed the experience and have learnt a lot. I appreciate all the support I've been given,' I said. I shook his hand. I said goodbye to all the great staff I had worked with and left.

Carole and I then spent just over two weeks touring Europe. It was a carefree and enjoyable time before we moved to England. It was the first time we travelled without Sheldon and Samantha. After our European tour I boarded with an English family in Howard Drive, Letchworth, the sister of an engineer at Kenfig that I worked with. He remains a friend and regular sender of many emails today. I lived with them for about a week in their house close to the plant before I organised a suitable house.

For the next four months we settled into a small semi-detached house in Biggleswade, Bedfordshire. It wasn't quite the quality of our house in South Wales but it was comfortable. I worked as a product development engineer at the Borg Warner Research and Development centre, and a part of the manufacturing plant, producing Jaguar, Rover and other transmissions mentioned earlier. It was a strange coincidence that the previous tenants that had just moved out were also from Toowoomba and lived just around the corner from our Toowoomba house. We soon made friends with the neighbours and Sheldon and Samantha found new playmates. I thought Sheldon was often the leader in making the new acquaintances but found out he would send Samantha to make the introductions..

In July, Carole and I attended a CBI scholar reunion dinner in London at the luxurious Connaught Hotel in Mayfair. It was a memorable night because all the scholars from around the world gathered with partners for a grand dinner. Carole and me were met by a traditionally dressed 'greeter' on arrival who ushered us to the entry of the huge and highly ornate dining hall filled with people. To our surprise he announced in a resonating and loud voice as we entered.

'Mr and Mrs Harland from Australia!'

'Crikey, how's that for an entrance? I feel like bloody royalty!' I whispered to Carole.

She was obviously chuffed with the formality of the occasion and had a wide smile while we were guided to our beautifully decorated table. We went to the Empire Disco afterwards with three other

Australian and nineteen Latin American scholars. It was a very memorable night that left us with eighty pence and exhaustion. We approached a taxi.

'We only have eighty pence, how far will that get us to College Hall?'

'It'll get ya halfway,' the driver replied in his cockney accent.

We walked the rest of the way arm-in-arm, breathing in the cold night air as we wove our way down cold and deserted streets to our accommodation in College Hall at the University of London, before returning to Biggleswade. It was a memorable night.

Sheldon and Samantha went to different schools in Biggleswade and poor Sheldon was unintentionally placed in a very embarrassing situation. The Wales school had casual clothing and we sent him off to his first day at school in Biggleswade in an Aussie orange t-shirt emblazoned with, 'Football, meat pies, kangaroos and Holden cars' without understanding a strict school uniform was required. The t-shirt was the result of a General Motors promotional campaign for the Australian-made Holden car. Somehow that wasn't understood, and Sheldon came home upset and embarrassed. A mad rush ensued to dress him more appropriately. He didn't enjoy school at Biggleswade. Samantha just went about her schooling quietly but happily.

Meanwhile, I was really enjoying my work at the Borg Warner Letchworth centre because I had to configure the best set-up for a lock-up converter, a new innovation at the time in the latest six-cylinder Volvo sedan, to improve performance and fuel efficiency. I also had to determine upgrades required in the Hillman transmission to make it capable of handling a four-cylinder BMW torque and horse power along with a few other small projects. I spent many hours test driving the Volvo during fuel consumption trials at the Motor Industry Research Association (MIRA) test track at Nuneaton near Birmingham, and felt very much at home with high-speed driving around the banked speed track. Speed was limited to one-hundred-miles-per- hour during the day and was unlimited at night or on special days.

'Have ya scored a hundred-mile-an-hour lap yet?' one of the technicians asked me.

'Is it okay to do it? You'd have to exceed one hundred on the straights to get an average of a hundred,' I replied.

'Go for it. You don't come all this way not to try. No one notices your speed on the straights' he said encouragingly.

Off I went with pedal to the metal and on my third lap I achieved my one- hundred-mile-an-hour lap average. It didn't seem like work at all because I was enjoying it so much.

It was also exciting to have Derek Gardner, the designer of the six-wheel Elf Tyrell Formula One racing car, become my boss when he was appointed as the director of the design centre while I was there. The scholarship year boosted my professional confidence. I learned that the skills I gained at the Foundry allowed me to work quite competently in the new work environments I was faced with. In fact, it showed me that Australian engineers, working in smaller sized companies, producing lower volumes, were exposed to many different product development and quality problems, and had to be a 'jack of all trades'. It provided valuable experience.

I found that in this high-volume production environment, most engineers were very specialised and highly competent in their area of responsibility and worked at a higher technical level. However, they had a much narrower field of experience as a result.

I'd tried hard to trust, respect and listen to the people on the shop floor during my career. This was strongly reinforced during my stay at Letchworth, when a senior development engineer had a new four-speed, special-build, BMW transmission assembled ready for dynamometer trials. He instructed Eddie, the workshop manager, to urgently run the test. He then headed off to the Nuneaton test track for the day to do tests on another project involving a Jaguar. He left strict instructions that the test must be done that day because the project was at risk of running behind schedule and important. Eddie came to me after the engineer had left and said, 'I've a prototype transmission for an urgent test but it's too tight to run. No one is here to check it, would you come and have a look at it?'

'No problem,' I responded and headed out to the dyno lab. Eddie had the transmission on a bench. I tried to turn it over while moving the gear selector through the four speeds.

'It's way too tight, I wouldn't run it on the dyno as it will seize for sure,' I said while I tried in vain to rotate the main shaft.

Assembling prototype engines at the Foundry taught me that everything assembled correctly must turn freely by hand. After feeling the unusual tightness while rotating the prototype transmission by hand, I authorised Eddie to abort the dyno test. The engineer returned late in the day. He was furious when he learnt the test hadn't been run as directed and instructed Eddie to run it immediately. He stormed through the door into the design office and walked angrily to my desk and said, 'Who in the hell gave you authority to make decisions on my project? You'd no right to interfere. I'm working with a tight schedule. It's none of your business.'

I was about to tell him why I reasoned the test shouldn't proceed when he just turned and angrily stormed back out to the test laboratory. *Good luck dickhead*, I cheekily mused to myself. Ten minutes after the test run commenced that evening, the prototype transmission seized up. It was reduced to scrap metal and the business opportunity was lost. The engineer concerned just moved to the next project making no apology to Eddie or me.

As I mentioned earlier when I described the employee's final check of the Volvo transmission, I came to view such an event as a powerful demonstration of decisions made on intellect alone as opposed to decisions made on an experienced 'gut feel' that is actually spiritually guided and aligned with truth.

I remember reading a library book on a Norwegian cruise ship with Carole when we sailed around Hawaii in 2002. The book was about a 'Mr X' who had a spiritual gift. He took a job as maintenance engineer on a large freighter ship. He apparently ignored the preventative maintenance schedule and each day would walk the ship and simply point out any work required. He was treated sceptically initially. However, the high degree of accuracy in diagnosis and the resultant efficiencies soon fostered support. We all have this intuitive power. It only needs to be reactivated to make life joyful.

Eddie and his team were extremely skilful. They could bring a car into the workshop, remove the transmission and make changes to it and have the car available again for testing in just under an hour. They were a very committed team. It was a privilege to have worked with them. I used to love walking past the many dyno rooms where engines of different makes were cycling the prototype transmissions through all load and road conditions simulated by the programming of the computerised dyno. The bellow of the twelve-cylinder Jaguar engine under a full power cycle used to make the hairs on the back of my neck stand up, as mentioned earlier, which I now believe is simply one's soul stirring. Before my experience I'd relate such hair raising events with fear, now I consider them reassurance from spirit.

I successfully completed both my projects when I received advice from CBI that my late request to work at the Yorkshire Crompton Parkinson Electric motor factory was approved. When I heard of the posting I almost cancelled this option because I was enjoying my R&D work so much, but the training opportunity beckoned and I agreed to move the family to Yorkshire. The day I left, the R&D engineer who admonished me for stopping his BMW transmission dyno test presented me with a prototype valve body from the original Volvo 264 GL prototype transmission I worked on. I treasure it and keep it in my office. I took it as his subtle apology.

During our stay in Biggleswade, Sheldon and I would visit the motor racing at Silverstone and often watch the antique planes fly at the Old Warden Aerodrome not far from where we lived.

We said our goodbyes to our neighbours. It was a cold, foggy and drizzling day when Carole and I drove north with the Cortina's heater on full blast. We made a lunch stop and finally arrived at dusk at our brand new two-storey house at Burley in Wharfdale in October. I can only describe the workmanship on the house as disgusting. I was shocked at the lack of a quality finish throughout the house. I had a high respect for the British tradespeople at Toowoomba Foundry.

After surveying all the faults I said to Carole, 'All the good tradies must have left for Australia.'

A heavy fog enveloped the neighbourhood, but on the following Saturday morning I woke up and was startled because the morning was fog-free.

'There's a bloody mountain in front of us! Who would've imagined that?' I yelled as Carole quickly appeared from under the bedcovers and gave a shriek of laughter. Sheldon and Samantha came running in followed by Dulcie after hearing our shrieks. They couldn't stop talking about the mountain that had suddenly appeared.

Samantha and Sheldon started school and we soon realised Samantha wasn't being accepted at her school. Her nan used to get upset watching her in the school playground that was opposite our house. She was dressed in her winter red tartan coat with a hood and nan christened her 'Little Red Riding Hood'. She was always sitting alone and not participating with any playmates. It was the only time Samantha didn't enjoy her schooling.

I started at the very old Crompton Parkinson electric motor factory, in Guisley, Yorkshire. Its equipment was way outdated and I worked with two industrial engineers from the Hawker Siddeley Aerospace Group to define the cost benefits on a planned capital investment in new CNC (Computer Numerical Controlled) machinery for a planned modernisation program. It mostly involved a time and motion study of existing practices, so an accurate comparison with the new CNC equipment could be made to accurately quantify the benefits and justify any capital investment. My area of responsibility was reviewing the machining of the many electric motor end shields and shafts. A young Scotsman worked the vertical boring machine that drilled and machined the wide range of motor end shields. I introduced myself to him and explained what I was doing. Then, over a couple of weeks, I timed his various operations on the many different-sized end shields. I had been doing it for a few weeks when I was urgently called into the managing director's office. On entering he said, 'Doug, I'm going to move you to the light bulb factory for a while, because the union is threatening to go on strike if you keep timing the Scot. They're accusing us of checking up on him, which is nonsense.'

'That's crazy,' I replied. 'I'll do whatever you say as I'm not here to create problems for you, I just want to learn.'

After a few days I returned to the site and approached the young Scot who I had been monitoring. I stopped beside him and he became highly emotional and sputtered angrily, 'You've been checking up on me and telling management, I know that's how you people work.'

'Matey, if I was checking up on you I would've reported you for taking a newspaper and having a shit for forty minutes each day.'

I then became more conciliatory.

'I'm here to learn and this is an opportunity to modernise this old factory. We simply need to know how much more efficient new CNC machinery would be so the investment can be justified. No one is checking up on anyone.'

He calmed down and didn't say much after that. I was able to resume the study and complete my task. All this time I still carried the idea that, one day, I'd pursue a career in motor racing, and watching racing at Silverstone always brought that feeling back.

We were all keen to see snow for the first time and to date it had eluded us – much to our surprise because we all believed incorrectly it snowed regularly across Britain. Winter descended and my first challenge was de-icing a thickly iced windscreen on days when I drove the car to work. I watched with amusement in the factory carpark when some people tried to access their car with all the locks frozen. Cigarette lighters and matches were lit beside the car lock while they vainly tried to melt the ice. Unknowingly, I had oiled all the locks in Wales during summer because they were so sticky and tight, and this stopped mine from freezing.

'Doug, come 'ere quick,' was my first prompt to see snow. Everyone in the office knew I had never seen snow and were keen to show me. I ran to the window and staff gathered around me to be with the Aussie seeing his first snow. Snow was beginning to fall and I was enthralled. A car approached the rise of a humped bridge over a railway line in view from the window, and it was moving in a strange manner.

Nearing the top of the hump, I was surprised when the car lazily turned sideways and slid down the hill bumping into others coming up. All of the cars were sliding to the bottom of the street.

'Bloody black ice!' someone yelled. 'Better be careful driving home.'

In less than half an hour a salt truck was spraying the road for traction.

It was during this time that Sheldon made me immensely proud of him. One cold Saturday morning in late November I was walking down a lane framed by beautiful old English oaks. It was thick with autumn leaves blowing in the wind. I decided to take Sheldon for a walk to a local village, Menston, to get some fresh air. He was walking in front of me with his thick mop of blond hair blowing in the wind and was neatly dressed in a mustard-coloured woollen pullover Dulcie had knitted for him in Wales, along with brown corduroy pants. He was kicking up leaves with his hands in his pockets and watching them fly away when an old stooped man came slowly walking toward him. He was dressed in a tweed jacket and grey trousers with a grey cap on his head and appeared to be quite forlorn.

Sheldon reached a spot a few feet in front of the man. He looked up directly into his eyes and said in his Aussie accent, 'Good morning sir, it's a beautiful day isn't it.'

The man appeared quite taken aback. I saw his shoulders lift, his eyes light up and he gave a beaming smile and replied, 'Yes it is thanks.' He looked back when he walked past Sheldon.

I wondered, *Where on earth did that come from? You lit that sad man's spirit up.* I walked up to Sheldon after the man smiled at me as he passed. I ruffled his hair with my hand.

'That was very good of you Sheldon.' I too felt lighter in spirit and immensely proud.

In November I was called by CBI and told that my last training day would be the 6th January 1978. Coincidentally, around this time Mum's estate had been finalised and we could afford to fund half of a world cruise on P&O's *Canberra* to return to Australia. It was leaving Southampton in late January. It proved to be six weeks of bliss.

It was so enjoyable that we would've been happy to sail past Sydney and stay on board. We only ever saw light snow during our stay. We were frustrated to learn that the day the *Canberra* departed Southampton, record snowfalls fell across Britain including deep snow in London.

Sheldon and Samantha were highly excited when we boarded the *Canberra* and loved the cruise experience. Most days they'd be away from Carole and me for hours as they participated in many of the activities that usually had educational themes. They both loved the 'dessert trolley' loaded with a huge array of tempting sweets that the waiters would wheel to the table after dinner. When we neared Australia, Sheldon said to Carole, 'Can we have one of those at home when we get back to Australia?' to which the whole table burst into laughter.

Sailing to Australia yielded some interesting and scary experiences. The first was during a stopover at Cristóbal before we entered the Panama Canal. Carole and I with the kids teamed up with another family on board. An introductory film about the port that we were shown on board told us to stay out of a particularly unsafe area of Cristóbal. Unbeknown to us, we accidentally ended up in that very suburb. People were coming out to look at us and staring in a way that made us extremely uncomfortable.

'Let's get out of here! I think we've walked into a dangerous area,' I whispered.

Rodney, the other father quickly responded.

'We shouldn't be here. We need to get the kids back to the ship.'

We all became nervous and turned the strollers around to head back to the ship. Suddenly we saw a policeman chasing two local boys. They were heading straight for us.

'Shit, he's got a gun!' I yelled, referring to the policeman. The barrel of the gun was about a foot long and it was obviously a very old model. The policeman waved it in the air as they ran toward us.

We started to push the strollers as fast as we could. In the next instant one runner was within a few feet of us when the policeman grabbed him and pushed him against the wall right beside us with the long barrel shoved against his chin yelling in a language none of us understood. We were relieved to get back to the ship without incident. We paid a lot more attention to future destination information talks before disembarking. We enjoyed travelling through the Panama Canal.

In San Francisco we did a bus day trip on the seventeen-mile drive to Carmel and stopped at Seal Rock.

Sheldon was chasing squirrels while we watched the seals lazing in the sun. We considered squirrels cute. It was a novelty seeing them running around. Sheldon caught one and it bit him on the finger drawing blood. Carole and I didn't have any concerns about it as we walked up to the bus driver.

'My son was just bitten by a squirrel and we need a band aid,' I said.

'Oh no!' he exclaimed. 'Everyone on the bus!' His obvious concern caused great alarm with Carole and me.

'What's the matter?' I asked.

'Rabies!' was all he said.

Carole and I were filled with dread. Even Samantha looked deeply concerned.

'You mustn't play with wild animals here. You tourists just don't understand the danger; we need to get medical help immediately.'

Everyone piled into the bus and we headed to the local fire station. The alarm of the attending officer made me feel physically ill. Carole and I were extremely scared for Sheldon. The attending staff were obviously afraid of legal liability and I was surprised and quite shocked when Carole and I had to treat the wound and bandage it. This was unheard of in Australia. It made me think that the legal system in the USA was out of control. Everyone suing at the drop of a hat. It was too bloody litigious. I hoped Sheldon would be okay.

A local biologist was contacted by phone by a very helpful policewoman who happened to be at the station. We were partly relieved when she explained he was sure that area had been free of rabies for almost a decade.

'How long does it take for the symptoms to appear?' I queried.

'Any time up to five years,' was the worrying response.

We returned to the ship and took Sheldon straight to the doctor who gave him a tetanus injection. He reassured us somewhat when he said, 'He'll probably be okay.'

Sheldon was watched closely over the next five years when he had any sign of sickness. It was late when we returned to the *Canberra* and it sailed at about 1.30am. A wild storm unleashed when we sailed out of San Francisco Bay into the Pacific Ocean. Luckily, almost all passengers were in bed after a big day on shore. We didn't know the commodore couldn't transfer the pilot to the pilot boat safely. He made the decision to bring the *Canberra* beam-side to the heavy sea to allow the pilot to disembark on the leeward side in calm water, free of wind. The *Canberra* was sitting almost becalmed when three large waves hit it. Carole and the children and I were in our bunk beds when suddenly the ship listed, almost throwing us out of bed and sending items on our dressing table crashing to the floor.

'Just a rough sea, don't panic,' I said to calm everyone.

We were all thrust wide awake and Carole was looking alarmed.

Something doesn't feel right.

I had just finished speaking when a second wave hit. Our cupboard doors flew open as our chair cartwheeled down the cabin. We could hear crockery crashing in the kitchen and other items crashing outside.

'That's *not* bloody normal, stay here. I'll check it out.'

I leapt out of bed. A third wave soon hit, making the ship list dramatically. I was thrown violently back on the bunk. Carole and the children were looking wide-eyed and frightened.

'I don't know what's going on. Stay here while I find out and come back. I won't be long,' I tried to say reassuringly.

I was met outside with large ashtrays rolling around the passageway and one clanging down the staircase. The door was open in a kitchen galley and all crockery and saucepans were spread all over the floor.

I rushed down two levels to the promenade deck to be met by a crew member running toward me yelling, 'We've hit a sand bank!'

Shit, something's wrong. I hurried to try and understand what was going on. The ship was stabilised and my concerns eased as I felt it getting underway again as I entered the entertainment room. I was shocked to see all the heavy lounge chairs stacked up to the ceiling on one side and all the orchestra instruments flung all over the floor. It was obvious the ship had listed badly. I walked briskly through the shopping area to see all the merchandise on the floor and expensive glassware smashed. The carpet in the restaurant was flooded. I noted a porthole was open and dripping in sea water. I felt the ship steady further and get underway more smoothly, so I felt confident we'd be okay. The PA system switched on, 'This is the commodore speaking. We apologise to all passengers for the rough conditions. While we were disembarking the pilot we were hit by large waves and we're now safely underway. There is no cause for concern.'

This broadcast reassured me all was well so I hurried back to the cabin to be greeted by a very relieved family. We were told later by a crew member the *Canberra* had listed a huge twenty-eight degrees. The commodore would be facing an enquiry in Britain on the ship's return.

When we arrived at Sydney's beautiful harbour we were met by my brother Graham and his wife, as well as Carole's sister and brother-in-law. It was great to see Graham and his family waiting for us when the ship berthed in Sydney in late February 1978. It was an unexpected surprise. Graham wasn't only a brother but a dear friend. Dulcie travelled overseas often after this adventure and had two new relationships. She was diagnosed with dementia and was placed in a home in 2011, where she died a short time later. I never heard Dulcie pay a compliment to Carole, she chose to only criticise her, something I found really sad.

I returned to the Foundry with a new confidence and the knowledge that our processes and product were in fact world-class. I decided once more it was a great place to work in spite of many areas needing modernising and improvement.

I was sure our marriage was tracking well but I was soon to find out differently.

I was thirty-one when I ended the enjoyable UK scholarship year and returned home in late February 1978. It was nine years before my revelational experience. I was a different person from the one who was to travel twice to the UK in June 1994, and later in March 1998, many years after my spiritual experience. I then saw things in a different light.

CHAPTER 12
FEELINGS VS EMOTIONS

All my life up until my extraordinary revelation of the spiritual dimension to life, I believed feelings was just another word for emotions. This misunderstanding was clarified as a result of the experience.

I now know there is a very important difference. I believe when we're centred in our feelings we're truly self-empowered. We're the recipient of divine or spiritual guidance and we're honouring our truth and our spiritual path. However, when we're emotional I believe we're in a victim state arising from our personality/ego. We're avoiding personal responsibility and pursuing self-interest. I now see it as the heart versus the head.

During my state of heightened awareness I remember being in awe of the things I could feel. I wrote earlier about the night I felt a day pass. Prior to the experience, in my younger days I considered some of my greatest 'rushes' were having the Sprite sliding around corners with the rev counter needle in the red. This was easily surpassed when I sat in my lounge room in wonder during the spiritually heightened period. I was actually feeling the wind in the jacaranda tree leaves outside the lounge window which was closed, something I'd have derided as impossible prior to my experience.

It was an unbelievably beautiful feeling. I again wondered how many Indigenous people just felt these things on a regular basis, as mentioned earlier. I believe this life-giving force exists in all living and inanimate things; I believe it to be God. It's no coincidence that Indigenous people all around the world recognised spirit in the various natural features and animals around them.

At an atomic level in all living and inanimate things, there is energy when the atoms and neutrons perform their timeless dance – I believe it's the energy of God. We took Indigenous people away from their hearts and intuitive skills that would have led them to a knowledge-based understanding of spirit developed over centuries through feeling. We force-fed their minds with an intellectual process of faith and belief in a book written centuries ago when poorly evolved patriarchal governance ruled the day. We took them from actual real experiences that are felt, and become knowledge, to the focus on a book that's an intellectual exercise based on belief and faith.

I love the quote in Neale Donald Walsch's book series *Conversations with God:* 'In order to truly know God you have to be out of your mind.' Also the comment: 'Feeling is the language of the soul.'[14]

The other interesting goal I mentioned earlier was to trust my feelings to navigate my hire car to each destination in the UK. I found I had a very high success rate. My experiences following both my attempts to leave the Foundry, mentioned earlier, to me are other practical examples of feelings shaping one's life.

Our education systems predominantly teach us about intellect. I've come to believe this lacks important balance in developing a human being. It's unfortunate that many people in leadership roles have only experienced intellectual study in relation to their chosen career – experience enhances character.

I remember in my early days of training during my cadetship I was spending time working a Herbert 9C 30 large turret lathe for the first time in the machine shop. I was machining large vee grooves in cast iron pulleys on the largest diesel engine made on site.

The pulley had six deep vee grooves for a belt drive and lots of spigot diameters to allow it to locate precisely on the engine flywheel to accommodate tail shaft and other drives. The lathe was before computer controlled (CNC) lathes were introduced in the factory so I had to remember the many stops and settings while each of the many tools were wound in and out by hand to produce the numerous and varied machined surfaces.

I worked on the large batch on a Thursday and Friday. The process became second nature to me and almost robotic by the time I finished work on Friday afternoon and went home for the weekend. When I came back to work on Monday morning I panicked because I couldn't remember the many settings. I rushed to the area supervisor Bill, who was Carole's uncle.

---

14   ND Walsch, *Conversations with God – Book 1*, Hodder & Staughton, London, UK, 2000, p. 3.

'I can't remember all the stops. I need you to show me again so I remember.'

'Just calm down Doug. Start the process again. Trust your feelings. It will all come back.' He waved me back to the 9C 30.

I did as he said. It all came back without me thinking about it. When I became general manager I decided I must learn to trust my intuitive abilities and those of employees; it can result in great business decisions.

After leading the rapid turnaround of the Foundry, which I'll describe later, retired employees often visited to tour the facility to witness the many changes that had taken place. Some past directors and senior managers visited and most commented favourably on the new technology, quality and plant cleanliness. My memory is that these were 'intellectually' focussed. When a retired quality manager revisited the site, on meeting me after the tour he was constantly shaking his head.

'I can't believe the feeling; I didn't think this place could ever feel like this,' he kept repeating.

He was a highly experienced man who regularly worked intuitively as he solved many product and factory problems. He was often derided by more analytical managers when he couldn't articulate an explanation as to what he actually did to remedy the various issues because he'd worked intuitively. I was deeply touched by his observation. I wanted to punch the air and yell, 'Yes!' but restrained myself.

There is a great relevant quote attributed to Einstein: 'The intuitive mind is a sacred gift, the intellectual mind is a faithful servant; we have created a society that honours the servant and has forgotten the gift.'[15] I do repeat it, but I strongly feel we need to get back in touch with our intuitive side. Considering the volatile state of the world, we need to do it urgently in my view, because it's the vehicle for one's integrity and authenticity. To me, it's wisdom versus intellectualism, a subject I've spoken on at many public events.

I also know that when I'm fearful, it's more difficult to discern what I am feeling and receive the clarity it brings. Often I'm acting on a feeling before I've thought about it. I also now understand it's important to have awareness of what's actually happening in the present moment to keep you in your feelings rather

---

15   Attributed to Einstein, Science, Philosophical and Religion Conference on Science, Philosophy and Religion in their relation to the Democratic Way of Life at the Jewish Theological Seminary of America, New York (9-11 September 1940). Contested as quote by Bob Samples based on Einstein's thoughts.

than a focus on a past or future issue. I love the quote attributed to A. A. Milne: 'Yesterday is history, tomorrow is a mystery, but today is a gift, that's why we call it the present.'[16]

Understanding the difference between my emotions and feelings gave me a greater sense of responsibility when I opened my mouth. I now believe that when anyone becomes highly emotional in a communication it's simply highlighting, and telling those present, that they have a personal investment or unresolved issues in the process. The greater good isn't the priority in this instance.

I find it very sobering when I get emotional now. I always ask myself: what's the personal investment I've got in the process unfolding? I also believe in the 'mirror principle'. This suggests that if someone is highly emotional and verbally criticising a person, then they're publicly proclaiming the very behavioural issue they dislike about themselves, albeit unconsciously. They see themselves reflected in the person they're criticising. Knowing this about oneself can result in a lot more personal responsibility when one opens one's mouth. It sure stopped a lot of my emotional outbursts. It triggered a lot of soul searching when I had this particular realisation.

I occasionally still get emotional about things, but rarely over people. It's usually technology-related. It's mostly about frustrating computer problems or self- imposed time pressures which can stimulate me to throw the odd tantrum.

All human beings get emotional from time to time. There is nothing right or wrong about it, it's simply being human. To assist spiritual development, I believe we have to develop self-awareness when we're emotional. We need to understand and acknowledge it, and consistently work with it and aim to reduce our emotional behaviour over time. For me, learning to overcome emotional outbursts helps one to operate more in one's feelings, be more self-empowered and more inclined to embrace personal responsibility. It's important not to beat ourselves up for simply being human at those times. I also believe the more we accept and operate as a soul with a body, rather than the reverse, we're better situated to become a more distant observer of ourselves, and, as a result, less emotional. Emotion has a different energy to feeling. It's the energy of a victim, it blames, justifies, denies and has a 'poor little old me' foundation. My son Sheldon used to call out emotive behaviour by saying, 'Stop the whiney voice!'

---

16   AA Milne, *Winnie-the-Pooh*, Penguin Putman Incorporation, New York NY USA, 1992, Np.

To me, emotion is triggered by old baggage we've not addressed. Some of it is unconscious and we need professional or mentored assistance to identify it and deal with it. It's just another part of the human journey.

I guess, put simply, we all need to avoid emotionally-based victim behaviours, driving us to continually blame or criticise people or circumstances, deny wrongdoings or justify our inappropriate actions. I'm finding that people are becoming increasingly hypersensitive and can be offended too easily. I love the quote attributed to Ken Keyes Jr. in his book *Handbook to Higher Consciousness:* 'You add suffering to the world just as much when you take offence as when you give offence.'[17]

This was the first book I read when I started my reading frenzy. I believe our intellectually-focussed society is driving us away from accepting our gut feeling as a decision-making tool in relation to decisions in business or life. In fact, during my studies at our local university, one civil engineering lecturer was most emphatic that an engineer must never use 'gut feeling' in making engineering decisions. Yet, in my professional association with many engineers and company chief executive officers, I found the opposite view. Most openly state that they regularly rely on their gut feeling. 'If something doesn't feel right, then investigate it further.' While general manager, I remember an occasion where I ignored my feelings and it cost the company $300,000.

I feel many 'new age' proponents have given feelings a bad name, because many have the philosophy of 'if it feels good, do it,' when in fact they're referring to sensation-based urges, which are driven by emotion or addictions, and are often not feelings at all.

There is a popular view that anything related to the heart, meaning in this instance the soul rather than the muscle, is based on emotionalism. This view is patronising in the extreme. I believe the heart is the home of one's true character, and is the generator of our values, whether of courage, trust, honesty, integrity, respectfulness, caring, tenacity, sincerity, enthusiasm and genuine commitment to a task.

The heart also provides a true sense of justice, generosity of spirit and all the other qualities that successfully carry a human being through the rigors and challenges of business and life in general. Simply

---

[17] K Keyes Jr, *Handbook to Higher Consciousness*, 6th Edition, Love Line Books, Coos Bay. OR, USA, 1st September 1985, Chapter 3, The Law of Higher Consciousness. Np.

put, I believe the heart is the home of our truth and integrity – it's the platform of our authenticity. It's the source of inner strength.

If the heart is the home of truth, what then is the mind? The mind is a miracle, the source of tremendous intellectual reasoning ability. However, it's also the home of our personality and fears. It's the launching pad for control, ego, mistrust, constant comparisons, insecurities, self-doubt, self-criticism, greed and the need for secrecy.

I came to believe that when I'm in my feelings my mind is the servant of spirit, and when emotional, or on power and control trips, my mind is the servant of my personality and ego. I also understand we need a balance of both the head and the heart in our daily encounters. Trusting spirit's guidance is a sure way to stay in your feelings. Another way of putting it is that when emotional, we're resisting, forcing, fighting and seeking control, while in our feelings we're trusting spirit and allowing issues to unfold before us.

I was interested to read in the book *Conversations with God* that the brain is like our computer, whereas our mind actually resides in every molecule of our body.[18] Maybe that's one for the scientists and the medical profession to look at. I feel our constant drive to quantify all things, ensure guaranteed outcomes and only accept ideas if they can be scientifically proven has driven the human race away from its heart, and into what I call intellectualism instead of wisdom. With the significant challenges facing the human race today, it's my view that we need heaps more wisdom and much less intellectualism. I believe the current rapid rate of technological development, without the overview of wisdom based on integrity, is likely to result in dangerous outcomes.

Planet Earth, our life support system, is currently experiencing pressures that are not sustainable. During my time as CEO of the Infrastructure Sustainability Council of Australia (ISCA), I learnt that we're using resources as though we've got 1.7 planets to exploit. We all need to take heed to find a new way of conducting commerce and living that's more equitable and sustainable. We're all one and connected to each other and connected to all living and inanimate things. We're stretching planet Earth to breaking point.

I believe everything is God, all that ever was, never was, and all that will be.

Everything is this divine energy. That includes us!

---

18   ND Walsch, *Conversations with God – Book 3*, Hodder and Stoughton, London, UK, 1998, p. 170

CHAPTER 13
LEARNING ABOUT ENERGY

As I've said, I believe all living things are interconnected, and that all life is important and interdependent. I've not been able to really validate this feeling of life's interdependence from an intellectual viewpoint except through energy. I came to know all was energy during that period of heightened awareness. Sitting in my Harristown High School class during a physics presentation in 1963, my teacher Mister Robinson walked in and with great authority, as was his nature, announced excitedly, 'Today we're going to be studying the new physics – quantum physics.'

Full of expectation, we all went silent. All eyes were on the teacher when he said, 'Scientist Max Planck has discovered Newton's theory didn't work in all cases when he was studying heating and cooling effects of black and white bodies. Our society has been shaped by Newtonian physics and now we've reason to rethink some of our assumptions. Max Planck is the father of quantum theory.'[19]

I screwed up my nose thinking, *What's all this about?* I was about to return to my pad where I was drawing a sports car.

'You won't find it in your physics book; it's a new science. Quantum physics has determined everything is energy, and energy is delivered in small packets. Little else is known about it but scientists believe it's the way of the future. It will result in a lot of new inventions.'

That ended the discussion on this new theory. We all felt deflated and left wondering why that was so

---

[19] MKEL Planck, Nobel Prize for Physics, 1918, www.britannica.com/biography/Max-Planck.

special and what its practical application was. Many years later I was attending the funeral of a Foundry employee in a small country church and the minister was full of fire and brimstone. I don't remember what religious faith it was. 'I notice many people in this church for the first time, it's not good enough to satisfy the lord – you need to come to church every Sunday to find salvation,' the stern-

faced minister proclaimed part way during the service.

I was most disinterested in his fear-based sermon. I was checking out other attendees when he said in the middle of his ramblings that I had tuned out of, 'There are those amongst us who believe we're all energy, that's the working of the devil. It must be ignored.'

I suddenly became attentive.

What planet are you on mate? My physics teacher isn't off with the devil, he's just following science. What's it got to do with the devil?

Later in life I knew mystics had been saying all is energy long before the discovery by contemporary science. To me it's another example of intuitive thinking surpassing intellectually-based thinking in gaining an understanding of universal truths.

My understanding is that quantum physics recognises that an observer can affect the experiment, as opposed to Newtonian physics which presupposes the observer has no affect.[20] I believe that because the essence of a human being is simply a unique 'ball' of energy (the soul) with a body encased inside, why wouldn't this energy field affect and interact, or mesh with, whatever other energies are around it if everything is energy? I believe everything living and every material is made from the same God- given universal energy 'stuff' and that at an absolute energy level we're all the same. A rock, plant or a human would be indiscernible. When the frequency of vibration of each entity is raised the different forms of matter appear – a rock vibrating at a lower frequency than a human. *Conversations with God Book 3*, supports this understanding.[21] In addition, in his book *A New Earth*, Eckhart Tolle writes, 'What we perceive as physical matter is energy vibrating (moving) at a particular range of frequencies.'[22]

---

[20] Professor B McCosker, Quantum Physics, Lecture, audio recording, Griffiths University, Brisbane, c.   1987.

[21] ND Walsch, *Conversations with God Book 3*, Hodder and Stoughton, London, 1998, pp. 177, 178, 179.

[22] E Tolle, *A New Earth*, (10th Anniversary Edition), Penguin, London, UK, 2016, p. 146.

Again, a quote attributed to Einstein:

> Everything is energy and that is all there is to it. Match the frequency of the reality you want and you cannot help but get that reality. It can be no other way. This is not philosophy. This is physics.[23]

If we believe in an interconnectedness of all things, the often quoted spiritual saying that what we do to others we also do to ourselves makes sense. If we are all one at an absolute energy level, then our energy is impacted by surrounding events. We're often just unaware of it at the human level and how our behaviours impact our spiritual journey, or our karma as many put it. I was given an audio recording of a lecture given at Griffith University in Brisbane by a Professor McCosker, circa 1988. He was head of physics at a NSW university and decided if he was to understand quantum physics he had to study the observer. He then decided he had to study himself. His search for self took him to India where he claimed he witnessed a man levitating, in defiance of gravity. He apparently posted the photo above his desk and became regarded as a radical by his peers. He left the university.

In the lecture he said, 'Isaac Newton was only twenty-three years old when he determined the mathematical formulae for universal relationships that has become the foundation of modern mathematics, physics and science. Newton made two key assumptions, firstly that the observer has no effect on the experiment, and secondly that everything is deterministic.'

I took this to mean that everything could be explained scientifically, and most likely, mathematically. He then said, 'Newton had the remarkable foresight at that young age to realise that he had provided the science platform for a future mechanistic and materialistic society.'[24]

I found this statement profound coming from such a young man. Newton was obviously a man of vision.

Sometime later I was participating in a personal development course. I sat beside a lady who was the personal assistant to a physics professor at a Brisbane university. We chatted over the weekend and somehow quantum physics came up.

---

[23] Attributed to Einstein but it is highly contested. Conjecture considers Darryl Anka as the source based on channelling from a spiritual being named Bashar.

[24] Professor. B McCosker, Quantum Physics, Lecture, audio recording, Griffith University, Brisbane, c. 1987.

'My boss has spent his life researching and trying to find the fifth force. I keep wanting to tell him maybe it's God but I value my job. He's not into spirituality,' she said.

I replied, 'I couldn't agree more, it seems very logical.'

The scientific search for a fifth elusive force was news to me. I was aware of the four universal forces being gravity, electromagnetism, and the strong and weak nuclear force. I hadn't considered God as a fifth force, but this entity's presence must impact all things inanimate and alive. It sounded very logical to me.

Maybe quantum physics will reveal this eventually and science and spirituality, or at least what's now considered paranormal, will become friends. I see so many people getting passionate, and some highly pious, about creation versus evolution, each believing they're right when in fact I believe they both are. Even Pope Francis, in 2017, stated publically he believes in the Big Bang theory[25].

I've the feeling that this awesome, loving, 'pure energy', omniscient life-form that I came briefly in contact with could be capable of anything. Why not a Big Bang to kick off the miraculous, expansive and endless material world as we now know it, combined with slowly evolving life? Either way, I believe the truths of the universe, such as the infinite nature of it in both outer space and atomic areas, are beyond the current capability of the human brain. I often wonder if science will ever find the 'smallest particle'.

Logic and science tells me that Gondwana took eons to evolve to the continents we know now. So to me, it's no mystery that life evolved similarly after it was created by this loving, super intelligent, higher power.

It was Christmas 1989, two years after the truth seminar, when Carole, the children and I went to Burleigh Heads on the Gold Coast for a beach holiday. We'd become friends with Pirio, a Finnish lady. She did the Truth Seminar with me. We visited her at a holistic healing centre in an old picture theatre on the main highway where she was working. It was operated by a local doctor open to alternative healing practices. We exchanged pleasantries, then she asked, 'We'll be holding a group workshop in a couple of days involving some massage and it's a great way to relax into a holiday. Would you like to join us?'

'Sounds good. I'm feeling a bit drained. It's been a real busy and challenging time leading up to this break,' I replied and Carole agreed.

---

[25]   Pope Francis, Address in the plenary session of the Pontifical Academy of Sciences, clementine hall Vatican, May 2nd 2019.

It had been a period of high tension at the Foundry leading up to the break and my head felt 'clouded'. We arrived on the day and there we about six other people participating. After some conversation the doctor called the group together.

'We're going to do a group head massage for all those interested. We'll all sit on chairs in a circle and Pirio and I will alternatively massage your heads. If you're comfortable with this then grab a chair and form a circle.'

We all did this and the doctor and Pirio started on opposite sides of the circle spending about a minute on a person before moving to the next. The doctor gave me a massage and it felt good and she moved on. Pirio arrived at my chair and started massaging my head by rotating her fingers in a circle. She was close to moving to the next person when a huge energy discharge like a lightning bolt left my head.

'Did you feel that? That was a huge release,' Pirio exclaimed excitedly.

'Yes, my head feels great; all the heaviness has gone. . . It's amazing.'

I've had several head massages since then but have never felt the huge energy discharge that occurred that day. My head felt just like it did on the morning of the revelational experience. I was again amazed how my state of being (my energy) could change in an instant. I didn't know I'd have many energy experiences as my life unfolded.

We have much to learn about energy.

CHAPTER 14
FOUNDRY SPIRITUAL EXPERIENCES

My father's death was the first time I started to believe the soul was energy and that it was really who we are, as mentioned earlier. I just knew there was an invisible force that left his body at death.

After I returned from Britain in late February 1978, I was working as a design engineer at the Foundry and had the responsibility to design a 122-foot-diameter rotary boom travelling irrigator for watering crops. I completed the project in three months and it went into production. Before I started the design, and following my analysis of watering patterns, I approached the works director.

'We need to move to a fixed boom machine rather than a rotary unit because it provides more even water distribution and a dry runway for the machine,' I said.

'Stop analysing the bloody thing. Just start designing a rotary machine, that's what's selling in the market. We need this machine now,' he responded angrily, leaving no doubt I was to forget the idea of a fixed boom machine. We were lagging the market. His impatience took over.

I designed the rotary unit and a couple of months after its production release the opposition brought out their fixed boom machines. I was promoted to chief tooling engineer and another designer converted the irrigator to a fixed boom design at significant cost. This stood me in good stead, because when I became GM of the Foundry I was determined to actually listen and 'hear' the employees after that misguided directive.

In mid-1978 I decided to take up go-karting and purchased a cart with money from my mother's estate, and raced it at a local track. I was surprised how much time and money it was costing me each month and was considering selling it.

One day Carole said, 'I play golf with a fellow and his wife who are interested in sponsoring your kart. I could invite them around to talk about it.'

I agreed and he came to the next race meeting to see what was involved. I had my first feelings of discomfort with him around Carole.

Weeks passed and it became obvious to me something was going on with Carole and the fellow. It came to a head one night and the truth of the relationship came to light. I was in total shock and devastated once more. I had Carole move out into a unit in the city. This time I sat with Sheldon and Samantha and explained their mum would be living separately from us for a while. I felt distressed at the look on each of their faces when I broke the news. We've never spoken of the incident since. I often wonder how it impacted them later in life.

I still loved Carole and we began counselling. I received a concerning unsolicited call during this time from a woman who didn't leave her name, warning me to keep an eye on another male golfer. I had decided to leave Carole as a result until a very persistent counsellor in a number of sessions got me to acknowledge I still loved her. She convinced me to give the marriage another try. We were separated for approximately seven months before we reconciled. I know Sheldon and Samantha were happy to see their mother return and for us to become a family unit once more. After 1978 we had many good years together.

In 1989 I was working with a recently appointed foundry manager, Andrew, to reduce casting rejection rates. Andrew was Polish and overseas foundry representatives who visited often commented that our moulding sand-grain size was much finer than world foundries. They claimed a coarser grain size would reduce our rejection rate even though our performance was considered excellent considering the wide and varied range of products produced daily.

'I'd like to try a test run using sand specs found in European foundries,' Andrew said enthusiastically as he entered my office late one afternoon.

'The Europeans have been telling us to change our grain-size distribution for years, so I agree, let's give it a shot to see what happens,' I encouraged.

The fine sand mined locally gave the Foundry a high-quality casting finish that the Foundry was renowned for, particularly in Europe, as mentioned earlier. In excess of 150 tonnes of mixed sand was held in the huge sand bins feeding the high-output automatic moulding line. Over a few days Andrew and his team slowly changed the grain distribution with the addition of some imported sand. When the molten ladle operators poured the molten iron into the mould pouring heads incorporating the coarser grain spread, small beads of metal started to spit into the air, some flying quite high. These molten iron droplets had a temperature just below 1300 degrees centigrade. I was working at my desk when the phone rang, it was Andrew.

'Greg Paix has just been burnt badly on his head, he was pouring a mould when it spat violently and he was startled. He whipped his head back so quickly his hard hat fell off and the molten bead of metal landed on his head. The guys have called the ambulance. They're tending to him now.'

Greg was a young pourer, relatively new to the task. He was working closely with his father, Eddie, who was operating the electric induction furnaces that melted the iron. I immediately went to the ambulance to see it leaving. I drove with Andrew to the hospital. Greg had a round wound just over a centimetre in diameter where the molten metal droplet landed and the hair had burnt away in the area impacted.

'It's cooked meat right to his skull; the hair will never grow back in the burnt area. He'll have a permanent bald spot,' the doctor said.

Greg was released that evening and I visited him at his parents' home. Eddie and his wife were, understandably, not happy. When I arrived they were quite angry that Greg had been hurt. I talked with them and explained the circumstances leading to the incident. They could see it was an unfortunate accident.

Greg soon returned to work and confirmed the doctor's diagnosis that he'd have a permanent bald spot. After chatting with Greg I was feeling bad about what had transpired to a good young employee. I went home from work one evening with it still weighing on my mind.

I went into the sunroom and started a meditation with Greg's incident sitting heavily on my mind. Suddenly I felt a strong will for him to get better. It came suddenly and was stronger than I had ever felt before. I was only meditating for a short time when a huge and strong energy flow discharged from my gut. I *just knew* instantly that Greg would be okay. I've never spoken of this to anyone and it was a short time later while doing my morning walk that Eddie approached me.

'Good news, Greg's head has healed totally. The doctor cannot explain it, all the hair has returned quickly and unexpectedly.'

'That's fantastic,' I replied, feeling much relief. I could see Eddie's concerns had left him.

After this I was a little confused when another serious injury was suffered by an employee I knew well, and no feeling of an energy flow occurred – I rationalised it must have been meant to be and was part of that person's spiritual journey and my own spiritual path.

Three years later, in 1992, I had been promoted to factory manager and was talking with the night shift supervisor in my office late one evening. He was an extremely honest man. A very open discussion turned to personal issues when a huge energy flow passed between us.

'Did you feel that?' I asked. 'That was pure honesty between us.'

I looked up and he'd gone. I think the incident frightened him and we never spoke of it again. I had come to know that when two people are engaged in a totally open and honest discussion with no guarded words, that an energy flow can occur between the two souls and is felt by the participants.

Not long after this experience I was told by the managing director that directors from a Brisbane-based customer were visiting and I was to take part in the discussions. Three directors from the company arrived the next day and a meeting was held in the boardroom where it was announced one key director was retiring. A factory tour was then conducted and I ended up guiding the retiring director. We became separated from the main group. The director started dropping words in the conversation that I'd describe as religious by nature. When I didn't react adversely to them he started to tell me his story.

'I had become an alcoholic from the stress of the business. My life went down the toilet to the stage where I ended up passed out in a suburban street gutter one night.'

I immediately stopped the tour.

'Let's go back to my office where we can talk privately,' I said.

I sat down at my desk and swivelled my chair so I was sitting directly opposite the director. I always had my desk against a wall so I didn't have to engage with people across a desk. He started.

'The evening when I was passed out in the gutter, a Christian gentleman came along. He picked me up and took me to a charismatic church gathering. During the healing part of the service, I was overcome by such a strong feeling of love and was healed of my addiction. I was born again.'

'I can relate to that totally because I had a similar experience also,' I said.

He then went on to say, 'I joined a Christian group and headed off to Russia with them, where I healed a very sick small boy. It was so awesome and miraculous I decided I had no more interest in my corporate venture as I wanted to follow my new spiritual path.'

It was obvious he was having trouble containing his excitement over this awesome event in his life and our discussion went deeper and wider. Suddenly, a long powerful surge of energy flowed between us both. He immediately broke into the conversation.

'Wow – feel anything?' he said. 'That was truth passing between us'

I nodded in agreement and said how I wished I could communicate this way to all people. It was one more special moment.

Sadly, I've only felt this once more. That was during a communication with my wife Carole. I often felt so frustrated that even after this experience, I could not, and still can't, always say what I feel. People are so cautious and unconsciously fearful in their conversations. To feel this energy flow and know there are no masks between you and the person you're talking to is truly a joyous sensation.

I've now come to believe that, at a soul or spirit level, truth is always communicated between people. When two people are communicating, if the words are not in sync with the truth, then the 'bad' or uncomfortable feeling about the communication arises within one about the other party. This feeling isn't easily felt if we're hyped up, 'jabbering', or fixated on a 'busy' head. We need to be calm or centred, as many would put it. In other words we need to be in our feelings, not in our heads to feel and discern it accurately. Often the feeling is as faint as a gentle breeze, so much so one is unaware of it unless one is tuned in and open to it. I find in most cases, as mentioned previously, I've acted on a feeling before I had time to really think about it. I believe, also as previously mentioned, that living in the present moment will enhance one's ability to be in touch with one's feelings.

I believe decisions made in our feelings (not emotions) are guided, and often may not appear logical; however, events often unfold that make them logical later. Due to the divine guidance, the feeling is looking into the future. It may not always be an outcome that you want, but I believe it's always one that you need on your spiritual journey through life.

During my role as factory manager, a shop foreman came into my office.

'Hi Doug, I just want to talk to you about the future of Harry the press operator. He's gone to seed and is obviously bored with his job. I think it's time to let him go and terminate his employment.'

I knew Harry well. It didn't feel right to sack him.

'Isn't there some other job we could move him to? He's a very experienced employee. He was very dedicated and knows the tooling inside out. If it were me I'd be bored shitless also doing that job for over thirty years.'

I gave it some consideration.

'What about training Harry to operate the new computerised tooling store we're about to implement?'

'He's a bit old to learn computers but I'd be willing to give it a try,' the foreman responded in support, which pleased me. I wasn't an advocate for terminating old and widely experienced employees.

The tools covered a wide range of manufacturing processes in the fabrication shop: intricate press dies, punch blocks, robot and manual welding fixtures, spiral pipe welder mandrels, pressure testing equipment and many machinery spare parts, galvanising hangers and shop consumables. I arranged for him to be relocated to the tooling store under construction and about to be computerised for the first time to improve its efficiency. Harry was an elderly employee who knew the tools intimately. He freaked out at the idea of operating the computerised inventory system, which was still in development.

I then instructed a senior training officer to sit with him for as long as it took. I recommended using Harry's advice and ideas to structure the managing software system during its development to ensure it was practical and suited to the needs of the area. The employee finally settled down with the very supportive trainer's constant reassurance and support, contributed practically to the software design and seemed to start enjoying himself.

After a month of his training I was stopped in a city street by an elderly lady I didn't know.

'You don't know me, but I'm Harry's wife. I'm extremely grateful that Harry is actually coming home excited for the first time in years as a result of his new skills and challenges. He's a much happier person. I just wanted to thank you,' she said.

I was bowled over by this unsolicited feedback. It felt really great to know this simple decision had made such a difference to Harry's life. I often wondered that if I hadn't had my revelational experience, it would have been a different, more 'traditional', outcome.

These unusual energy experiences were a precursor to many more I'd experience after I became general manager.

CHAPTER 15

THE FOUNDRY FLOUNDERS –
THE YEARS OF FINANCIAL LOSS

The Griffiths family, owners of the Southern Cross organisation, had borrowed heavily in Swiss francs to upgrade the factory in 1987. This was following The Pope's consultancy. The Australian Hawke government floated the Australian dollar in 1983, and unfavourable market exchange rate volatility following this borrowing of capital resulted in the family holding a debt they couldn't service. In 1987, a Melbourne-based firm, National Consolidated Limited (NCL), bought a forty-eight percent share of the business and after 116 years the company reluctantly moved from family ownership to a semi-public company. It went fully public in 1990 when NCL acquired the remaining fifty-two percent holding.

The years 1987 to 1993 were tumultuous times at the Foundry, with a new general manager appointed each year as the board tried to find a leader capable of turning the ailing business back to profit. A continuous focus on budgets, cost-cutting and redundancies left employees in fear. Morale was low. The business was moving to a state of dereliction and neglect each year from a lack of investment. While this focus was maintained, confidence in the business was lost. In 1989 I was approached by the general manager to undertake an interview by a national consultancy firm to determine my suitability as a future GM. The interview took place and I was called to the GM's office the following day,

'The consultant said that you're not suitable as a potential general manager for the Foundry because you don't read *The Financial Review*.'

The Fin Review, as it's referred to, is a daily business newspaper in Australia. I was taken aback by his remark because it seemed the only way these people viewed a future for the organisation was by takeover bids to build the company. Turning the business around through organic growth wasn't considered possible. The organisation comprised the marketing company Southern Cross and the manufacturing company Toowoomba Foundry. In its heyday, when it was the largest manufacturing organisation in the Southern Hemisphere, Southern Cross product was well known throughout Australia, South Africa and Asia.

Shortly after this discussion, the deputy to the GM approached me. He was highly intellectual with a superiority complex. I regarded him as having little common sense. He looked me in the eye.

'Anyone who meditates is just not GM material – you need to look for another job.'

Before I could answer he turned his back and walked off.

You ignorant prick. I was fuming as he strutted away. Within a couple of weeks, the Foundry foreman Andrew was called to the GM's office and told he was to sit upstairs to develop recommendations for productivity improvements.

Andrew presented his first report to the GM who threw it in the bin in front of him without opening it. It became obvious he wanted to get rid of Andrew and wasn't prepared to sack him. The ploy worked and Andrew and his wife returned to Poland.

The end-of-financial-year results were finalised and a $1.2 million loss was posted for the organisation. A program to make many employees redundant to save $1.2 million in salaries and wages was soon implemented. I was told I had to terminate an engineering employee with forty years of experience. He had designed the extensive supporting infrastructure for the modernisation of the Foundry. I saw him as invaluable to the Foundry's future. His experience and knowledge were extensive.

'You can't sack Ian. He's the only person familiar with the design of all the GF line's associated equipment.'

'Okay, I won't.' It was a rapid and surprised response by the GM.

I left his office feeling pleased thinking, *that was easy.*

The day of reckoning came. All employees to be made redundant were to be given their notice at

11.50am, just before lunch. A heartless process, they were to be presented with a prepared envelope, told to pack their belongings and escorted from the premises just after 12.00 noon. At 11.45am I was shocked to be called to the GM's office. I was handed an envelope for Ian.

'You said you weren't going to make Ian redundant,' I pleaded.

'I lied,' was his sick and unemotional response.

You dishonest bastard. I was enraged, but said nothing. I felt my stomach churn as I told Ian of his redundancy and angry that he had no time to say goodbye to his many workmates after forty years of dedicated service. He seemed to understand it wasn't my doing and remained respectful to me even though he was obviously in shock. That night I visited him at his home to assist him with issues around his superannuation and potential future job opportunities when his wife entered the room and asked, 'Who are you?'

'I'd like you to meet Doug Harl . . .' Ian started.

'You're the hatchet man – … get out of my house!' she yelled angrily, interrupting Ian.

'Doug, you'd better leave,' he said quickly and softly.

I felt terrible that a cherished employee could be treated this way. I held no malice toward his wife because I understood her emotions entirely. It had a real impact on me and I felt impotent. A month or so later I was called to the GM's office again.

'You've gone to seed; I want you out in three months. I'm cancelling your Qantas Club membership, stopping your fuel allowance. You'll spend your remaining time in charge of maintenance.'

I said nothing and left the office.

You bloody arsehole, you wouldn't know how to run a shithouse let alone a manufacturing facility.

I duly moved to the much-neglected maintenance department and remained positive as was my nature. I took time to ponder.

If I didn't have that spiritual experience behind me I'd probably be scared out of my wits by now.

At the time I was forty-four and only had $18,000 in my super fund and a mortgage on our house. I immediately started a survey of the status of all equipment and prepared a detailed estimate of the cost of bringing the equipment back to a reasonable standard electrically and mechanically. Maintenance costs had continually been cut and the equipment was in poor condition. I also arranged the immediate repairs to two towers I found in a condition close to collapse; one supporting a large steel water tank was so badly rusted that it was in danger of falling and killing an employee who often worked under it. My efforts resulted in the GM calling me in one day.

'You've made some good changes; I'll extend the time that I want you out by a few months.'

Again I made no response as I left. I was in the department for about six months when the half-year financial results came out and the forecast was for a similar loss as the previous year.

Soon after, the GM and his deputy were dismissed, and another GM was appointed. I was promoted to factory manager again. The allowances were reinstated along with a welcome salary increase. It was our fifth GM in five years. Needless to say, with each appointment the fear level in employees increased while they wondered who would be next to lose their job. It was 1991. I warmed to the new GM because he had a likeable personality and had wide experience in manufacturing in Britain. The Southern Cross corporation was losing $200,000 a month, and I was informed the Foundry's contribution to the loss was $500,000 a year. I was shocked to see him downing a couple of glasses of whiskey before each time a head office director visited. I realised he was fearful about his position.

He was the only GM who refused to use consultants.

'They knew bugger all about business and were overpaid. We need to find the fix.'

Each GM before him always hired a consultancy firm.

He taught me a lot about the management of unions which was to help me later in my career. I remember one story he shared with me from when he was the CEO of a large automotive company in England employing a few thousand people. It was a tactic I chose not to use.

'There was a serious HR issue with the manufacturing union in the UK, I didn't know how to approach it,' he said.

'What was the issue?' I enquired.

'It was bad enough that I was nervous about addressing it. A lot of senior union officials had been ushered to the boardroom. I was procrastinating trying to think of a way to approach the meeting to diffuse the obvious tension before I met 'em. I had a sudden idea and walked confidently to the door of the boardroom and stopped, looked in and said to them, "Guys, before I start there is something I wish to share with you," when they all looked up expectantly I let out the loudest fart I could.'

'All the officials were looking at me really seriously before I farted. They couldn't stop laughing afterwards and the meeting went off without any tension with much humour, and the issue was resolved.'

That was an example of his unusual sense of humour. When 1992 arrived and the company was still losing money, the managing director of Southern Cross started exerting his authority over the GM and I became a sandwich in the middle because each encouraged me to take sides with them. It was the time I successfully applied for an alternate job and refused it at the acceptance meeting as mentioned earlier.

Head office commissioned a consultancy firm, GPR (I never found out what GPR stood for), in an attempt to find a way forward for the ailing company. Over a dozen people arrived on site and started interrogating every process in the organisation. It was an expensive exercise for the company. This period was an uncomfortable time. It wasn't long before the managing director of Southern Cross announced that the Southern Cross marketing arm and fabrication shop would be sold off by National Consolidated Limited and he'd remain MD of Southern Cross. The Foundry was to become a stand- alone business unit remaining as a division of NCL. The GM resigned and a transitional GM was appointed to ensure due diligence during the split. His name was Bill Hawes.

Bill was a New Yorker who had led the large consulting team of GPR. He was the sixth GM in six years.

The Foundry was still in turmoil and future prospects were grim. I didn't know Bill was about to transition to the 'other side'.

CHAPTER 16

SALE OF THE FOUNDRY - REDUNDANCIES

The sale process commenced and a director from head office arrived. I was called to a meeting with him because I'd been given responsibility for the management of the factory under Bill's leadership. He was sitting at a desk in a white shirt and red tie. Bill and I sat down on the opposite side of the table when he started a tirade. Spittle flew through the air while he spoke!

'This bloody place gives me the absolute fucking shits! I'll be glad to get rid of it. It'll never be any good. The board has decided to put it up for sale, but God knows who'd ever want to buy it. Clearly we need further redundancies before that happens. Doug, I'm giving you the job of managing it.'

Bill and I looked at each other,

There sure is no love for the Foundry, was my thinking.

'Bill, I'll decide the numbers shortly with the managing director. You'll have to get the managers to identify the employees to be listed,' he added.

Bill gave each manager the required number, and the unpleasant job of finalising the list began. The director had no faith in the employees of the Foundry and many consultants called them inbred and regarded them as having poor ability. I was determined there would be no repeat of the heartless previous sackings. Having accepted the responsibility for terminating the employment of a large number of people, I sat with each employee and their manager to clearly explain the reasons why they were being let go. I allowed them whatever time was needed to say goodbye to their workmates. We also gave a commitment to assist in finding a new job and offered counselling if needed. Some discussions lasted only five minutes and others up to two hours. The benefit of the personal meeting became obvious, because all parted with a friendly handshake and an understanding of the poor state of the company as well as the reasons for their dismissal. Warnings that sabotage may occur if they were not escorted from the premises proved unfounded.

It was interesting that more union members than non-members were made redundant. This was accepted by the Metal Workers Union. Our supervisors had listed every disciplinary note, regular absenteeism and behavioural issues. The final decision on who was to be made redundant was made by all supervisors coming together giving similar appraisals. It was not an individual's choice.

It was a draining experience!

The Foundry was put up for sale and Bill and myself, with the new title of operations manager, sat down to discuss the future. It was now August 1993. Bill opened the discussion in his heavy New York accent.

'I now plan to stay until May next year. Originally I was going to leave in July when the company split was complete. I like the style of the new managing director, Doug Curlewis. I think I can learn much from him. He has a very professional, frank and focussed approach to corporate management. Also I'm going to recommend you to be GM when I leave. I plan to send you to Harvard for six months to develop you professionally for the position.'

'That's fantastic. I hold Harvard in high regard. I used to read their monthly business reviews. They really are leaders in thought. Will the new MD support my appointment?' I replied enthusiastically.

'He'll follow my recommendation. What do you think we should do to get this place on track?' he then asked.

'We need a strategic plan. Not another bloody budget to shape the company. We need to get a group of employees off site for a few days to workshop the issues and develop a one-year action plan as part of a five-year plan. I know of a good facilitator, Dr Peter Long, who knows the company. He's facilitated other workshops.'

'Let's do it. I'll arrange a venue. You speak to Peter.'

I was sure Bill would book a low-cost local venue for the workshop. I was shocked when he told me we'd hold it in a four-star luxury Netanya beachfront resort at Noosa. We'd all been conditioned totally to 'lack' thinking. 'Abundance' thinking was something I was determined to bring back into the company. Even so, I too was feeling uneasy about the travel and accommodation costs of this luxury venue. I knew from an energy standpoint it was important to think in terms of abundance, but I was having difficulty breaking years of conditioning.

Bill, originally a school teacher in the US, had worked as a business consultant all around the world. His efforts in Russia and nearby countries had resulted in a personal invitation for him to meet the Pope one-on-one at the Vatican. He told me it was a highlight of his career. He mentioned the he and his partner Jeanine decided to leave New York in the early 1990s when parents started buying bulletproof vests for their children to provide protection against random street shootings.

Bill had based himself at Broadbeach on the Gold Coast, a popular holiday destination beside the ocean with beautiful and extensive white sand beaches, about two and a half hours' drive from Toowoomba. He went back to be with his Chinese partner Jeanine twice a week and spent the weekends there. It was my understanding that he chose to base himself there because Jeanine had Chinese friends nearby for support. He loved the relaxed lifestyle and the beautiful beaches the Gold Coast offered.

It was during this time that Jeanine, a refugee from Chairman Mao's era of purging academics, decided to return to China for the first time to visit relatives, while Bill was in his transitional caretaker role at Toowoomba Foundry. She hung a jade Buddha around Bill's neck on a leather strap before leaving and told him not to remove it while she was away because it was to keep him safe. Bill wanted to get a gold chain for it but Jeanine apparently kept saying it was a symbol of humility and a gold chain would be too pretentious for what it represented.

Jeanine then left for China, apparently leaving Bill on his own for the first time since they were together. This occurred soon after Doug Curlewis's new appointment to the NCL Board. NCL was a $204-million Australian corporation that focussed on manufacturing, and the new owner by default of Toowoomba Foundry through the full acquisition of the Southern Cross Corporation. Doug was managing director, and he was committed to world-class manufacturing and saw the company was in need of good leadership. I later viewed his appointment occurring at the same time I was appointed GM as a nice piece of synchronicity. Doug taught me a lot.

The Foundry urgently needed a new electric induction melt furnace. Bill asked for a capital investment proposal for the board agenda, which was to be finalised in a few days' time.

I had already developed a very detailed proposal, with engineering requiring a $2.7-million investment in new equipment; however, the company was losing $500,000 a year and was in poor shape. Doug Curlewis told Bill he wouldn't consider it, and would only make $300,000 available. Second hand furnaces became the only option. In spite of my protests to Bill that this amount was nowhere near enough, it became clear it was $300,000 or nothing for the loss-making Foundry.

Back in 1991, two furnaces had become available at Malco's Sydney foundry when they transferred their manufacturing to Toowoomba Foundry. I had pressured the financial director at that time to allow me to attend an auction of the furnaces when Malco closed their foundry He wouldn't hear of it, saying we couldn't afford to buy them because Malco's CEO insisted we had to buy both. After the auction I found out the furnaces were sold separately. Both realised a meagre price of $21,000, which stunned the engineering team and me. One furnace went to a steel-making company on the Gold Coast and the other to a foundry in Bendigo, Victoria, and was never installed. The critical high-voltage electrical control and switch gear, which was kept in a sealed shipping container, was later moved out into the weather by a new accountant in that business, so the company could store records in the container. This proved to be nearly disastrous for the furnace by the time we finally acquired it.

So by 1993 we were faced with a limited budget and a need for increased capacity. I recommended the purchase of the rusty unit in Bendigo for $21,000 plus transportation costs to Toowoomba, following the board's approval of the $300,000 expenditure. The old furnace was thirty to forty percent less efficient electrically than modern furnaces, and therefore much more expensive to operate. It also housed the banned chemical polychlorinated biphenyl (PCB – a carcinogenic) in its capacitors, which would cost in excess of $150,000 to dispose of legally. These two negative factors were abhorrent to the engineering team and me. I urgently contacted the managing director of an Australian supplier of new furnaces and asked if he could do anything for $300,000 because we were in desperate need of the additional melt capacity.

It was a week before the board meeting when our recommendation for the old furnace was in the board papers. The MD of the furnace supplier rang me to let me know he could provide a good second-hand furnace body for $450,000, backed up by a brand new modular power cabinet. This offered many advantages that would yield major cost savings (in the order of $600,000 each year) as it would use 40 percent less electricity. It incorporated no PCB. Another advantage was that the power pack was compact, preassembled in a sealed modular cabinet with all new electrics, while the second-hand furnace electrics we purchased were all individually mounted in various banks in a large cage – it was like a large rusty Meccano set to clean up and put together. It needed time and space for its installation.

About five days before the board meeting, Bill was sick. I was carrying the responsibilities of the site manager. I tried unsuccessfully to contact Bill on the Gold Coast to let him know I needed to change the board papers. I then rang the new MD, Doug Curlewis, whom I had never met before, saying, 'I need you to pull the existing proposal from the board papers. I'll submit a new one incorporating an additional $150,000 investment. This will . . .' I was quickly interrupted.

'It's my first meeting with the board and you're asking me to change the papers a few days before the meeting?' he exploded. 'I've strong doubts that you lot know what you're doing, it's very unprofessional. Put me through to Bill.'

'He's not here. I cannot raise him either, he's still ill. He must have the phone off the hook. I think . . .' Doug just hung up.

The next morning, I was chairing a daily meeting with the leadership team in Bill's absence in the conference room when the phone rang. It was Doug demanding to speak to Bill Hawes because he couldn't raise him at his unit either, despite many attempts.

'I need to speak to Bill,' he demanded.

'Bill isn't here, he must still be ill. I've been unable to contact him too,' I replied.

'I have all board members on a teleconference call. Would you tell them what you recommended yesterday.'

'I believe I'm acting in the best interests of the company and I request the furnace papers be changed to a recommendation costing an additional $150,000.'

I was about to explain the benefits when the line went dead in my ear.

It was obvious I had upset him and the board

Probably not a good career move, I thought.

I was forty-six years old and facing an uncertain future – I was about to face my life's biggest challenge.

CHAPTER 17

BILL HAWES'S DEATH – I'M GENERAL MANAGER

I was able to finally make contact with Bill on a Saturday early in September 1993. He sounded sick.

'I'm still unwell, I tried to come up Friday but I vomited in the cab and had to go back to the unit. I'm sure I'll be fine by Sunday, so I'll come up Sunday afternoon. We can get together to discuss your new proposal then. I'm planning to visit Doug in Melbourne on Monday before the board meeting on Tuesday,' he said.

He then became very personal and his tone changed to one of friendship.

'Doug, I've been very hard on you. I hope I haven't offended you,' he said,

'Not at all, you said not to take it personally and I haven't,' I replied. There was something that seemed strange to me in the unusually kind feeling of his response when he said, 'Thanks Doug, I didn't mean any harm.'

I put the phone down and couldn't understand what I was feeling, but something was different. I come to realise later Bill was unconsciously saying goodbye to me. It was my last conversation with Bill because he was unknowingly experiencing serious heart issues. A fortnight earlier he had said to the financial controller and me, 'You Aussies don't know what real life is like. You live in a cake walk. You wouldn't last five minutes in New York. I'm goin' to toughen you up and I ask that you don't take it personally.'

'Fine,' I said, 'I won't.'

One example of his toughening-up process was when the accountant and I were preparing the new furnace submission a month before he took ill. We'd worked on it for about two days when he came to us and said to me very aggressively while bending over with his face near mine, 'If that fucking proposal isn't on my desk within the next hour it'll go in the bin and stuff your bloody furnaces.'

He then stormed off leaving us in a flurry of activity.

Bill didn't arrive Sunday evening as promised. I couldn't raise him on the phone. I didn't worry about it too much, because I mulled that he was most likely still unwell and would drive up Monday morning. I arrived at work on Monday at about 7.20am and immediately felt concern about Bill. I had a meeting with a consultant hired by the board to bring change to the company and it started at 8am. Bill usually arrived at 8am at the latest. When the time came and Bill was still nowhere to be seen, I became quite anxious. I couldn't settle in the meeting. The consultant observed my continuous pacing in the room and the fact I wasn't concentrating. He said, 'You're concerned about Bill, aren't you?'

'I'm feeling very concerned, I'm probably panicking but I'm thinking of calling the police at the Coast to see if he's okay. I offered to drive down on the weekend to support him, but he said he was being looked after by friends.' This proved untrue later.

I couldn't settle so I placed a call to the GM of another foundry who I knew well, because the foundry was at the Coast not far from Bill's unit, and I planned to get him to send an employee to check up on Bill. He was overseas, so I then phoned my niece's husband, a police officer at the Gold Coast, to ask him to make enquiries at the address I provided. Barely ten minutes had lapsed when he rang back to tell me a report had come in that morning that Bill was found dead in his unit. Bill's unexpected and untimely passing led me to another beautiful spiritual experience.

I rang Doug Curlewis immediately, and a director in Brisbane who contacted the police. The police gave the director Bill's personal contact diary. The Brisbane director and I rang all contacts to find where Jeanine was so she could be told of Bill's death. Both business and family contacts were spoken to without success. We were able to determine she was five days into her journey to a remote part of China where she was going to meet relatives, but still hadn't reached her destination. The Brisbane director finally raised Jeanine's aunt in the USA, and she said, 'I know where Jeanine is heading. I'll send an urgent telegram to her, but I'm not optimistic that it will reach her very quickly, if at all. It's a public holiday here in the United States and where she's going is very remote.' I think it was the July 4th holiday.

I never saw the telegram, but I understand it read, 'Jeanine, your husband Bill has passed away. You need to return to Australia urgently.'

Through some miracle, most likely the result of people reading the sad contents, it reached Jeanine at a remote railway station in China twenty-four hours later, before she arrived at her destination. Bill's mother, Mary, was also phoned along with his brother, Bob, both of whom had no idea where Jeanine was headed. Mary was upset that she couldn't get the closure a funeral would bring because she couldn't make the trip to Australia. She lived in South Amboy, New Jersey.

It took many days for Jeanine to reach the Gold Coast. She was exhausted, distressed and drained. I was given the responsibility of helping her, something I was anxious to do. She was with her Chinese friends at the Mongolian Restaurant at Miami on the Coast when I met her. I gave her a hug and tried to console her as best I could.

Sometime after I drove her to the unit where Bill passed away and all their belongings were. Jeanine immediately broke down on entering the unit and started searching for something. She then spoke in a distressed and anxious tone, 'I gave Bill a jade Buddha to protect him while I was in China. It's not here. I need to find it.'

'The police have all his personal belongings. I'll drive you to the station. It's not far from here.'

We drove to the police station and all his personal belongings were handed over to Jeanine. The Buddha wasn't amongst them. This caused Jeanine to become more upset as we returned and entered the unit. The police said some money had been stolen and we were discussing if the Buddha was also stolen. Jeanine suddenly said, 'I need to go to the Broadbeach shopping centre. We need to go now.'

I didn't understand why she suddenly wanted to go shopping, but I didn't question her, because of the urgency in her voice.

'I'll lock up and we'll go.'

We drove along the highway and I hesitantly asked, 'What's it you need Jeanine?'

'I need to go to the jewellery shop there.'

I was thinking, *Why on Earth does she want to go to a jewellery shop at this time?*

It all became clear on arrival, we hurriedly walked to the shop and on entering she rushed to the counter.

'My partner brought a jade Budda in here to have a gold chain put on it, do you have it?'

'Yes, I know it, I'll fetch it for you.' He rummaged through a drawer while I explained the situation to him. The jeweller produced the Buddha with a gold chain fitted at Bill's request and said, 'I'm so sorry to hear of your loss, there is no charge.'

Jeanine kept shaking her head in disbelief and was highly distressed as we left. She was continually crying and saying, 'I told Bill not to get a gold chain, it's not right, he should've kept the leather strap. Why didn't he listen? It was for his protection!'

We then returned to the unit and started going through Bill's belongings to work out what to do with the extremely huge collection of books he had. Bill was an avid reader, and always had a new book on the go. He apparently read a new book each day. Bill's mother told me this some months later when the Foundry manager and I visited her in South Amboy to help bring closure.

'When Bill was a young lad at South Amboy just south of New York, he was reading on the porch one day when the house across the road caught fire,' she said. 'The fire-brigade and crowds came, the fire was extinguished. In spite of me constantly pestering Bill, his eyes didn't leave the book. After the fire, Bill didn't know about the excitement that happened across the road. He went into another world when he was reading. How many young men would do that? I can't understand his intensity to this day.'

While Jeanine calmed herself initially, as the day went on she suddenly became distraught to the point of being hysterical. I knew something was seriously wrong but couldn't get her to articulate it. I hugged her and she cried and wailed. I pleaded with her to tell me what was troubling her. After lots of coaxing she sobbed, 'I want to commit suicide now that Bill's gone, I don't want to live any longer. But my family will disown me and burn all photos of me and my belongings to destroy any memories of me. I want my family to love and remember me. I don't know what to do.'

I was totally convinced she meant it because I hadn't seen anyone so distraught. I immediately took her out of the unit and walked her to the Surfers Paradise beach with my arm around her. We walked up and down for hours, and I became very emotionally involved. It was a beautiful sunny afternoon and the crashing waves provided a peaceful environment. Seagulls became our constant companions while we walked along the pristine white sand. I told her about my spiritual experience and how important it was for her to live, and that time would help heal the hurt. Nothing I said seemed to make a difference until

I started talking about living for the moment, and not worrying about the future. An old Buddhist story suddenly came to mind. Afterwards I wondered where it came from. I decided later it was guided and was what Jeanine needed. I started the story, 'A Buddhist monk was walking on a path beside a steep cliff one day. He met a warlord coming the other way who was intent on robbing him. After robbing him, the warlord threw the monk over the edge of the very steep cliff. On the way down, in spite of his imminent death he remained totally calm and admired the beauty of wildflowers growing on the cliff face as he passed by and eventually died on impact in peace.'

'That's a beautiful story.' Jeanine replied.

She immediately calmed right down. All the emotion seemed to disappear. I suggested she visit a Buddhist centre and said, 'I'm sure one is here at the Coast.'

I had the feeling the Buddhist religion gave her peace. I still cannot understand how that story had such a calming impact.

It was getting dark so we returned to the unit to sort out some more belongings and to collect our things. I drove her to her Chinese friend's restaurant. They put on a great spread until we all decided it had been a big day and it was time to retire to bed. I was glad she had these kind friends for support. They also said they'd take Jeanine to a Buddhist centre near Brisbane the next day. During the meal Jeanine spoke of her short China experience.

'The China I left was an extremely caring one, but the China I found on my visit was heartless.'

'What do you mean?' I said.

'I was on a railway station platform in a small village deep in China when the telegram was given to me. When I read it I was really upset and I went into a panic. Somehow all the clothes in my suitcase spilled on the platform. I was shocked that even though the platform was lined with people, both men and women just stared at me – not a single person came to help. In the old China everyone would have helped!'

I was exhausted. I came to learn later, with another incident involving my brother Graham having open heart surgery, that one must not get involved emotionally because it drains your energy. My head was spinning, my legs and body ached. I hadn't arranged any accommodation. It was a great effort just to drive around. I drove up and down the full length of the Coast in the old white company Ford Falcon Ghia looking for a motel, but all were booked out. Sometime, well after midnight, I drove into an old run-down motel displaying a dull and partially-lit vacancy sign. I parked the Ford and walked over crunchy gravel to a reception office in darkness. I rang the night bell.

I was extremely relieved when a light came on and the owner appeared at the front office door in her pyjamas looking half asleep. It was obvious I had woken her.

'Do you have a room for the night?' I asked while she opened the door.

An untidy and old office with papers everywhere materialised in the dull light behind her. She gave a nod and a grunt, saying nothing as she gave me a key to the unit. She pointed in the direction of the unit, again without saying a word as it seemed like too much effort. The run-down state of the lodgings didn't please, but at least I had a bed.

When I entered the unit I could see why it was available. It was dimly lit, the walls were faded and marked by too many bags brushing past them, and the bedspread was faded and tired. *At least the sheets and pillows look fresh and clean.* I showered, and tried unsuccessfully to meditate to calm myself. I then went to bed and attempted to sleep. My head was spinning and was full of 'head noise' while pondering the day's events. I ached from the exhausting day. I lay there wondering how I was ever going to get some sleep and be fit to face Jeanine tomorrow, when suddenly, in the dark, I felt someone place their hands on both sides of my face from behind. I immediately felt perfect peace surge through my body, and my head cleared instantly. My body suddenly felt great. The feeling of exhaustion vanished in seconds. I unwittingly turned my head sideways to speak.

'Thanks Carole,' I started to say when I abruptly realised I wasn't at home but in a motel, in bed alone. I lay awake for a while grasping the idea that I had just been healed by spirit. A new energy flowed into me. I relaxed and was just about to close my eyes when a sexual feeling came around me and I felt the top buttons on my pyjama top being undone. It gave me a start. I dismissed it, thinking that an old lost spirit that was a frustrated lover, or had been addicted to sex, had passed away in this room. I just ignored this presence and went into a very peaceful sleep.

I awoke feeling totally refreshed the next morning in both wonder and amusement at what had happened during the night. I was amazed how spirit could change my state of being (my energy) so rapidly and how we need to understand and learn how to raise our collective consciousness so these happenings become 'normal'. Once again I was thinking as I drove away in a very positive state of mind after this unique event.

If only our medical professionals would recognise and study the energy aspect of human beings. Medicine needs to recognise the truth that we have a soul and its implications.

Jeanine was in a much more settled state as her very supportive and encouraging friends were obviously having an impact. After organising the fate of Bill's belongings, I hugged her and said goodbye to her and her friends and returned to Toowoomba. Her friends were taking her to the Buddhist centre and then planned to make funeral arrangements. Thankfully, Jeanine had given up the idea of suicide.

When I returned to the Foundry, I was met by the financial controller.

'Head office rang and the board didn't consider the new furnace proposal but they did approve the cheap, second-hand unit.'

I knew this was an indication of the lack of confidence the board had in the business, because the previous GM and others, including the directors, believed Toowoomba Foundry was past help and had no future.

Soon after, Doug Curlewis rang me.

'I'm making you acting GM because Bill made the recommendation to me. I'll talk about it when I meet you in Toowoomba. You can drive me to the Coast to attend Bill's funeral. I'm not at all pleased with you over your last-minute request for a change to the board papers, particularly because it was my first board meeting.'

It was the day before Bill's funeral when Doug arrived on site. He soon arranged a meeting with me in my office. He was quite bombastic and as we sat opposite each other at my round table, he started grilling me in a very 'in your face' manner.

'I'm making you acting general manager, I know nothing about you. You pissed me off immensely with that second furnace proposal.'

'I just acted on the situation as I saw it. While it was unusual, I was acting in the best interests of the company.' He then responded generously with a more conciliatory tone in his voice.

'Maybe I should've been a bit more flexible. It was a pity it was my first board meeting as the new managing director.'

While I was a bit taken aback by his bombastic style, I soon liked the nature of him. I openly answered the many questions he rapidly fired at me. After about three quarters of an hour he jumped to his feet on the other side of my round table, and grinning widely he reached across the table and put out his hand.

'Congratulations!'

'What's that for?' I said with a sudden sense of curiosity.

'You're not acting anymore; I'm making you general manager!' He said it with a beaming smile. I reported to ten different people in my twelve-year term as GM. I still remember Doug with the highest regard and respect.

That night when I went home I said to Carole, 'I've just been made GM. Seeing how I'm the seventh in seven years I'll at least be assured of a year's employment.'

Carole laughed. She was obviously pleased with my promotion.

That night, Doug Curlewis took me and a few members of management out to dinner where we came to know each other more intimately. The next day, before we left for the funeral, Doug turned to me and said, 'I'll not tolerate a loss anymore, it's unacceptable. I'm setting you a profit target of $200,000. It's not negotiable.'

'I'll give you $400,000.' It came out of my mouth without any hesitation.

Shit, where did that come from? I questioned.

Doug gave me a huge grin and said, 'That's what I like to hear,' as we walked to the carpark. I drove Doug to Bill's funeral service at the Gold Coast and noted he was eyeing off the tired state of the Foundry's old Ford. He authorised a new car for me a week later.

As I wrote earlier, I'd turned down a lucrative job offer in a picturesque valley to inherit a mess! Even the Melbourne NCL board and the previous MD were calling it a hopeless case!

The board would soon be mystified as to how a rapid turnaround, with excellent financial results, actually happened.

None of us were expecting nine months later at financial year end a sales increase of 230% to $23.3m and an EBIT of $2.6m. $300,000 of it being generated by leasing unused factory space.

CHAPTER 18
CLOSURE FOR BILL'S MOTHER

The funeral went off well. Bill was available for viewing. Jeanine arranged some Buddhist chanting music, which made the service extremely peaceful. Everyone attending commented it was the most peaceful funeral they had attended. Jeanine returned to the USA to be near relatives in Los Angeles. She let me know months later by letter that she was teaching the American-born Chinese the Chinese language.

Before I deal with the goings-on that happened when Doug Curlewis and I returned to the Foundry, I'll move the story ahead twelve months to when I was able to give Bill's mother, Mary, and his brother, Bob, some closure.

In June 1994, I planned to visit Bill's mother and Jeanine on my return from attending the major foundry exhibition, GIFA, at Dusseldorf, Germany. About four months earlier, in February 1994, I was in a local bookshop when a book caught my attention. I've long since passed the book on but it was about a Mother Meera. It was a story about a man's spiritual awakening after visiting a spiritual healer, Mother Meera, in Dornburg-Thalheim, Germany. The man attended Darshan held by Mother Meera, where one kneels in front of her. She then places her hand on one's head as she undoes 'spiritual knots' on a white spiritual line running from your toes to the head. He described that during the thirty-second, hands-on period of Darshan, he had a few days of physical experience. I considered it amazing that he apparently went into a spiritual realm where time didn't exist. I remembered Einstein's comment that time is just an illusion.[26] My reading of various spiritual books also substantiated this phenomenon and that everything that ever happened or will happen is happening now – the present moment is all there is. My trip to Dusseldorf for the foundry exhibition had been approved, so I decided I'd see if I could book a Darshan session.

I wrote a letter to the German address in the book providing my schedule. A letter returned promptly, accepting me. I was booked in for Saturday 11th June 1994 at 7pm. The manufacturing manager Wayne Day, or 'Daisy' as we called him, and I flew from Australia to the UK for industry visits and meetings. We then flew to Dusseldorf to attend the exhibition. The weekend booked for Darshan in Dornburg was free so Daisy went to Berlin as a tourist as I set off to what I thought was Dornburg in the district of Thaliem in the state of Hesse. I had accommodation booked at Limburg, a village twenty minutes' drive from Dornburg. I set off by train, but I'd booked my trip to Dornburg BAD, (I learnt later that BAD is commonly attached to the name of a town that is named after its founder or patron.) which unbeknown to me was a five hour drive from Limburg. I arrived late evening in a huge old pre-war railway station at Leipzig which my map indicated was only a one hour drive from Dornburg. The Leipzig Hauptbahnhof, built in 1915, was reportedly the largest railway station in the world with 26 platforms. I barely had the time to take in its enormous cast iron and ornate structures as I struggled to find someone who could speak English to give me directions. It was getting late. When the terminal started to empty I decided to walk outside. On the opposite side of the street I saw a guy closing the doors of a hire car shop. I ran across to him, 'Can you help me please? I need to get to Limburg.'

I was sure it was only a short drive away. I was relieved when he spoke English but startled when he said, 'Limburg? That's five hours drive from here, it's a long drive. Sure you can hire a car; you just caught me. I was just closing. Come inside.'

I was shocked. He produced a map and I realised I'd travelled to the wrong Dornburg. I hired a car and set off full of apprehension as it was the first time I'd driven on the right hand side, and it was dark. I arrived safely very late in the night at the Limburg hotel after being totally lost at one stage of my journey.

On Saturday evening I drove to Mother Meera's house for Darshan. Many people were sitting and

---

26   A Einstein, This quote is contested, but it claims to indicate a possible origin of it is a letter from Einstein to the family of a personal friend Michele Besso, sent a few days after his death.

standing quietly around the grounds waiting. One American girl was sitting on the ground in the middle of all the waiting people in a traditional crossed-leg meditation pose with her eyes closed. I shook my head thinking, *wanker*, and sat down and waited for an official to call us. A lady of Indian origin dressed in a colourful sari eventually came out near the appointed time. In a no-nonsense manner she described what would take place and how we were to behave.

'Please make your way quietly into the room and please don't talk,' she said as she indicated the way to enter.

The American girl quickly hopped up and walked straight to the lady saying words to the effect of, 'It must be soo wonderful doing this amazing work here and . . .' She was cut off abruptly by the lady.

'No, it's bloody hard work organising you lot, so go inside. Remain quiet.'

I was chuffed. *That's good, these are no-nonsense people; I already have a respect for them.*

The room was crowded with people. We all sat on the carpeted floor. My turn came and I walked to Mother Meera and knelt in front of her as she placed her hands on my head for about thirty seconds. I felt a warm sensation and that was all. I returned to my spot and sat until everyone had Darshan, noticing one lady shake quite violently while having it, but standing up with a very peaceful look on her face. I drove back to the hotel and slept soundly.

The next day I went for a walk along the nearby river and came across stalls selling German sausages and sauerkraut. A German band was playing traditional music. I sat in the sun watching them while eating my sausage. I saw an old cathedral nearby and noticed people were checking it out. I walked up to have a look. I picked up a brochure at the front door when I entered and learnt it was the Cathedral of Limburg.

I walked around the church; it contained beautiful hand-carved woodwork throughout, and an array of intricate stained glass windows. I stopped near the ornate wood alter to admire something that caught my eye. Suddenly a huge energy flow started pouring through me, it was beautiful and like being in a divine shower. It was the same feeling I had at the truth seminar. It lasted about twenty seconds. It left me feeling great and that spirit was close by. It felt so peaceful. I contemplated, *They must be good people that come to this church.*

I had many more such experiences later in my life. They started during Maryann's Truth Seminar and

I often wonder if my visit to Mother Meera further opened that channel for me. I returned to Dusseldorf with another treasured memory.

The exhibition finished and Daisy and I flew from Dusseldorf to Heathrow with very long transition delays, then to New York. We arrived late in the evening at our hotel. Daisy immediately turned on every light as he opened up all the curtains and blinds to check out New York. We were only on the second floor so I said, 'Well Daisy, you've probably made us a great target for a random shooter out there.'

'What? What do you mean?'

'Bill told me people get randomly shot in New York.'

'Shit,' was all Daisy said. He hurriedly shut all the blinds and curtains.

I arranged for a limo to drive us to South Amboy, New Jersey and we went to bed just after 1am. I set the alarm for 4am to get ready for an early morning pick-up because we had to return to catch our flight to LA. Feeling very sleep-deprived we met the limo driver before daybreak who drove us to South Amboy to meet Bill's mother Mary and have breakfast with her. It was 26th June 1994, nine months after Bill's passing.

On our arrival, we pulled up in front of a modest house. I knocked on the door. It opened and I immediately knew it was Bill's mother Mary who greeted us. 'Doug is it?' she asked tentatively.

'Yes, at last we meet.' With that we hugged and I introduced her to Daisy.

We started to walk in when Mary saw the limo driver standing by the car.

'Are you joining us for breakfast?' she asked him.

The driver obviously hadn't experienced such a friendly request before and was looking around to see who Mary was talking to. It took a while to sink in and he said, 'Who me?'

'Of course, it's a special day,' Mary responded cheerfully and the driver hurried up the stairs just as Bill's brother Bob appeared and introduced himself.

Mary had prepared a great breakfast. We talked and talked until it was time to leave for the airport. The driver kept thanking Mary for the great breakfast. It was an extremely enjoyable experience. Because we'd not slept for a couple of days we were both extremely tired and finding it difficult to concentrate.

'I'm so very grateful for your visit; it's helped me to get closure. God bless you both,' were her parting words to us. We hugged her before we walked down the stairs to leave. Bob was also overcome with emotion as we walked down the steps to the limo.

Mary showed great hospitality. She obviously shocked the driver by asking him to have breakfast with us. The driver had never met such a friendly group or enjoyed such a well prepared, home-cooked breakfast. He was very touched and appreciative of his inclusion because he kept talking about it constantly while driving to the airport.

We arrived at John F. Kennedy International Airport just in time to catch a flight to LA to meet with Jeanine. We'd gone several days without any real sleep and my meeting and dinner with Jeanine was a disaster because I could barely stay awake. We flew economy class and being tall, I find it difficult to sleep on planes when flying economy, particularly in daylight. Jeanine had driven for over an hour to the meeting.

'You're much too tired, I shouldn't have come,' she said. 'You need to go to bed.' I struggled to finish my meal and we hugged as we said goodbye. We really needed to have planned a stopover so I could spend quality time with her.

In 1997 our letters to Jeanine were returned unopened and I've since lost track of her. I hope she's okay.

CHAPTER 19

WE MADE A PLAN

On returning to the Foundry after Bill's funeral in September 1993, I was officially appointed General Manager of Toowoomba Foundry. The date was October 1st 1993. Doug Curlewis and I sat down to discuss what to do next. A $5.5 million fire sale price had been placed on the Foundry because the board just wanted to get rid of its burden company. The board had also transferred many liabilities from Southern Cross to the lost cause of the Foundry to make the Southern Cross sale more attractive. The managing director of Southern Cross was publically saying he'd buy the old Foundry for a 'song' after the split and dedicate it to making Southern Cross product only.

I'd made a push for a management buyout when we first met. Doug flatly refused to consider it.

'I won't consider or support it. You'll all lose your homes, forget about it,' he said.

I wasn't experienced sufficiently at the time to get around the situation even though I'd met with interested investors.

We sat at my round office table after Doug toured the plant and he said, 'What do you plan to do next?'

'We need to get a strategic planning session underway urgently,' I said, 'to identify what we need to do in the next twelve months and in the next five years. I've spoken to Bill about this and we've a venue booked in a week's time.'

'No way, you won't have time to put all the data together needed to make informed decisions. You need more time.'

'We know the issues. We're ready now to do it, it's important,' I protested.

We haggled for a while as I argued the case. After some toing and froing Doug eventually relented and approved it, saying, 'Okay, but you'd better be right.'

Preparations for the planning session continued.

Meanwhile, I had to fly to New Zealand to present at a national foundry conference. I was the Queensland and national president of the Australian Foundry Institute (AFI). I left immediately after my presentation to lead the three-day Noosa planning session. I engaged Dr Peter Long, an HR consultant, to facilitate the session because I knew him as an experienced and able presenter. Peter became a personal friend and confidant. During the flight home from New Zealand I contracted asthma, an illness I'd never had before. My spiritual experiences convinced me it was just my fear blocking off my airways. So there I was, sucking on an odd-shaped huge plastic Ventolin apparatus my local doctor had prescribed during the planning sessions.

'I want to make the Foundry the best in the world!' I said in an early session between puffs.

I knew this was possible because my overseas experiences had shown we were a world leader in casting quality. This was met with huge cynicism and some ridicule but we decided to be the last Australian foundry standing. Unfortunately and sadly it was ultimately not to be.

I was determined to build an inclusive culture, and over thirty employees from all areas, including some experienced shop floor operators, attended the three-day sessions. All the wives journeyed up for a celebration dinner on the last night.

Many of the Foundry's managers were uncomfortable about the money invested in the planning session because abundance thinking had been crushed by a continuous and relentless focus on bottom line issues only. I left Noosa with a strong feeling that everything was going to be okay. My asthma disappeared on the last day, when the fear left me. The Foundry had stood the test of time for 122 years by the time I became GM in 1993. I was determined to make the business sustainable. Five key business issues were identified to be addressed and I placed these under an umbrella strategy of 'Rebuild, Optimise and Grow.' A mission was developed to provide focus: 'Our mission is to be the preferred manufacturer of superior quality machined ferrous castings through exemplary customer service.'

Within twelve months, three major customers and other small ones told us we were their preferred supplier because of our quality and strong customer service focus. As general manager of the factory I had a number of deep-seated personal goals. I was determined to be a leader, and not a manager. My overseas travels had built confidence in my leadership abilities and I knew strong leadership was needed.

Total transparency would be the order of the day – no hidden agendas. People must be allowed to say what they felt without retribution. I wanted to eliminate fear from the workforce as far as possible. I believe a non-threatening environment breeds creativity, loyalty and a strong commitment and responsiveness to market changes. Employees are more innovative and creative when devoid of fear. These are essential qualities for success in these rapidly changing and uncertain times. Mistakes would be tolerated. It's the pathway to truth in a business and employees quickly relate to it. They embrace it.

My experience made me aware that many CEOs punished people for mistakes, yet they made many themselves.

'I've learnt so much from my mistakes I'm thinking of making a few more,' I used to say at many of my employee sessions.

To me it's simply recognising employees are human beings and not machines. I'd made many mistakes through my career.

Training would be a priority and considered as an investment rather than a cost. The budget wouldn't be a strategic document but a secondary milestone document. I felt the three financial controllers that I worked with struggled to understand why I had little interest in the budget during the year except to see at the end of the month how we were tracking. It would be one element of the most important focus, which was a strategic plan developed by the leadership team and selected employees. Budget management was devolved to the shop floor areas where possible and these sections were only responsible for issues they could control. When it was implemented, this achieved some great cost savings. There was a sense of ownership when supervisors recognised the cost of the materials and labour under their control. They became less wasteful.

The third financial controller appointed during my time as general manager was Gordon Piets. I really enjoyed working with Gordon. He had worked as chief accountant for a large British corporation. In Australia he worked as an accountant for several years to Australia's richest man, Kerry Packer. He was then appointed to eliminate corruption in the Port Moresby Council in New Guinea. Progress was being made until his wife, in a supermarket, was threatened with a machete by two large locals. He immediately moved back to Australia where I was able to hire him. He facilitated the devolvement of budget responsibilities extremely well. He also had a great sense of humour and told me he crashed a Tiger Moth aeroplane in England while showing off in front of his mother. His work and humour proved very empowering for many shop managers and supervisors.

I aimed to have real-time reporting an all key business indicators. The closest we achieved was daily updating and this was a major tool in the company's transformation. We had a very competent, self-trained and practical IT manager, Glen, who could give me any data or statistic required.

Traditionally, an expense item would be unexpectedly high in a month. This would prompt the works director to reprimand the relevant supervisor who could never accurately identify what caused the increase during the month. Daily reporting identified an issue the next day. Supervisors and their operators could easily remember and identify yesterday's issue and so became part of the solution to prevent a reoccurrence. It facilitated non-punitive management and management by conversation rather than admonishment. Employees felt empowered when their suggestions for solutions were sought and implemented.

I know some saw this style I embraced as weak leadership, particularly as the culture in the years prior to my leadership had become quite punitive. Some previous managers thought nothing of heavily criticising and admonishing staff in front of others. I was doing what I felt was the right thing. I was relaxed and enjoying the many positive changes happening because I knew spirit was assisting.

However, not all agreed, as one reporting manager stated, 'You're a weak manager; you need to be much tougher when dealing with people.'

'The results are demonstrating I'm doing okay,' was my measured response.

Why's it so strange for people to understand that coming from love rather than constant fear is far more powerful?

I held no malice and just felt he didn't understand my unusual approach. He ultimately became my biggest supporter. It was interesting that he was the a direct report to me who worked mostly in his feelings. Short meetings of the leadership team each morning ensured everyone was 'on the same page' and the focus was on solving problems in a timely manner. It kept the leadership team focussed on 'today's' issues. It was the nearest I could get everyone to working in 'the present moment'.

Continuous improvement would also be the order of the day, no matter how small the improvement. I was determined no employee would be asked to do any task I wouldn't do, and any undesirable conditions were to be dealt with promptly. I had an ambition to move from a component supplier constantly driven by price, to a marketer of our own branded product, using research and development (R&D) as a vehicle to achieve the transition. The experience I had during my time in the Product Designs Office of Southern Cross in relation to engine, pump and irrigation equipment development became valuable, as did my time working in the R&D section of Borg Warner UK on automatic transmission development. It made me appreciate the importance of product and brand development, and the market power it provided to an organisation's future.

A consultant assisting me to develop job descriptions asked me to explain to him how I defined the difference between a manager and a leader. I went home that night, and drawing on my spiritual view of the world, I came up with the following.

Management is about compliance. It's analytical and external to the person. Its effectiveness can be easily audited. It's a journey of the mind and is clearly defined by institutions of learning. It's predominantly an intellectual process. Its major impediments are ego, power and control trips and rampant intellectualism. Its positive attribute is reason through considered use of intelligence, resulting from practical 'life' education.

Leadership is about creating. It's qualitative and internal to the person. Its subtleties are elusive and difficult to define. It's a journey of the soul, defined by self-realisation and self-determination. It's a spiritual process (not religious). Its most challenging aspect is not abrogating personal responsibility to the 'universe', but taking personal responsibility with accountability through using as much wisdom, honesty and integrity as possible.

I've come to believe that the best leaders, consciously or unconsciously, are working at the level of their very essence, are spiritually driven whether they realise it or not, and as a result, are respected for their integrity. My personal experience revealed to me the importance of coming from one's very essence in daily activities and tuning into the guidance available to us all if we just embrace it. In summary, I believe if a business remains unchanged for twelve months it's most likely being managed, not led. Integrity-based leadership is about authenticity and transparency.

On arriving back to the Foundry from Noosa, I walked from the carpark to the office entrance looking at its peeling paint, I then looked at the factory with its dented walls with numerous nail holes and peeling dark red paint, with rusting obsolete appendages clinging to it. I viewed the rubbish lying down near the distant boiler house. *There are so many challenges in this unloved workplace, where do I start?*

Knock over one thing at a time Douglas and don't panic.

I took a deep breath and marched through the door trying to ooze confidence, drawing strength from my spiritual experience.

CHAPTER 20
THE TURNAROUND BEGINS

The old second-hand induction furnace was installed during the Christmas break within budget. The additional profit it generated recovered the investment in the first month of its operation. A very enjoyable and productive relationship developed between Doug and me, most likely assisted by the fact the company made a profit of $20,000 in the first month. Up to fifteen work centres were broken down because of cost cutting, so my first directive was to get them all working and earning money. This strategy helped yield the small profit.

It was after my first month's report was lodged that Doug rang me one day to make a demand. 'I've been going through the financials from before the split and you only had 192 people, now you have 224 on the books. That's not on. I need you to cut staff by thirty-two.'

'That figure didn't include casuals,' I insisted.

'There are no casuals listed here.'

'They were left out to make the people numbers appear better and were treated as an expense,' I explained.

'No way, I'm directing you to determine the names of thirty-two people from staff that are to be made redundant. It must come from the indirect area.'

'I refuse,' I said bluntly.

'If you don't do it I'll bloody well replace you with someone who will. This isn't negotiable.' The threatening tone and energy of his response made it clear it was me or someone else.

I took a deep breath and said sullenly, 'Okay, I'll look at it.'

I was really pissed because it seemed every managing director just looked at people numbers. They were obsessed with the need to get rid of them. I told no one and compiled the list at home. I outlined in detail the consequences of terminating each employee. I knew each intimately and understood their contribution. I emailed a report from home without involving my secretary because I wanted to keep this outrageous idea to myself when the team was starting to get well and truly 'fired up'.

A few weeks passed and the next month's profit report came in at a welcome $100,000. I suspect this totally unexpected great result, and the fact that we almost had reached his demanded annual profit in two months, tempered Doug's thinking. He rang me after reading the monthly report and said.

'I'll let you keep those people – you don't have to make them redundant.'

'Great,' I responded quietly, and hung up. It was the only time I was really pissed off at Doug. I destroyed my report and got on with leading the many changes needed. Profit was increasing each month by $100,000 in spite of the company's run-down state. The monthly profit peaked at $425,000 in January 1994 just after the old furnace installation. We had won a $4-million axle box order and our increased sales activity on the road was generating orders also. I had removed all travel restrictions. Employees were also cutting waste and were more committed to their work.

'$500,000 next month Doug?' Doug Curlewis asked expectantly when I phoned him to tell him of the excellent monthly result.

'No, I think we've plateaued, but it's great to be in this position.'

I felt very satisfied with what we'd all achieved. I was enjoying reshaping and reenergising the Foundry and its people.

Having demanded I deliver a profit at year end, Doug was ecstatic that the company was turning around so rapidly and exceeding profit well beyond his wildest expectations. He couldn't understand how it happened. The metal workers union delegate called it a miracle. Doug was always impressed by the enthusiasm of the leadership team and the people at Toowoomba Foundry.

'I can't understand your enthusiasm and the positive attitude of your team. You're up for a sale, you've a very onerous supply contract, the place was run down and people usually drop the ball and morale plummets under such circumstances,' he said during a visit.

It was a great feeling to finally have the bloody place in profit!

CHAPTER 21

MOTIVATING THE DOWNTRODDEN EMPLOYEES

The Foundry was still in a very neglected and derelict state. Employees were ashamed to admit they worked there. The employees were also very fearful of the future. Continuing redundancies each year had been the order of the day. The factory was sheeted in mostly dented corrugated iron with peeling dark red paint and it was dark and dirty inside. It had 365 roof leaks which often rusted trays of new product. I had John, the plumber, count the leaks. I realised we one for each day of the year. Numerous run- down or derelict, obsolete, structural appendages such as old towers were attached to the building in a rusting state. All fences were falling over. The five blue metal stone street gutter crossings were in such disrepair the wheel of a mother's car broke through one and the car was stuck in the gutter after she dropped her son off in the entry carpark.

Forklifts regularly bogged in the unsealed areas of the site and concrete floors in the factory were in gross disrepair. Morale was very low. Rags and soft drink cans were often left on the floor in walkways. Through continuous cost cutting in maintenance, between ten and fifteen key work centres would be broken down each day, as I mentioned earlier. The newest computer numerical controlled (CNC) lathe had major slide-way damage due to a lack of lubrication when maintenance programs fell to cost cutting. The accident rate was obscenely high. It was a frightening four times higher than the industry standard.

The marketing and sales area was in no better state. The managing director just prior to the split, who was now the MD of the Southern Cross sales and marketing business, had focussed only on the production of the company's own Southern Cross product in the period leading to the split. The contract work in the Foundry, involving a range of rail, agricultural and automotive customers external to the company, was neglected. Relationships got to the stage that as GM I had to personally apologise to one angry MD of an important international customer to convince him not to resource to another foundry.

The Melbourne-based NCL board was so convinced the Foundry would close after the company split eventuated, the supply contract to Southern Cross was onerous and unreasonable. They agreed to keep all the Southern Cross liabilities with the Foundry such as all unresolved product warranty issues. The Foundry was immediately put up for public sale at $5.5 million. As I said, it was regarded as a 'fire' sale. No offers were forthcoming.

However, due to the swift increase in profit in the next twelve months, the board refused an offer of $18 million. The board took it off the market. The change in strategy had resulted in a rapid and major turnaround in profitability

In the first eighteen months I flew all over Australia resolving the outstanding warranty claims inherited. The fourteen warranty claims included problems with large centre-pivot and travelling irrigators; centre-pivot irrigation systems in North Queensland on sugar cane and mango farms; drip-feed irrigation of olives in New South Wales with a failed crop; a flood lifter pump with cavitation problems on the Murray River; a solar pump installation in Western Australia; and a house with crumbling bricks in Queensland, a leftover from a brick company Southern Cross once owned. I achieved my personal goal of resolving most of these outstanding issues in the first twelve months at a significant cost, which also impacted on the Foundry's profit. A couple of claims subject to legal dispute dragged on over a few years and were finally resolved at a cost of $300,000. Fortunately these were covered by insurance policies.

In addition, the number of parts supplied to Southern Cross by the Foundry was in excess of 13,000. Unfortunately, the new supply contract was written to allow the order for quantities of parts to be as low as 'one-off' even though it took hours to set up machines for some parts and only minutes of cycle time to complete the operation – it was a recipe for disastrous losses.

To make matters worse, the contract stipulated that on the major product range of International Standard Organisation (ISO)-rated centrifugal pumps the profit margins, prior to the split, would be given as a full discount to Southern Cross in the first year. It would then reduce each year to zero in the fourth year. In addition, a new notional annual rent of $140,000 was paid to head office. (This national rent increased to $722,000 after new owners purchased the business in 2002). It was very obvious there was no love for Toowoomba Foundry. Staff numbers had been cut each year through constant redundancies so I took on both roles of operations manager and executive general manager for the first year. This proved exhausting and unsustainable after twelve months, so I appointed a manufacturing manager.

I'd managed to put my initial fear aside and settled down to face the daunting challenges. I drew strength from my spiritual experience. I was determined to drive out fear in the employees also. In the first year I spent many nights each week, and many weekends, walking the factory talking to the day shift, evening and late night shift people (called 'the lost tribe' by the night shift supervisor because they were rarely visited by management). I communicated the new strategy, saying 'yes' to initiatives they suggested hoping to encourage their empowerment, reassuring them their jobs were safe, and gaining their trust and confidence. One day Daisy met me walking through the factory,

'You're just a bloody yes man, you're saying yes to everything,' he said in his typical frank way.

'It's all needed so what else am I supposed to do?'

I felt vulnerable approving so many changes based on a gut feeling without the full understanding of some of the cost implications. Traditionally, a report or recommendation would have to be submitted to make many of the changes I instigated. However, a decision always felt okay. It allowed change to move extremely rapidly and did prove to be right. Pride was soon developing in the workforce, profitability was rising and customers were noticing and making complimentary comments. I'd adopted all employees as my family and I was committed to seeing they were well informed, trusted and empowered. I'd witnessed such bad treatment of employees in the previous years that I was determined it wasn't going to happen on my watch.

One night, the night shift foreman commented, when I walked in after a late night outing, 'Do you make your bloody bed in the Foundry?'

I lived within seven minutes' drive of the plant so it was easy to pop in regularly. Slowly, I felt I was gaining the trust and respect of the employees. This made me more determined not to let them, our customers, or our head office, down. Over the first two months I came to know each of the 224 employees personally and by name.

It was within the first year of becoming general manager that Dr Peter Long, the facilitator of our first strategic planning event that had led to a spectacular company turnaround, identified that I was taking on too much responsibility and not delegating appropriately. One day while on site I invited him to have lunch with me and he declined because he said he had another engagement. I was really surprised when I returned to my office and found a dozen small, black, stuffed monkey toys sitting on my round table and two larger grey haired ones. Peter soon appeared in the doorway with a wide smile.

'Doug, how do you like your monkeys? Each time someone comes into your office with a problem I want you to pick up a black monkey and decide who has the problem to solve after the meeting and give the monkey to that person. You've gotta learn to delegate more. It has to be clear who has the monkey on their back.'

'You crazy bugger, I'll give it a try – thanks Pete,' I replied.

The process of delegating monkeys proved most enjoyable and was completed with much humour. It greatly assisted me to delegate. The two larger grey-haired monkeys represented Doug Curlewis, the MD I reported to, and the chairman of the board. I still have three monkeys. Doug's international experience in manufacturing was a welcome contribution to our planning when he introduced us new measurable performance indicators.

I learnt a lot from Doug. He visited regularly, and was always complimentary about the positive approach all employees displayed and the great financial results. I remember the second time I took him into the factory for a tour and to talk to employees, something he always was keen to do. Our first stop was the core shop where I handed him over to Daisy to give Doug the tour. I left and went back to my office. Doug came into my office on his return.

'You know what? You're the first manager who's ever left me on a tour and not closely guarded me. What if they said bad things about you and how the place is run?' he said.

'I'm sure you'd tell me and I'd want to know so I could address them. Isn't honesty what our corporate values are about?'

One day while he was getting into his car to leave, I was saying goodbye when he turned to me.

'You're the most qualitative manager I've met, I don't understand what it is you're doing but please keep doing it,' he said with a wide grin and a laugh.

I never told anyone my deepest intent was to change the energy of the organisation through total openness and transparency because I'd realised working at a high level of integrity triggered powerful universal forces and synchronicity that can rapidly assist an organisation. True and authentic positive energy attracts positive things. I can also honestly say that at no time did I ever think about what was in my best interest during my twelve-year term as general manager. The only exception to this was when the chairman of the new owners told me in 2005 he was retiring me. He and I knew my refusal would mean instant dismissal.

Safety and customer service measures were two key performance areas Doug taught me. We embraced this totally. He was passionate about safety and the Foundry had a pitiful record in this area with injuries occurring almost daily. I made a commitment to attend every accident and the hospital with the employee if they were hospitalised. I did this for two reasons, one to reassure the employee their pay would continue as normal and they'd be fully supported. Hearing it directly from the GM was very comforting to them. The second reason was to maintain my personal awareness of the impact accidents had on my employees and their families to reinforce and stimulate my commitment to safety. I had the feeling some of my managers considered it interfering, but I had a strong feeling to do it for 'my family'.

We started using an internationally recognised measure called the Lost Time Injury Frequency Rate per million hours worked (LTIFR). Our first measured data yielded 150 plus – the Australian heavy manufacturing industry benchmark in 1993 was 40. A lost-time injury was defined as one serious enough that the employee couldn't return to work the next day. We also introduced a measure called the Medically Treated Injury Frequency Rate per million hours worked (MTIFR), which was an indication of the number of injuries requiring medical attention on the day of the injury but the employee was okay to work the next shift, to identify areas needing attention to reduce risk. We later introduced a third measure called the First Aid Injury Frequency Rate per million hours worked (FAIFR) to alert us to potential danger signs so we could be proactive to support early risk mitigation measures with data. The smallest first aid attention was recorded. These measures are now used by nearly all engineering and manufacturing businesses but their use was just gaining acceptance by most Australian manufacturers at the time. My feeling of connectedness to all employees as a result of my experience stimulated my commitment to them.

During our strategies to improve accident performance we started to benchmark global companies with exemplary performance. This highlighted gross corporate dishonesty. The safety officer found a foundry in the USA that achieved millions of hours free of injury and was featured in industry journals. The company was tracked down and it turned out the employees were mostly untrained and of Hispanic origins. Broken limbs were commonplace. The company had a doctor and hospital room on site so employees were given a training document to read while in bed so the injured employee 'attended' work each day and no lost time was officially recorded.

Two years into our change programs, I read that a foundry owned by a global automotive corporation in the UK had won safety awards and had an LTIFR of sixty. I was invited by the British Cast Iron Research Association (BCIRA) in the UK to present at an international foundry conference at Warwick University, in April 1995, on the successful and rapid regeneration of the Foundry. I decided I'd take the opportunity to benchmark foundries in the UK and Europe. I visited the automotive foundry and was immediately shocked by the very poor housekeeping. I immediately became suspicious of the score. After the tour I talked to the safety staff and found that the measure was based on 200,000 hours and not one million hours.

This meant the LTIFR number needed to be multiplied by five to convert it to the international measure of one million hours. Under UK national government legislation at the time, injuries that resulted in employees being three days off work were reportable to the government. This three day absence period was the criterion for the LTIFR number, not the one day international measure. The safety team was obviously embarrassed when they disclosed this information to me. We stopped benchmarking after these two findings and concentrated on keeping our results totally honest and continually improving. I'm sure executive bonuses drive this dishonest behaviour.

Our lowest LTIFR achieved during my term was eight. I attributed this dramatic improvement to the adoption of the DuPont safety training program. Its total focus on people interaction combined with simple and practical processes attracted me. This was in preference to the National Safety Council's five star safety program which required a library of procedural documents. We initially offered incentives each month if targets were reached and a TV or similar prize was drawn. This was stopped when some employees became critical of injured employees and we finally settled on a celebratory barbeque for all employees, cooked by management and supervisors. When key milestones were reached we'd issue free movie passes or a similar acknowledgement. Individual sections would be treated to a restaurant dinner with their wives when new improved safety milestones were reached in their work area. I was against bonus or incentive schemes because I'd witnessed many people in previous years work to the detriment of the company to secure their bonus. I've the view that selective individual bonus payments generate self-interest. A scheme that rewarded all employees equally was the system I embraced. It applied to me also.

At Christmas the company would present each employee with a 'Santa sack' loaded with goods. It recognised not only the employee but their wife or partner also. Most years I'd include a personally written Christmas card to each employee thanking them and highlighting a positive that they contributed.

I remember one morning I was doing my morning factory walk at about 10am. I stopped to speak to a machine shop employee. When I walked to his machine I was shocked to find him in a very distressed state.

'Hey John, what's the matter?' I said as John turned his eyes to me. His hands were shaking and he looked unsteady.

'I'm sorry . . .'

'No need to apologise John, turn the machine off.'

John switched off the multi-spindle drill and turned to me.

'Me wife's just had a nervous breakdown and isn't in a stable state of mind, my daughter's run off and I've just been diagnosed with cancer,' he paused. 'I just dunno what to do,' he said with tears in his eyes.

'You need to take it easy. I'll arrange a lift home for you. You can take all the time you need on full pay.'

'Thanks Doug, that's really appreciated,' he said while we were walking to the section manager.

I then had a new company policy introduced that required all employees who were absent from work to report directly to their supervisor before commencing work. There was some criticism because a small minority, and the union, had the view it was checking up on people taking 'sickies'.

A clear explanation as to why the policy was being implemented was provided at the next GM Brief. I made no apology that anyone just taking a day off would have to eyeball their supervisor on their return. It was supported by both unions involved following the explanation and became policy. Absenteeism wasn't high in the plant and was always under four percent and usually between 2.5 and three percent. Doug was also passionate about customer service and as a result we introduced another measure new to the leadership team called Delivery in Full on Time (DIFOT) and if the quantity of product delivered wasn't exact or it was delivered a day late to a customer it was a miss.

Structured daily reporting assisted both openness and in a significant reduction in employees fearing to speak up and express a view. It also provides the platform for management by conversation rather than more 'end of month' punitive styles as mentioned earlier. It generates trust and stimulates a genuine interest and focus in finding solutions.

Every minute of machine down-time was logged and charted over time so the areas needing attention, redesign or capital investment for continuous improvement programs were easily identified and addressed. Every reject casting was logged and the reason for the rejection and its costs was available, as one simply drilled further down into the database. I remember one day when I did my morning review of the data I noted $7,000 worth of rejects on a component in our major product family. I immediately knew an operator wasn't performing the quality checks during the machining process. I rang the shop manager.

'It's obvious to me gauging [measuring] checks weren't done on the brake-drums by the operator.'

'Her supervisor agrees, yet Christine's claiming they were. We're not prepared to say she's a liar,' he said.

I supported this approach. Faced with this dishonesty, I returned to my office to work out how the operator could be clearly brought to account. I rang the quality manager and explained the situation.

'Gary, would you set up one of the reject drums with the measuring gauges so I can ask Christine how the gauge read incorrectly?'

He set up a reject brake-drum with the measuring gauges used. I met with the operator.

'Christine, would you please show me how the gauges didn't measure properly? It's a very expensive failure of the gauges and I need to understand the problem so we can stop it happening again.'

Christine was very nervous while she handled the gauging equipment. It was obvious to both of us the gauge was never used in spite of her weakening continuous assurances that it was.

She resigned the next day and I remember thinking how accurate daily reporting and non-punitive management strategies can bring great accountability. The only employees subjected to immediate summary dismissal during my time as general manager were blatantly dishonest ones. It was a very small number.

Each employee was also trained in customer service and telephone answering. A cascade training system that we learnt from our DuPont safety training was adopted where I'd teach managers who reported to me, and then the training cascaded down until all employees were trained by their immediate manager or supervisor. The company had over seventy phones distributed across the plant and the training resulted in all being answered very professionally within four rings. Many phone answering awards were won in a head office corporate competition.

In 2000 head office agreed to invest $4 million in three robotic machining and assembly lines. This project highlighted to me a lesson in the ego-based power games sometimes played by corporate staff. I'd worked with our relevant people and developed a capital investment request. I sent it off to the head office, spoke in detail to the head accountant and communicated its urgent need to address rapid sales growth. He was to present it to the chairman for approval because it was within his authority. I was extremely busy and in Canada. The factory rang me to let me know head office hadn't approved the capital request. The need was urgent as we were experiencing growth of 40%.

I was in Winnipeg where our customer was based and, frustrated at the unnecessary delay, I decided to ring the head accountant Jerry.

'Hi Jerry, what's happening with the approval of the robotic machining lines?'

I was stunned by his response.

'It mustn't be really urgent because no one has chased me for it.'

Seething with anger over this blatant stupidity and ego-tripping I yelled.

'I fucking thought I was dealing with a mature person. It's now obvious I'm seriously mistaken. I give you my personal commitment that I'll ring you every fucking hour until it's signed.'

His flippant treatment of this request for capital approval, critical to meet the huge growth was a shock to me.

I immediately hung up. It wasn't only the Winnipeg cold that made me shiver. The approval was signed shortly after. This is one of many issues during my business life that left me convinced accountants had no place in running manufacturing or engineering businesses. Maybe I just dealt with too many with big egos.

The robotic lines were installed and production volumes ramped up quickly.

We had allowed a month to install each line. This proved to be super optimistic as each line installation took three months to reach full output. I never criticised staff when projects ran over time. My spiritual experience helped me to avoid forcing deadlines. I let them unfold at their natural pace, even if this was uncomfortable at times. The end result was always pleasing.

For quite a number of years while general manager of the Foundry, I'd lecture to mature part-time MBA students at the local university about business strategy and the company's rapid turnaround. In the final lecture I gave I emphasised that accountants are not equipped to effectively manage manufacturing or engineering businesses. I watched as several attendees slid down in their chairs and the university officer who contracted me gave me a dirty look!

I was never asked to present again. My view of avoiding accountants as managers in engineering or process businesses was endorsed during a visit to Japan when I met with the Japanese Management Association. It had also been the prevailing view during the many meetings I'd had in Germany. This could be one possible reason why these countries are excellent at engineering and manufacturing.

I was told recently by a retired CEO of a large German manufacturer that accountants are now moving into CEO roles – I wish them luck!

Around this time I attended a number of management retreats where business performance of all divisions and future strategies were reviewed. These events were arranged by head office in Melbourne. When recognition awards were handed out by the MD over a celebratory dinner I would get the Silent Achiever Award.

In around 2003 there was a bright young lad I'll call Billy who often had highly emotional outbursts at his supervisors, accompanied by very foul language, irrespective of the area in which he was placed. I'd spoken to him a few times on my rounds and he seemed a likeable and intelligent young man. His disrespectful behaviour reached a stage where the shop manager decided to terminate his employment. I made it my policy to do an exit interview with the manager of the employee and any employee who was recommended for dismissal. The metal workers union became involved because Billy was a member. They were strongly pushing to have Billy relocated to the company's despatch warehouse on a different part of the site. I supported Billy's dismissal in spite of the union demands. When, at the exit interview, I told him about my decision, Billy immediately began an emotional and abusive tirade directed at me.

'You fucking managers don't give a shit about young people like me; you're only interested in looking after your fucking selves. Go on, fucking sack me then.'

I then had a feeling he had been badly mistreated in his life. I returned his tirade using similar language. For some reason I decided to go hard in my response.

'Don't you tell me I don't care, I've been fucking working on a drug rehab centre for the last two years to help young people just like you. If you keep this up you'll end up in fucking jail and I'm sure the old inmates would like shagging that young bum of yours.'

Billy immediately broke down.

'That's what happened to me,' he cried with tears rolling down his cheeks.

My heart went out to him. Daisy and I quickly changed to being supportive.

'I'm really sorry to hear that Billy,' I said.

'Me mum burnt me with cigarettes,' he said while still crying, lifting his shirt to show the many scars. 'She sent me to a boarding school in Melbourne. That's where it happened. A pervert teacher abused me.'

'Billy, do you still wanna be this angry when you're old and in your sixties?'

'No . . . I wanna get rid of this anger.'

We talked more and I offered him as many free counselling sessions as he needed with a local psychologist. We then learned he recently had an altercation with the local police and was subject to a local bail order. If he didn't pay $1,000 by the end of the month he'd be jailed for a month.

'Leave it to me.' I left the room to meet with the union official.

The union was still pushing hard for Billy to be relocated to the warehouse, saying to me how they support their members and dismissing Billy was unjust. I met the official and explained what we'd just learnt.

'Why don't we each put in $500 for his bail money? He's been through enough and I don't want to see him in jail,' I said.

The union representative went very quiet.

'I don't have the authority to do that,' he said.

He returned to Brisbane and his concern for Billy was greatly diminished. I decided to pay the bail money out of my personal funds and arranged to meet him the following day at the city courthouse. I parked my car and walked up to the courthouse at the agreed time. Billy and his best friend came walking toward me.

'Thanks for doin' this,' Billy said without introducing his friend.

I walked up close to him to give him the cheque.

'We can't have you going to jail,' I said.

During this exchange with Billy I saw how distrustful he was of human beings because when I walked within a couple of feet of him, he stepped back quickly and thrust out his hand to receive the cheque. It was obvious he trusted no one but his friend. No one was allowed in his 'space'. I just wanted to give him a hug because I could feel his pain, but couldn't approach any closer than within one metre of him. The bail money was paid and Billy left the city after having about three sessions with the psychologist. He visited me to thank me for the support. He said he was getting on top of his anger issue. About a month later I received a phone call from an upset Billy.

'My mother told me she had arranged a job for me in Victoria and when I arrived I found it wasn't true. I've now run out of money to get back home and don't know what to do.'

'Could you give me $200 to get back home?'

I was initially suspicious but I decided to trust Billy. I transferred $300. Around six months later I received a second call from a very excited Billy,

'I've been working on getting my semi-trailer driver's licence in Albury. Next week I'll get it. I'll be able to drive B-doubles [a truck with two trailers].'

He was really looking forward to it and he sounded very happy. It seemed his life was getting on track. It was less than a month later I again received a phone call one night from a very distraught Billy in Albury, New South Wales.

'Me best friend was killed in a car crash a couple of days ago and today I did an illegal U-turn to buy a pizza and the cops saw me. I was upset and lost my temper with a cop so he booked me and I'm in big trouble with 'em again.'

Billy couldn't cope with anyone in authority making demands on him. It just brought back the painful memory. Coincidentally, I was planning to visit an automotive customer in Albury, a rural city close to where Billy was working, the next week. I arranged to meet Billy to see if I could assist somehow. However, he didn't show. I constantly rang his mobile phone during my visit but it didn't answer.

Billy has never answered my many calls to his mobile phone since. His phone has now been disconnected.

I often wonder what happened to Billy. Months later I was speaking to an employee on my morning rounds who was relatively close to Billy. He told me that before working at the Foundry, Billy had travelled to Melbourne with a small axe in his luggage to kill the man who abused him so he couldn't abuse any more boys. When he learned the man had died he said to the employee on his return, 'At least he can't hurt anyone anymore.'

Sadly, there are a lot of Billy's in this world. Where is the love that prevents this happening?

CHAPTER 22
THE BUSINESS TURNAROUND

I have no doubt the spectacular transformation of the business under my leadership would not have happened without the influence of my revelational experience. It helped me make key decisions rapidly using intuitive guidance, thus avoiding detailed intellectual analysis and formal proposals that often drag timeframes out.

I was keen to get real-time status reports of all pertinent business functions. That would keep a focus on what was happening in 'the here and now', an important spiritual need to try and keep people 'in the moment' as mentioned earlier. Our self-taught IT manager, Glen, was a whiz in setting up systems and while real-time reporting proved too difficult, we settled on daily reporting and Glen soon had the systems in place. The leadership team then knew the status of all aspects of the business each morning. Capital investment was extremely limited by the board and new CNC machinery was urgently needed. One day, Ken the tooling manager walked into my office.

'I know where we can get some excellent machine tools at low cost,' he said.

'Where? We sure need them and head office's capital expenditure allocation won't buy much.'

'In Osaka, Japan there's a street they call 'Machinery Mile', it's full of good quality second-hand machines. I can get info on what's available.'

'Do it,' I replied knowing well that I was about to approve Ken's visit to Japan without any written justification. My spiritual experience gave me a confidence in decision-making, allowing me to discard the normal bureaucratic processes of the past. It just felt right.

Ken flew to Japan and second-hand machines from Japan were sourced and installed. One multi-pallet Mitsui Seiki CNC machining centre had less than 150 hours of spindle running time logged. It cost less than half the US$1.2 million price for a new unit. A near-CNC lathe was bought also. The Japanese culture is very kind to machinery. The machines were as new, it was a much-needed triumph.

Some of the profit in the first year, which was well in excess of the budget, was invested in upgrading maintenance and the reliability of the plant. I also managed to sneak in an unauthorised and much-needed capex project. During the 'honeymoon' period of the rapid turnaround I wasn't exposed to close board scrutiny. I found I had a greater appetite for taking risks after my spiritual experience. However, it didn't take long for the need for more head office control to arrive.

To assist cultural change, monthly GM Briefs, based on total transparency, kept employees on every shift informed about the company's operation and performance. Transparency is yet another vehicle that allows spirit to operate in a business. The financial controller at the time came to see me.

'You can't tell employees how much money we're making; you'll have the unions demanding big pay increases,' he said.

'Don't worry about it, it'll be okay, I'll handle it,' I reassured him.

I was determined that total transparency would be a key value of my leadership.

The month's profit only became an issue once, during a period of very high profitability, when the metal workers union delegate spoke at a GM Brief because I encouraged employees to speak their mind.

'I guess we can all get a big pay rise now the Foundry's travelling so well, Doug,' he said wryly as all employees suddenly smiled.

'You can put it through in the next Enterprise Bargaining Agreement (EBA),' he continued.

When return on investment (ROI) was clearly explained to employees at the GM Brief in simple terms, along with the many risks and challenges faced by manufacturing in Australia when compared to 'armchair' investors in stocks, it became a non-issue. People relate to truth when they hear it.

To further assist cultural change, supervisors were empowered to spend moderate amounts of money to improve the housekeeping and organisation of their area. This resulted in a rapid change in the presentation of the factory. It helped build ownership.

I lost my need for control after the experience and relied on my daily walks to give guidance and approval on improvement projects. I had come to learn that a strong need for control is fear-based and can inhibit solid outcomes. I did find it difficult to relinquish control in some areas though. It can be hard letting go!

In September 1994 production was stopped for two days. All employees were taken off site and put through a Put People First event run by Time International. It was an entertaining program where an experienced facilitator challenged employees to think about their lives and the future. He introduced personal growth themes and psychology descriptors like 'transactional analysis' where employees learned the benefits of using the adult (mature, balanced and emphatic approach) 'tape' in their daily routine rather than the child (emotional and victim approach) or parent (authoritarian or controlling approach) 'tape' in their home and work environment. Many employees were looking for the company's catch and there was none. Some saw it as an entertaining day off. One supervisor marched into my office.

'Those bloody two days did bring changes to me and my home life. It was worthwhile. I just wanted to say thanks.' He turned and left as I was calling out.

'Great, I'm glad someone benefited from it!'

He disappeared. My spiritual experience left me confident that to make the company a success we had to get to the very essence of the many poorly treated and scared employees. Trust through honesty and integrity was to be the vehicle, along with this event which demonstrated we genuinely cared about them. It also gave them something 'without hooks' – the true spirit of giving.

Many others mentioned that it did bring a change to their approaches at home and at work, however all employees knew the company did something meaningful and enjoyable for them without expecting a payback. It further helped to develop trust and loyalty. Head office was concerned about the $150,000 total cost of the event and the loss of production; however, the unexpected financial results resulted in positive recognition of the company's performance by the MD and the Melbourne-based board.

The culture improved rapidly through a greater sense of involvement on the part of the employees. Ownership resulted. It also assisted the many continuous improvement and strategic change programs. Instead of a few managers being the custodians of decisions leading to change, many employees were contributing daily to changes. It prompted our sales manager, who visited many companies throughout Australia on a regular customer visit schedule, to walk in my office one day.

'I think it's amazing, each week I walk through the factory and I see significant change, while in the many customer companies I visit I don't see any changes over years,' he said.

I had a commitment to incremental change. Small changes happening each day amount to a visible major change at year end. It was more affordable.

The Metal Workers Union delegate couldn't believe how morale and factory presentation had changed so quickly and as I mentioned earlier, he considered it a miracle. To me it was the power of real empowerment, transparency, letting go of control and rapid intuitive decision-making. As I said earlier, sometimes it wasn't easy to relinquish control. I was determined to leave events to unfold before us instead of forcing outcomes. This approach also harnesses the help of spirit. Maryann also had the facility spiritually cleaned to rid it of the old energies. This assisted greatly in improving the feeling of the organisation. Each time I walked the factory I'd also clean its energy in my mind, something I'd learnt from my experience. Customers visiting the factory were soon very positive about the changes and spoke of this to employees, something I encouraged. This further increased employee pride.

Incremental, continuous improvement was now the order of the day. Small areas of the factory walls were resheeted, or painted, as profit permitted. Three acres of asbestos roofing was incrementally replaced with metal roofing and daylight panels installed. My instinctual daily verbal approvals to area managers for expenditure without written justification really accelerated the change process. My loss of fear from my revelational experience made each day a joy as I watched the rapid transformation of the factory unfold before my eyes. It changed the energy of the workplace and it felt better.

Lights were no longer required during the day. The dull uninspiring workplace became more pleasant. Concrete flooring and outside areas were also incrementally upgraded. Over the first few years, the factory atmosphere changed significantly for the better and all building improvement programs were virtually completed over ten years. Gardens were planted where rubbish and obsolete machinery was once stored. I was keen to have the energy of nature permeate the workplace, promoting well-being.

Over thirteen semi-trailer-loads of rubbish were scrapped or taken to landfill in the initial clean-up.

I was determined to rid the factory of old decaying energy. The plants, lawns and gardens did assist in bringing a new positive energy to the factory. The front entry garden, initially tended by keen employees and then by our cleaner and his family, became a winner in the industrial category of the September Toowoomba Carnival of Flowers competition. The site was bunded and stormwater interceptors were installed to ensure that in the event of a leaked chemical, none of it would reach the adjacent waterway. Five factory stormwater drains discharging to the local creek had their historically stained outlets steam cleaned and monitored for cleanliness weekly.

I'd come to learn nature must be treated with respect.

In 1996 the Federal Government of Australia introduced the Voluntary Greenhouse Challenge program to reduce emissions. I'd read NASA and other reports on the greenhouse effect, and the leadership team was keen to participate and be environmentally responsible. During the strategic planning session we decided we needed to be a company that was an industry leader in the environmental area and exceed legislative requirements. I was pleased when Doug Curlewis responded.

'We need to be more respectful to planet Earth.' I liked Doug's integrity.

In 1997 the Foundry became company number 150 nationally to sign up. We were handed a members' certificate at Parliament House, Canberra.

The national daily paper *The Australian* ran a major article on this small foundry business entering the challenge, because the journalist couldn't understand the benefit for such a small company. We were determined to meet or exceed the European emission reduction target of 10 percent between 1993 and 2003. While the motivation was to do the right thing for the environment, our participation in the program generated huge savings through energy reduction as well as significantly cutting emissions per tonne produced.

We initially saved around $250,000 a year. In 2005, new state-of-the-art melt furnaces generated additional annual savings of $800,000 when operating at full capacity. Ultimately, costs reduced by $1 million each year and emissions per tonne dropped by thirty-three percent.[27] Our total emissions increased because we doubled sales from $20 million to $38 million. However, it was much cleaner production. I

---

[27] *Report on Australia's Greenhouse Challenge Program (The first 100 enterprises)*, Greenhouse Challenge Office, Commonwealth of Australia, November 1997, p. 183.

was told by overseas industry people that we were possibly the first foundry in the world to achieve the ISO 140001 environmental certification and the first to achieve a regional environmental award.

I had a personal financial objective to build sales to $40 million to provide a revenue buffer over the high fixed costs of the Foundry operation. I could see a more sustainable future when sales finally reached $38 million.

One other key objective was to have a committed, competent, safe and well- rewarded workforce. I regarded them as my family and I was determined to look after them. This was at odds with some CEOs I knew who were constantly trying to cut wages and reduce employee entitlements as they focussed primarily on budgets and cost cutting. I was pleased that our employees were able to receive a four percent pay rise virtually every year I was GM. Each year we also increased the lowest paid employees' wages by an additional $1,000. Training became a major focus and a training officer was appointed. Each month we'd log 300-850 hours of training. The organisation had 135 work centres so detailed training and safety plans for each were developed over a period of approximately eight years. This program was shelved when new owners took control in 2002.

My extensive exposure to R&D programs during my career led me to understand the market power that manufacturing proprietary product provided, as opposed to being a component manufacturer where customers were mostly interested in price cutting.

Demands were usually driven by purchasing managers trying to achieve bonus payments. A few were often most unpleasant.

I remember the CEO of Volkswagen being hailed as an industry hero for his brutal cost cutting scheme in the 1990s. He called all his suppliers to a meeting and told them their supply contracts were null and void as of that moment. He then indicated only suppliers that reduced their component price by thirty percent would remain suppliers. I understand it damaged Volkswagen greatly. Unfortunately, it was copied and became the thirty percent cost-down mantra of many hard-nosed purchasing managers in the industry.

In March 1995 we won a $9-million export order to Japan for the supply of 42,000 truck-brake-drums a year. This product was marginally costed and I was prepared to have a thirty-percent total exposure to marginal sales for export. The volume increase and resultant technology upgrades resulted in export work fully absorbing all production fixed costs. During their second Toowoomba visit, a very senior executive from our Japanese customer spoke up.

'We need to see productivity improve and costs reduced. You need to aim for thirty percent cost reductions each year.'

'Does that mean we have to supply product free after three years?' I cheekily replied.

He blushed and stammered and lost the thrust of his argument. We never reduced the price.

In 1997 I was representing the Foundry on the superannuation committee and all employee pension accounts were with the mutual organisation AMP. On November 20th 1997, AMP demutualised and was publically listed. The share price increased significantly over the short term so, with the committee's support, I spoke to the financial director at head office and recommended we sell. He agreed and an $700,000 profit resulted.

I drove home in the BMW feeling very pleased with myself. However, not long after, stories of mums and dads losing great sums of money unfolded in the press and my view of the windfall changed.

The system sucks, I mused. *We contributed nothing and ravaged the savings of many ordinary families and hurt the retirement prospects of some. It's a spiritually corrupt process.*

This event made me think the share market was not an authentic system and needs to be devoid of speculative processes if we're to have an equitable social system. My spiritual experience shifted my views about what's authentic, fair and real. I've come to see this aspect of share trading as manipulative, greed-based and abhorrent. I have a similar view about CEO salaries and large banks.

An investment was made in computerised 3D modelling, which provided the capability to design and manufacture tooling for new product correctly the first time, conduct stress analysis and run computer simulations of the molten metal being cast. This increased the ability to manufacture new high-quality product in a much reduced timeframe.

This 3D technology platform accelerated further development and consistency of profit. Daylan, a doctor of materials, was hired to run the simulation software. A local and capable marketing lady Cath was also hired, to professionalise our marketing. An R&D department was formed.

That year was 1998, and between May and December we averaged the development of one new product every four days using the 3D technology platform. Eighty percent of the Australian market, traditionally held by a USA supplier, was won in six months. It was a tremendous feat by all involved and I was very proud of the leadership team and employees. The sales manager of the American supplier visited the Foundry to shake my hand and congratulate our team on the quality and rapid takeover of the market. The launch was supported by professional marketing material enhanced by exceptional service levels. This strategy resulted in customers reducing their stock holdings and receiving urgent out-of-schedule parts within twenty-four hours. We soon supplied many new original equipment manufacturers (OEMs) and aftermarket customers. The business was growing at thirty percent a year. Kenworth, Mack, Volvo, Iveco, Meritor and BPW became key customers.

Production numbers on truck and trailer brake-drums eventually went from around 7,000 a year to over 200,000 a year. Wheel hubs went from around 2,000 to 40,000 a year, with production opportunities unfolding in India to meet Canadian demand.

I now write of another piece of synchronicity that happened at this time around the death of a man I greatly respected.

Phil Chote, the works director that arranged for my salary to continue during my scholarship year in the UK, retired to Maroochydore on Queensland's north coast. It was near where Carole and I owned an investment unit. I took a week's holiday at our unit, something Carole and I did about every three months.

I had a strong unexpected urge to visit him during our May 1998 stay. I found his address in the phone book and arrived there to find there was no one home. The next- door neighbour saw me leaving.

'Are you looking for Mr Chote?' she called over the fence.

'Yes, I used to work under him at the Foundry and I just came to say hello.'

'I'm very sorry, but Mr Chote is in a local hospital. He's not well. He's dying.'

I went straight to the hospital in Buderim and it was great to chat with him. It was May 26th. He remembered me and told me that I had certainly kept my commitment well and he was proud of what my leadership had done to the company during my time as general manager. Many employees had retired to this area and Phil had obviously been kept up to date. It was reassuring to hear these words from a man whom I respected greatly. I later learned that Phil died three days after my visit on May 29th. I still feel a sense of awe when I reflect on these moments of 'universal synchronicity'.

The acquisition of the wheel marketing company Malco proved to be an interesting employee relations exercise. When I arrived at the Sydney plant for the first time, to announce the takeover, our financial controller Lalith and I addressed all employees. (Lalith relocated to Melbourne to assist his son's health issue and Gordon was then appointed.) Staying true to our values, we were totally transparent about plans to close their factory and how the transfer of their machining operation to Toowoomba was to be carried out. It was explained how the employee redundancies would be managed. Any questions were always answered honestly, honesty and integrity being one of our core values.

Weekly visits followed and each time all employees were briefed. One senior employee told me the men were impressed with our regular open communications and our obvious concern for their welfare. The night before closing the plant we paid for a dinner for all employees to say goodbye to each other. The next day we were loading trucks to remove the last of the remaining equipment and stock. I was extremely surprised that many employees stayed back until we loaded the last truck at around 6pm, when we'd previously told all employees they could leave at 10am. I was touched deeply and humbled when their quietly-mannered spokesperson shook my hand.

'Thank you for treating us with respect, it's something that's never happened before. We all wish you well for the future. We have enjoyed our short time with you,' he said. It once again reinforced my commitment to honesty.

We won the export contract to Japan and we started to learn Japanese customs because many government export workshops stressed this was most important.

In the end, we decided we'd be who we were but be totally honest. Our marketing department, at Cath's suggestion, instigated a policy of answering all communications within an hour. We often didn't have an answer to the query, but would let them know when it would be available and adhere to it. We were able to deliver our first containers of brake-drums into Japan only six months after our first communication. The Japanese customer told us the supply process traditionally took in excess of two years.

It was total, raw honesty, backed up by an immediate willingness to fix issues arising that made this possible. At first, the Japanese managers said we were very aggressive but after our relationship developed to one of trust, they openly said our quality and service were the best they had experienced. The speed and quality of the supply of product to the JIK Group for Isuzu trucks by Toowoomba Foundry was so ground-breaking it was written up in the *Tokyo Times*. A copy of the newspaper article was given to us, however it was never translated. We were not aggressive, just honest with a high service commitment. Some admissions we made when questioned by the Japanese quality auditors were embarrassing, but we were honest and committed to making the necessary upgrades or process modifications promptly. No games were played.

This project reinforced my belief that honesty is speed in business.

A business venture based on total honesty between both parties only focuses on the true needs of each in the relationship and is a very efficient business model. It's fast and also fun – one does feel vulnerable at times though!

The Japanese business was building over a few years when the Asian crises struck in February 1997 and adverse currency movements resulted in a thirty percent penalty against the Japanese customer under the terms of the supply agreement. The 1997-1998 Asian financial crisis began in Thailand and quickly spread to neighbouring countries. It began as the USA started to increase interest rates, resulting in reduced money flows into Asia and their currencies devalued. One of the four brake-drum products supplied was swiftly withdrawn. However, supply continued on the remaining three products, to our amazement, until around September. We decided the strength of our relationship was the reason all product wasn't withdrawn. At the next face-to-face meeting in Toowoomba I said to the team leader, 'Our close business relationship is greatly valued and appreciated, but if you need to discontinue supply due to the currency impact, I understand it is a necessary business decision on your part.'

'Thank you, we'll cease supply Harland San,' was his polite reply.

Supply was immediately cancelled when pipeline stock ran out. I really enjoyed the relationship we had with our Japanese customer and was surprised at our last meeting when the team leader turned to me.

'Our employees were worried you were going to take all of our production because your quality is better than ours and we've never experienced such good service,' Watanabe San said.

It was with sadness I dropped them off at Brisbane's airport. The relationship ended. They had become part of my 'family'. The domestic market was growing strongly so the loss of this customer had little impact.

Further product development followed, with the Toowoomba Wheel Product (TWP), Toowoomba Engine Product (TEP) and Toowoomba Water Product brands released to the market. The TEP brand mainstay was high-performance, small block- iron Chevy racing cylinder heads exported to our customer in Las Vegas. Peak volume one year was 12,000 units. The accuracy of the 3D technology resulted in 2.8-kilogram- lighter heads. A new efficient port shape yielded an additional twenty horse power over competitors. The Americans declared them the best performing small block-iron Chevy heads in the USA.

In the first weeks of learning the 3D technology platform, a differential manufacturer came with an Aston Martin differential case 3D model. He was pleading for us to make the casting because no one in Australia had been able to make it from the computerised model. The casting was due in four weeks for the project.

Ken, the tool shop manager, was approached and decided they'd have a go even though the 3D technology was new. They delivered a perfect casting in two weeks. It was with a touch of pride to know that when I watched the James Bond movie *Die Another Day,* the Aston MartinVanquish sliding around on the ice in the Arctic had a Foundry differential case.

I thought back to the many comments by consultants that the people of Toowoomba Foundry were too insulated and inbred to grow the company to a world- class level. It was so great to see their arrogant, quick and shallow appraisal of the workforce proved wrong. Treat people well, eliminate fear, and employees will soon be full of creativity and surprises.

I was exposed to constant change among the Melbourne-based head office people to whom I reported. This resulted in my reporting to ten different people, involving many managing directors, one chairman and two corporate executive general managers/CEOs during my twelve-year term as a director, executive GM and GM. A foundry was not seen as a good 'corporate fit'. I did not enjoy the test-prove cycle a couple put me through. Some constantly pressured me to remove members of my leadership team who had a trade background and replace them with managers holding academic degrees.

I formed the view from my spiritual event that it's almost a battle between the qualitative or experienced 'feeling-based employees' and the quantitative or 'intellectually-based employees.' What's not understood by those exposed to total intellectual study is that many of the trade or experienced-based managers have well- developed intuitive skills. That, coupled with their experience, results in 'wise heads' in many cases and plenty of 'rare sense', as my son Sheldon called common sense. This intuitive skill is spiritually based and powerful and is mostly unconscious, developing with practical experience. This critical balance, between the intellectual and intuitive skill developed by experienced employees, is rarely considered in organisational structural changes based on my many observations.

I have the view that when one is working purely intuitively, a door is opened and access to the greatest encyclopaedia in the universe becomes available – the universal mind as some would call it.

I did see areas where a higher qualified person with a degree may have moved some issues faster and more professionally. I was content to keep the continuous change programs moving forward and felt my ultimate vision for the Foundry would be achieved. The many positive rapid changes that occurred were a testimonial to their 'non-degreed' skill.

I'd been considering doing my MBA after my opportunity at Harvard was lost with Bill's death, but this thinking was dropped while I was attending a residential marketing course at Sydney's Macquarie University. While I was working on an assignment in a building adjacent to the campus's entry road, at around 6pm, I looked up and became curious as I watched a procession of premium-range Ford and GM cars driven by guys with white shirts, red ties and sunglasses. 'Who are these people driving in for classes?' I asked the tutor.

'They're the MBA external students arriving for their night class.'

I immediately made the decision to forget about an MBA. Instead I completed a mini MBA course at a winter school at Melbourne University. During the winter school I completed another Performax test and my 'D' for dominance had increased dramatically. The lecturer was most emphatic that one's scores would never change through one's lifetime. I didn't correct him. My spiritual experience sure helped my dominance – yet I always tried to exert my power by not using it.

The development of exports to Japan combined with the growth of Toowoomba Wheel Product increased the factory volumes significantly, improving profitability. The huge increase in product volume greatly assisted head office support in capital investment. Exports of aluminium smelter product to Mozambique, Chevy racing heads to USA and truck and trailer wheel product to Canada followed. When the first pallet of brake-drum castings, taken straight off our production line, was received by the Canadian customer, I received a disturbing phone call from their sales manager.

'I'm not happy with your sample shipment. You've specially processed these like the Chinese do and the finish is too good. We need to see your actual production samples.'

'That's what these are. They came straight off our production line. They haven't been specially treated. I'll send you a container load along with some sample hubs.'

We talked further and it was obvious he was still cynical when our conversation ended. We sent a full container of product along with truck hubs and when they arrived he rang me.

'I'm astounded by the high quality. I've never seen such good-looking wheel product. The packaging is also great.'

Our product achieved the reputation as 'bulletproof' in a very short time span among Canadian truckers. The Canadian market soon developed and it was a great surprise to receive an unsolicited email from the purchasing manager of Volvo Trucks, Toronto, because we hadn't dealt with them. He congratulated the factory and its employees on the excellent quality of the wheel product. He saw the product at one of our Canadian distributers.

I again felt very proud of the Foundry employees when I read the email to them at a GM Brief.

It became evident some employees were not completing important production documentation correctly and quantities were sometimes miscounted and other important production documentation not completed correctly. We decided to perform a literacy and numeracy test on all factory employees. When I raised it at a GM briefing a significant amount of negative feedback came from the employees and union delegates. The main reason was the fear of exposure and possible embarrassment.

Ross the HR and training manager had developed high-quality but simple practical tests that encompassed all the major literacy and numeracy requirements in the factory. After the employees' concerns were taken on board, it was decided to go ahead with the tests.

As another Foundry and corporate core value was respect and dignity, I didn't want the dignity of employees to be impacted. Therefore, we had each employee perform the test alone and in the privacy of the special room. The employee was given as much time as needed to complete the test. Only the HR department and I would have access to the results, thus ensuring the preservation of the dignity of all who attended and the avoidance of any embarrassment. Trust had been developed and the tests were soon underway. It was a surprise revelation that thirty to forty percent of employees had either a literacy or numeracy issue and some had both. Night classes with a retired school teacher were organised. Many older employees expressed their gratitude for this opportunity.

A local psychologist was also contacted and made available to any employee who wanted to discuss personal issues.

Each employee was also trained in customer service and telephone answering and we won awards for it. Seventy phones would always be answered politely and within four rings, as mentioned earlier. I was pleased to receive many positive comments from customers about out prompt phone answering. The cascade training system that we'd learnt from the DuPont safety training was adopted until all employees from me down were trained.

After 130 years of bearing the name, in October 2001 Toowoomba Foundry was renamed Toowoomba Metal Technologies. One reason for this emerged from a meeting with the Federal industry minister at the time, I was pushing a case for support in manufacturing in my role as Queensland president and national vice president of the Australian Industry Group (AIGroup). The minister looked at me.

'What business do you represent?' he asked.

'Toowoomba Foundry,' I responded.

Waving his arm in dismissal in front of him, the Minister replied, 'Our focus is on the new economy, like IT, biotech and other high-tech industries. Old economy companies like foundries will fade away with production moving to countries like China.'

The fact that state-of-the-art 3D software and new economy technology were entrenched in the cast metals industry was lost. I worked as a consultant after leaving the Foundry and was commissioned to survey the ferrous (iron and steel) foundry industry in my home state of Queensland. All in the industry were shocked to learn it generated a significant $600 million in sales. Additionally, if the non-ferrous (aluminium and brass) foundries were included it was close to a staggering $1 billion. The industry was virtually unknown to politicians and written off as having 'old economy' practices. It employed 2,000 people at the time and over ten percent were apprentices.

Australian government has a policy of not picking winners, but leaving change in strategic areas to the 'market'. I believe the government needs to shape the country's future. China is a great example of the government leading long-term strategies that breed rapid social change. I do not support their inhumane approach, however.

Company boards don't like surprises, and as the green sand foundry process is one with the most variables of any manufacturing process, it still requires intuitive judgments or some 'art and craft'. For this reason, it's not popular with many boards in Western countries, yet every country has a need for cast metal product. It's essential to living. The other decision to change the Foundry name was cemented in my mind after the first visit by John Condos, the Australian managing director of Volvo Trucks. After touring the plant he turned to me and said, 'Can I speak frankly with you?'

'I encourage open and frank discussion with everyone, so please feel free to speak your mind.'

'You have to get rid of that bloody Toowoomba Foundry name. You've such a clean factory and state-of-the-art technology here – you need to call it Toowoomba Technologies. I had in my mind I was coming to visit some dark and dirty foundry. It's been an eye-opener. The use of modern technology is amazing.'

The name was changed to Toowoomba Metal Technologies following unanimous agreement at the next strategic planning session. One hundred and thirty years of tradition was put aside on October 1st 2001 when the company traded under the new name, proudly referred to as TMT by employees.

The culture developed very positively. Employee pride had returned. Sales had increased from $10 million to $38 million and the company had won many awards by the time it was sold to the new owners in 2002.

After the sale the chairman rang me.

'I wish you all the best with the new owners. I think we've sold the wrong company. We invested $40 million in our textile division and it's losing $3 million a year. We invested $4 million in the Foundry and you're bloody making $3 million a year!'

I knew I was in trouble at the first board meeting with the new owners when I was asked to remove safety results as the first item in my monthly report and replace it with profit results. I soon learnt after the ownership change that the land and buildings had been sold to a developer. I then knew the Foundry's days were numbered on the Toowoomba site. I invited the new CEO to our annual strategic planning session in order to provide him with a strategic view of the organisation. When the day ended we walked to my car to return to the factory and the CEO turned to me, 'That was just a bloody talkfest and a waste of time. You won't be doing that again,' he said dryly.

The power of employee alignment through involvement was totally missed and I knew we were in trouble. There is a quotation by Gita Bellin about alignment that I like:

The impossible is possible when people align with you. When you do things with people, not against them, the amazing resources of the Higher Self within are mobilised.

Involving employees in a genuine way opens the door for spirit to assist. Sometime later, he visited the factory unannounced through the back door to catch us out because he couldn't relate to a relaxed and happy culture; he liked to have employees in fear to 'keep them on their toes'. Each visit by him to another company in the group resulted in a redundancy and, naturally, there was huge fear in their employees. He was also shocked by the frankness displayed at the Foundry's management meetings and expressed his surprise to me. He was obviously not familiar with totally honest and open meetings.

I was no longer setting the energy for the organisation and important decisions were being taken by the CEO, using my reports without my involvement. I knew my time was running out. The energy had changed.

I was fired in 2005, along with our business development manager, by the chairman and the company closed in 2012 after 141 years of activity. It was all about a real estate deal. I learnt later that the plan was to source cast product from Asia and move the machining to a company site in Ballarat Victoria.

On the night of my termination I slept soundly while my family couldn't. I was proud of my leadership contribution and satisfied with the company's development. I was sad for all the employees. I focussed my energy on bringing the circumstances around my untimely departure to account. Carole and I spent several months documenting evidence and preparing for the court case. I'm sure without the benefit of my spiritual experience I'd have been a complete wreck. I was very touched when, shortly after my termination, around 130 Foundry employees comprising managers, supervisors and operators gave me a great send-off night at a local hall. It was a treasured moment.

I was still gutted by the decision and went through a grieving process while we prepared the legal documentation. I was frustrated that future plans I had for the company were now history. The grieving process particularly hit me one day a month or so after my dismissal, when I was sitting in a second-floor shopping centre café having coffee with Carole overlooking the entrance of the centre. A pattern shop employee on his day off walked in full view on the pathway leading into the centre and I felt a huge surge of sadness that I'd not be saying hello again on my daily rounds. It probably took twelve months to two years to readjust properly. I greatly missed the people who became my extended family. I really enjoy catching up with them at the annual Foundry reunions generously organised by two past employees.

I'd implemented total transparency and an open culture based on real values, exemplary customer service, daily reporting, the 3D technology platform, and product R&D. Quality had always been a foundation stone for the company. Honesty, integrity, respect and dignity were our core values promoted and actively practiced across the organisation.

One phone call I was proud of was a phone call from the regional director of the State Development Department based in Toowoomba.

'Hi Doug, I'm just ringing to let you know the Foundry is now ranked as the preferred employer in the city,' he said.

It was something I really cherished because foundries are not noted for attracting employees. We also had visits from Ford and GM foundry managers and other large competitors to gain an understanding of what we'd done to achieve the industry-leading performance.

I was also chuffed when a lawyer acquaintance said to me at a function, 'What do you feed your people on?'

'What do you mean?' I said.

'I and few associates go to the Spotted Cow pub each Friday afternoon after work, and two of your guys in TMT uniforms spend each Friday afternoon working out how to improve the bloody place! I wish my people would do that!'

The foundry was about to achieve a $3.8 million profit on $38m sales while paying $722 rent, and to celebrate, they fired me!

CHAPTER 23

BROTHER GRAHAM

When we were growing up, Graham and I were always playing pranks on each other and, being six years younger, I usually came off second best. We always maintained a strong friendship. My sister Daphne was twelve years older than me and often absent in my life so the same closeness never developed.

In later years Graham had some hard life experiences, starting with a triple heart bypass, a fall off a hotel roof during a major renovation and finally a very serious motorbike accident that resulted in the loss of use of his right arm and caused his retirement. It was a Saturday afternoon in May 1997, ten years after my experience. I received a call from Graham's son Mark who had been riding his motorbike ahead of him in a picturesque valley with winding roads near a Queensland country town, Esk.

'Dad's been in a terrible head-on accident, emergency services have arrived in a helicopter and are trying to stabilise him. He's not good and they're going to take him to the Brisbane General Hospital. Can you tell Mum?'

I rushed across to Graham's wife to break the news and get organised to go to the hospital.

'I'll go home to pack. You do the same and I'll come back to take you to Brisbane.'

Within two hours we arrived at the hospital to be greeted by a caring orderly at the entrance. Graham's other son John had also joined us.

'Are you the Harland family?' he queried softly but clearly. We nodded silently with apprehension when he went on to say, 'Come with me to a private room, the chopper is on its way, it took a long while to stabilise Graham on the ground at Esk Hospital. It will arrive within half an hour. Have a coffee. Try and relax.'

'Thank you,' was all we could say.

'Graham will be unrecognisable and unresponsive. He won't know you because he's been placed in an induced coma. He's in a very serious condition and will go straight into tests ready for surgery. You'll not be able to be with him until much later.' He left.

'The chopper will be landing in five minutes,' was his next announcement when his head appeared through the semi-opened door.

We all raced to the roof helipad, watching nervously as the chopper landed and shut down. The paramedics started readying Graham for the trip to the hospital. We all stood there silently filled with apprehension while the rotor blades slowly came to a stop and the cargo door opened. Graham was wheeled past us with son Mark following along. All I remember was a much enlarged chest, black and blue from severe bruising, a black eye and a pale swollen face. He was wrapped in a silver thermal blanket. It was unusual, but Mark was allowed in the chopper by the paramedics because he had remained free of emotion and helpful, however on seeing us he broke down crying when he let go of his pent-up emotions.

It was the next morning before we could be with Graham and we started a routine of bedside visits. This was ten years after my spiritual experience and I'd learnt that when one gets emotional that energy can be felt by people you're with. If you're upset then they can feel that also. Only one person was allowed to be with him so we each stayed beside him until we started to get emotional when the next person would go in. That way Graham was only feeling positive feelings. I talked to him during my visits because I was sure at a soul level he could hear me. I know his wife deemed that strange and funny.

When he came out of the coma he kept hallucinating,

'Ainsley and John visited today. We had a barbeque on the balcony, it was nice,' was one trip into his imagined world. We were instructed to continually tell him what was real and what wasn't. The doctor said he was at a ten out of twelve in relation to his level of brain damage.

I had been willing my energy to Graham each day he was in intensive care. I was continually moving into an emotional state. I channelled energy very easily and powerfully when in my 'love bubble' immediately after the experience in 1987, so I was trying to replicate the energy channel. Instead, because of my regular emotional state I was simply beaming my own energy away. When it became obvious Graham was going to survive I decided to return to work in Toowoomba.

I was really exhausted when I walked to the car, my body ached all over. When I hopped in I found it was a huge effort to push in the BMW's clutch, change gears and drive. I had given my own energy rather than channel universal energy.

We and the doctors were all concerned he'd have major brain damage, but he surprised everyone weeks later when his normal brain function returned. Months passed and he healed but he had lost the use of his right arm, which hung limply beside him. It wasn't long before he asked the doctors to remove this dead weight with no feeling that he was carrying. He'd cut it or burn it without knowing he had an injury. He also has twenty-four-hour phantom pain that buckles him over regularly. He is a person with a high pain tolerance. I'm in constant wonder at how he's tolerated it over the many years.

After three years he finally persuaded a doctor to remove the dead arm. He immediately accepted the change, much to the surprise of the doctor. While writing this section Graham was diagnosed with terminal leukaemia. He was responding to chemotherapy and exceeding all doctors' expectations, and we didn't know how much longer he would be with us. Each time the phone rang late at night I would think it may be about Graham.

Then in July 2017 I was shocked by a late night call to learn, not about Graham, but about the unexpected death of my much-loved son, Sheldon.

CHAPTER 24

LEO'S ACCIDENT

I've included my account of the first and only fatality in the factory during my leadership because it became a spiritually uplifting experience for all involved, in spite of the sadness and great feeling of loss. Leo O'Leary, a much respected 'factory elder', passed away, the result of a workplace incident, on September 13th 2001. This event tested my commitment to truth. I was determined to walk my talk and be 100 percent honest during the daunting processes I knew would emerge. It proved to be the best course of action, serving the interests of all involved. This open approach helped bring closure to both factory people and many family members.

During my term as general manager of Toowoomba Metal Technologies, I always ensured that when I was on site I walked the factory a minimum of twice a day and chatted to employees. During the afternoon walk, before I left the factory for home, this usually meant a stop to talk to Leo, a key senior operator in our machine shop. I learnt after Leo's fatal accident that he was an accomplished polocrosse player, was quite well off, and that he enjoyed his work immensely at the Foundry. I believe Leo was a person who wasn't into 'retirement'.

I always enjoyed speaking with him because he had an easy-going personality. Leo was always forthright in telling me if there was an issue in the factory that needed addressing. He was always clear about what he had to say without being critical. Often, I'd stop at his work centre and after small talk, I'd 'talk shop'.

'I think this is a bit rough, Doug,' he might say after enlightening me about a shop issue. Then he'd offer suggestions as to how the issue might be addressed.

This was something I always appreciated because many others would raise problems with me, but rarely solutions. It was in contrast to one confrontation I was involved with in relation to a new enterprise bargaining agreement (EBA). This was a wage and condition review that set pay issues for the next three-year term. A new employee I hadn't met who had a strong background in unions was working on the molten iron pouring line. I was on my daily factory walk and when I approached him to introduce myself to him he saw me heading his way. He turned and quickly walked towards me looking aggressive.

'You're a fucking liar, that's all bullshit what you said at the GM briefing yesterday. It's all lies.' His whole body was trembling.

This bloke thinks I'm going to sack him on the spot.

I didn't react emotionally, but responded in my feelings by warmly shaking his hand. He looked stunned.

'That took a lot of guts,' I said. 'I'd like more employees to say what they really feel, but I wish you'd tone down the delivery a bit. What have I supposedly lied about?'

We then talked. He told me what he decided I'd lied about. I was able to convince him he was grossly misreading my intent and we soon parted amicably. I often spoke with him on my walks after the confrontation. He left the company after a couple of months. I decided he was a product of a company with an appalling culture. My spiritual experience assisted me to remain calm in confrontations of this nature. I know it assisted employees to speak openly without fear of retribution. Thankfully, the vast majority of discussions were polite and respectful.

I didn't find out until after Leo's death that we'd come together when I was a kid when Leo was best man at my cousin's wedding in a country town. It was two days after the September 11 attack in 2001 when I and other employees were still trying to understand and absorb the enormity of the terrorist strike. I was in my office, meeting with two state representatives of the Australian Metal Workers Union (AMWU). We were discussing wage bargaining, when a machine shop employee entered my office and said, 'Leo's been in a serious accident, the ambulance is just arriving to take him to hospital.'

I immediately excused myself, and grabbed my hard hat and safety glasses. I headed for the shop floor to find Leo being loaded into an ambulance in a factory driveway. The concerned look on the ambulance officers and employees filled me with dread. I went to the back of the ambulance and saw Leo lying on his back. He was unconscious. A machine shop employee came to me.

'A brake-drum come out of the chuck on the LC50. It hit the glass safety window which flew out and hit Leo in the face,' he said.

I turned to ask the attending ambulance officer, 'What's happened to Leo?'

'He has a major trauma on the back of his head.'

I still couldn't grasp what had happened until an employee said, 'The safety glass pushed Leo's head back against the robot's brass jaw that was parked behind Leo's head.'

I immediately understood what had happened. I knew it would have wreaked terrible havoc with Leo's skull.

I rushed to our HR manager when the ambulance left. After getting the address I drove to Mrs O'Leary's house to take her to the hospital. No one was home so I headed for the local hospital and found his wife Doreen already at Leo's bedside in the emergency department. She welcomed me and we were soon joined by his daughters Natalie and later on, Leanne. I realised we were going to lose Leo and that scared me. I put my fear aside as I tried my best to comfort the family. People were trying to locate the other daughters because the outcome had become obvious. The duty nurse then entered and asked, 'Who are you?'

'I'm the general manager of the Foundry,' I replied.

'You need to leave. It's not appropriate that you be here,' she said curtly.

I walked to a waiting room feeling bad that I'd unintentionally intruded on the family.

I was relieved when Doreen, with Natalie accompanying her, came to the waiting room. 'It's okay Doug, come back with us, you're welcome to stay,' she said.

I returned to Leo's bedside and was standing with Doreen with my arm on her shoulder. Natalie, on the other side of the bed, was very upset and crying. I was looking at her.

What can I do to help Natalie? She's so young and this is probably the first time she's faced death.

Immediately after my thought I suddenly felt totally drained. I knew I was about to pass out on the floor. It happened so quickly I struggled to understand what was going on, and I staggered back to the visitors room feeling very dizzy and close to collapse. I had to put one hand on the walls as I walked to steady myself. It was like my energy had just been sucked out of me. When I arrived in the empty room I immediately cleaned my aura, as I'd been taught by Maryann. After a few minutes I felt well enough, but very tired and drained. I returned to the bedside a little confused and wondering what had happened. Both Natalie and Doreen, now calm, were bringing some humour into the situation.

'Leo was never in a hurry to do anything,' was one comment that almost brought a smile to my face, and I felt all the tension ease.

Maryann explained to me later that my energy had been transferred to Natalie. During this transition process I realised the O'Leary family had a great spiritual maturity and we stayed together until Leo's body had finally rested. I hugged all the family and said goodbye, promising to stay in close communication. The next few hours are a little blurry. I remember confirming my secretary had rang head office and I called Mark in Melbourne, who I now reported to, to let him know what happened.

I did the rounds of the traumatised factory people when I returned from the hospital. The HR officer Ross had arranged counsellors to come and assist employees. The safety manager told me that the occupational health and safety authorities quarantined the work centre. I met with them to assure them nothing would be touched and we'd cooperate fully with their requirements. We always maintained a totally transparent relationship with the safety authorities in all dealings, as we did with the environmental authorities. I met employees to let them know they were free to go home if they wished and to not work if they were too upset.

I was feeling exhausted from the day's events when I was finally able to meet with employees directly involved to get a first-hand understanding of the incident. When I approached the shop's first aid attendant, Ross Hills, I could see he was obviously in shock. He had witnessed the incident.

'Are you okay? Would you like to see a counsellor?' I asked.

'I think so. Yes, I'd like to see one.'

'I was told you saw the accident happen,' I said.

'Yes, I saw Leo standing beside the LC50 in the robot drum cell. It was making an extremely loud noise. I yelled at Leo to run but he just stood there and I couldn't understand why. I was looking at Leo when he was hit and fell to the floor. Then a cloud rose from Leo's body and disappeared up a tunnel of white light, right up into the factory roof.'

Ross's account was unexpected.

'I ran to Leo's side but I just knew there was nothing I could do. I just stood there beside him.'

I knew from my experience this would be a life-changing event for Ross because he had seen Leo's soul leave his body.

'Ross, you're privileged to have witnessed Leo's soul leaving his body. It'll change your life. Let's go and find a counsellor for you to talk to. It'll help you to feel better and understand what's happened.'

Apparently other employees had pushed Ross aside as they attempted to help Leo. They decided Ross was frozen by shock. They had called the ambulance and cleared a path for it to efficiently access an area close to the work centre.

Three psychologists arrived soon after Leo had been taken by the ambulance. Rooms were provided for privacy and they started meeting with employees seeking counselling. Our HR manager had arranged this. I was with Ross and introduced him to a counsellor.

'I saw Leo get hit and fall to the floor. Then I saw a cloud rise out of his body. It went up into the roof in a tunnel of white light,' he said.

'No, you didn't see that, it was just the shock and you imagined it and . . . ' I cut into the counsellor's comment.

'I had a similar spiritual experience some time ago. Ross didn't imagine it, I'm sure it will change his life. He was privileged to see it.'

She looked at me quizzically. We walked away.

Back in my office I said, 'I don't think any of the counsellors can help you.'

'Okay,' was all Ross said.

'Why don't you go home to your wife? I'll drive you if you like,' I said.

'No I'll be okay,' Ross replied. He left for home.

I rang the local university fibre composites section to let them know what happened. I then asked how we could make a 'bulletproof' machine tool guard to prevent such an event from reoccurring. They suggested that fibre composites weren't the answer. They recommended I contact a ballistics specialist on the Gold Coast.

Somewhere in all this I was interviewed by a local television station, confirming the loss of a valued employee. The station had been monitoring the emergency services radio frequency.

I then visited an employee with responsibilities in safety. I was shocked when I saw him. His eyes had what seemed to be very large white poker chips in them, spreading them wide. I blinked and his eyes looked normal. I realised I'd seen his great fear. I had other experiences of seeing various kinds of 'thought images' in other people.

I met with a female executive a year before this event with Leo. It was following a group meeting. She seemed to be dragging an issue on after taking me to discuss it in a more quiet area. I wondered why she was labouring the issue, which I thought we had dealt with. Suddenly an image of her with exaggerated pouting lips and closed eyes appeared in the air between us. I immediately knew the sexual nature of the 'agenda' and took my leave. I mentioned earlier my unusual experience while talking with Sandra, the lady I met on entering the Inner Energy Centre for the first time, where light beams shone out of her eyes.

I was, and remain, amazed how such an image could materialise in mid-air. I had no control over them, they just happened. I've not had another experience of it since then. This is another area ripe for study. In my view, these images are energy, but how they can materialise into a 3D image, I've no idea.

Leo's death was a very emotional time for me. As I sat with the employees and their families I came to realise just how respected Leo was and how he was regarded as a confidant and father figure. I returned to the factory to meet with the night shift. Production had virtually stopped because most employees were huddled in groups while they tried to come to grips with the loss of a respected workmate. I felt that was appropriate given the circumstances. The board chairman in Melbourne rang me.

'I've put this matter in the hands of the Brisbane office of our law firm. You're to comply with their directives,' he said.

The law firm's representative rang shortly after to say he'd meet me on site the next day. I wondered how we'd ever get the great momentum back that we had prior to the incident. I went home exhausted. I'd broken down in tears a couple of times with employees when I met with them. I appreciated the support they gave to me. It had been a long day.

The next morning I walked through the factory to speak to as many employees as possible. I called a GM Brief to let all employees know what had happened. I stressed the need to leave the scene untouched while the workplace health and safety authorities conducted their investigation. The first visitor to the factory next morning was the managing director of Craig International Ballistics at the Gold Coast, who arrived early. He was keen to assist us to find a failsafe guarding system on the large Japanese lathe.

After a thorough briefing and site inspection outside the quarantine fenced area, he indicated the type of materials that may be suitable.

I asked, 'How much will it cost?'

'We can work that out later,' he replied.

We reviewed the guarding on a similar Japanese CNC lathe. He then returned to the Gold Coast to start penetration and deformation ballistic tests by firing bullets with much greater kinetic energy than anything another failure could generate, at a range of possible material combinations. I visited Leo's wife Doreen. The remaining daughters living away from Toowoomba had now arrived. I let her know that if she needed anything from us, to just ask. I told her the whole factory was in mourning and the supervisors were numb with shock.

'We're going to cancel the safety milestone barbeque scheduled for this month as a token of respect,' I said.

'Leo really enjoyed the safety barbeques. Please don't cancel it, Leo wouldn't want that. Would it be okay if family members could attend?' Doreen insisted.

'Certainly, that would be welcomed.'

The safety barbeques were designed to celebrate safety achievements. The managers and supervisors cooked lunch or dinner for all three shifts. This decision resulted in an extremely uplifting and healing event for all employees and the family. It greatly assisted closure.

'Many supervisors were having trouble managing their grief and one is experiencing feelings of guilt because he feels somehow he should've prevented it,' I said to Doreen.

'Bring them here to my home to meet the family and talk together,' Doreen generously suggested.

I returned to the Foundry to arrange the visit, deeply touched by the family's supportive approach. The Brisbane-based lawyer was the next visitor.

'I'll need statements from all relevant employees. Nothing is to be provided to the safety authorities apart from the mandatory notification form and statements. You're not to speak with them. I remind you that head office has given our firm the responsibility to manage the incident.'

'I'm not happy with that because it's against our corporate values; we always work in a transparent manner with authorities,' I protested.

He was a good man, with whom I felt at ease, and he was just following his firm's normal procedure. I finally agreed – I had no choice but to comply. When the authorities rang me, I told them all communications had to be solely through the law firm. I immediately felt that their suspicions and anger were aroused. I cursed the fact I couldn't be totally open with them. I left the lawyer to take statements and immediately phoned the chairman.

'I'm not comfortable following the lawyers' direction to withhold all information from the safety authorities. It's against our values. I'm asking your approval for me to release any documents requested by the safety authorities.'

'Doug, you need to do whatever the lawyers tell you.' Our conversation ended.

I visited the safety manager in his office.

'The lawyer has insisted I must not supply any additional documents requested by the safety authorities. I'm totally unhappy with that. I rang the chairman and he confirmed that I need to follow the lawyer's directives. It's against our corporate values of honesty and transparency. Irrespective of the outcome I really want the authorities to have whatever they request. I don't care if we're in the shit.'

'That's a bugger,' he replied, as I walked out of his office.

Some days later he came to me and said with a smile, 'Doug, no instruction had been given to me, so I provided everything to the safety authorities that they requested.'

A feeling of great vulnerability swept over me at this disclosure but I said, 'I really appreciate that, I'll probably be in the shit but at least we've done the right thing. Thanks.'

I walked away.

Shit, I'm not looking forward to the lawyers' or head office's reaction. You might be unemployed soon Douglas.

My feeling of vulnerability increased further. A friend in Brisbane, who had a close relative working in the Brisbane office of the state government's department responsible for occupational health and safety, confided to me that a prosecution was being demanded by senior officers in that department. I kept this to myself because I felt the key people involved directly in the accident were already in significant fear as a result of the serious nature of the event. I was frustrated that the lead safety agency in our state was passing judgement so quickly with no knowledge of the facts, and had an attitude that automatically assumed that industry were the 'bad guys'. I wasn't looking forward to the coroner's inquest.

I was only interested in the truth, no matter the outcome, something the spiritual experience embedded in me. Head office wasn't pleased at my indiscretion and neither was the law firm. The lawyer was quite shocked at this disclosure, but I kept my job. We then focussed on the issues to hand. I remember many occasions where being willing to be vulnerable and open in approach resolved an issue in regard to environmental complaints that were potentially damaging to the company. This approach enhanced the community's respect for the organisation. Maryann often used a quote: 'The vulnerability of honesty is the doorway to personal freedom.' I sure as hell felt vulnerable!

CHAPTER 25
AFTER LEO'S ACCIDENT

We were losing critical production with a major work centre quarantined after Leo's accident. Arrangements were put in place to maintain service levels, as far as practical, on less productive work centres. Our customer service staff were busy keeping our customers posted and negotiating revised deliveries on a daily basis. All customers cooperated totally. It was a stressful time for all involved. I was still concerned for Ross, the first aid attendant who'd seen the accident happen. A day after the accident he still appeared to be in great shock. Both the manufacturing manager and machine shop manager came to me and said it looked like 'he wasn't at home'.

Daisy then said to me, 'I'm worried about Ross, something's not right. I don't know what we can do.'

That something was still very obvious to me also.

The day passed with more counselling before Maryann arrived unannounced to support me and offer any assistance, after hearing of the event when a family member rang her. Maryann had been a crisis counsellor for over forty years and I always appreciated her very practical assistance and wisdom, because she came from a much deeper spiritual perspective. She met with a number of managers and supervisors and whatever she said, or did, obviously helped each one. I met with her.

'We're all still concerned about our first aid attendant, Ross. He witnessed the accident and still seems to be in shock.'

'Bring him here. I'll see if I can assist.'

Ross walked into the area outside my office and I introduced him to Maryann.

'Could I use the privacy of your office for a moment?' Maryann asked.

She and Ross went into my office and Maryann closed the door. A few moments later he came out looking normal and more relaxed.

When I asked Maryann what had happened she simply said, matter-of-factly, 'He was still out of his body from shock. I just put him back in.'

I spent the rest of the second day speaking to employees and head office. In the afternoon some supervisors and I left for Doreen's home to meet with the family. We were warmly welcomed.

Over a cup of tea and cake we learnt about Leo's habits from the family. The supervisors all spoke about what had transpired and their feelings about it. It was a much needed healing for all concerned. We were all greatly impressed by the warmth and understanding the family projected. While it was the first accident Leo had during his time at the Foundry, the family humorously informed us that he was quite accident prone at home.

I drove back to the factory with Daisy and he turned to me and said, 'I felt so down before the meeting that I wondered how I could ever get motivated again and stop the feelings of guilt and frustration. That sit-down with the family lifted a great weight off my shoulders. I know all the other supervisors there told me they felt the same. I really feel now we can get goin' again.'

I spoke to Doreen about the funeral arrangements and let her know that the company would cover all costs. My decision wasn't popular with the law firm who told me it could be interpreted as an admission of guilt and responsibility. I took responsibility for the decision as being the right thing to do for a longstanding, valued and trusted employee, who'd lost his life in the factory.

Leo's accident, occurring two days after September 11th, posed a travel problem for his brother. Leo's brother, the Reverend Father Ray O'Leary, was originally a highly respected Catholic priest in Toowoomba, before then being based in the USA. Flight restrictions in the USA after 9/11 delayed his travel plans and the funeral was deferred until Leo's brother could attend to conduct the service on September 18th.

I felt very privileged later when Doreen and her daughter Natalie approached me to ask me to deliver the eulogy. I set about writing a fitting tribute to Leo. Leo's brother finally made it to Australia and funeral arrangements were finalised. I'd completed the eulogy and was at home where Maryann and Carole were chatting with me on the afternoon of Leo's funeral. Maryann looked at her watch and remarked.

'It's time to go. Are you okay?'

She had driven from Brisbane to support me, something for which I was very appreciative.

'I'm fine.'

Maryann led the way out and, just as she was exiting through the laundry door, my legs went to jelly. She immediately spotted it and turned around and said, 'You're not okay.'

She then came to me and started touching me lightly on my head, chest and back and I immediately went very calm. She had never displayed this gift to me before. I marvelled at her understanding and abilities regarding our personal energy and the energies around us. How she understood them and worked with them amazed me.

We arrived at the grand St Patrick's Cathedral to find it was packed, with standing room only. I sat in the back row with Carole and Maryann. Leo's daughter Natalie must have seen me arrive as she walked back to us from the front of the church.

'Doug, we'd like you to come and sit with the family.'

I walked to the front with her and sat in the middle of all family members.

On doing so I felt the huge amount of emotion around me and felt I was drowning in it.

I'm never going to be able to deliver the eulogy. How will I ever calm myself?

Maryann, still up the rear of the church, obviously spotted I was in trouble. She came and sat close beside me. Somehow she calmed me.

Leo's brother, the Reverend Father Ray, conducted the service. I think about twelve priests were seated behind him because he was greatly respected in the local church hierarchy. It was then my turn to give the eulogy. When I stood in front of the large crowd, I was fearful in the first few moments that I wasn't going to be able to speak. I took a deep breath. I'm sure Maryann did something, because I settled and delivered it without faulting.

'Firstly, I thank Doreen and Leo's family for the kindness and support given to me, and the opportunity to genuinely communicate a eulogy for Leo; I feel it a privilege and an honour,' I began.

I won't include the rest of the eulogy here but it can be read as an appendix at the end of the book.

I ended the eulogy with, 'I feel I have lost a member of my family.'

The service finished and the Foundry workers had formed a guard of honour outside the church as the pall bearers moved Leo's coffin to the waiting hearse. Just as the pall bearers exited the church, three F111 jets roared directly over the procession. I appreciated the moment.

What a beautiful coincidence and spectacular precision in universal synchronicity. What a very fitting tribute to Leo's formal departure.

It confirmed my feeling that spirit was well and truly present. I was again extremely touched and grateful when the family requested I be a pall bearer for Leo, representing Natalie.

It took me back to the continual synchronous moments I had with my revelational experience. While I was waiting for the funeral procession to the cemetery to start outside the cathedral, an elderly and gentle-mannered priest, who was seated close to the alter during the service, approached me and said, 'Thank you for the beautiful eulogy, would you be so kind to talk to a youth group I work with?'

I took an immediate liking to him and his gentle manner.

'I'd be pleased to do it . . .' I was interrupted as his head turned away from me. His attention was turned to two younger priests. One had grabbed his arm and was leading him away while looking at me suspiciously without saying a word. I immediately knew I wouldn't be presenting to the youth group and sure enough the request never came. When I saw the large number of priests in the church at the start of the service, I wondered if I should delete my reference to priests in the eulogy but decided not to because I believed it to be truth.

The cemetery service was equally well attended and once again I found myself in a sea of emotion. Once again Maryann stepped to my side and I was able to calm down.

Carole decided to return home with family. Leo's family, grandchildren and workmates placed items meaningful to Leo in the grave during the service.

After the funeral, I sat at home reflecting on the precision of the synchronicity of the F111 flypast as the funeral procession left the church, and thought about the synchronicity of my visit to Phil Chote. Knowing spirit is with you can still bring joy in the most difficult of times.

A few days after Leo's funeral, the managing director of the ballistics company rang to invite us to his Gold Coast facility to review his findings regarding a new guard design. It was an impressive facility. We walked past professional displays of army helmets and bulletproof vests to a strongly reinforced long room where an 8mm gun barrel was set up. A small section of one of the proposed machine guard sections was mounted on sand bags at the end of a basement tunnel about the length of a cricket pitch. Safety requirements were explained. The operator shouted, 'Clear target area!' We all fell in behind him ready for the test firing.

An 8mm barrel was triggered and a bullet smashed into the guard sample.

'Wham!' The report echoed throughout the bunker as the bullet smashed into the guarding sample, which we all inspected. A magnum 10mm barrel was then mounted and loaded. While the 8mm round gave a loud noise, the magnum round yielded an ear-splitting boom when fired at the guard sample. The guarding design recommended was simple and obviously well and truly strong enough. The managing director noted their data demonstrated it would withstand one million times more impact energy than we could generate in the brake-drum lathe. We walked back to the office with the sample and I shook his hand.

'Thanks, I appreciate your support and prompt response. What do we owe you?'

I was humbled by his very kind response.

'I've no intention of charging for this service considering the circumstances. I wish you all the best and hope it all works out for you.'

With that he bid us goodbye. It was in total contrast to the blatantly excessive fees charged by the law firm.

Our engineering staff immediately started on the new guard design for the CNC Okuma LC50 lathe and another similar machine, each costing around $10,000. We subsequently sent the managing director of the ballistics company a framed acknowledgement. I wrote a letter to Okuma Japan recommending a viewing window upgrade with no response.

With the funeral behind us, the safety barbeque was due and it went ahead. It was a hugely uplifting experience for all. Forty O'Leary family members arrived and all were taken to the accident scene to provide a complete understanding of how Leo was lost. Many family members were impressed with the modern robotic technology controlling multiple CNC machines and vision systems, which this fifty-nine-year-old man had mastered. I was told it also helped gain closure for some family members. The family then sat with all employees chatting with them while eating their hamburgers. It was held indoors in the huge, unused, heritage-listed timber canteen building originally used to feed 1,000 employees in the company's heyday. It was where Puggy launched me in my Puggy dream.

A more formal part commenced. I welcomed the family and Leo's brother, Father Ray, gave a very moving and uplifting speech, followed by speeches from Leo's daughters and grandchildren. The coming together of the family and employees was a great healing event. After the barbeque, the factory's momentum soon picked up again. Production ramped up to previous levels. I later received a number of beautiful personal letters from various family members and the grandchildren, which I greatly appreciated and treasure and often reread. I was extremely humbled by the family's personal thank- you to me in a notice in the local paper thanking the hospital staff and all involved.

The next phase was the coroner's two-day inquest, held on September 9th 2002, almost twelve months to the day after the accident. I was nervous on the day of the hearing but ready to accept whatever outcome occurred. Many witnesses gave their statement, as I did. I was much relieved when the coroner declared it an accident and no penalties were awarded against the company. I was surprised when the safety authority conducting the investigation was criticised by the coroner for using the same hydraulic company that serviced our machine to review the hydraulics performance and maintenance, rather than an independent company.

I left the court room and passed by the regional director of safety, whom I'd respected and worked with prior to the accident. I was shocked when he gave me a strong warning with a veiled threat about what would happen if any future incident occurred. I immediately lost respect for the man. I was saddened by his strong reaction to the final verdict of the coroner. I also felt very proud of the professionalism of our engineering, maintenance and production employees, because we were able to table both an in-house and an independent safety audit, with all issues addressed. Training records for Leo and other operators were tabled, along with full up-to-date maintenance records for the robot cell.

The final mark of respect for Leo was a ceremony in the front street garden area of the factory where a memorial plaque was unveiled in front of an olive tree provided by a maintenance employee. Family members and employees stood around while a simple unveiling ceremony took place. After the closure of the Foundry, the O'Leary family maintained the garden area; the plaque and olive tree were relocated in 2017 when a multinational hardware chain built a megastore when the Foundry was demolished and the site redeveloped.

When the chairman of the new owners terminated my employment on July 19th 2005 with twenty minutes' notice, I was extremely touched and humbled the next morning. I answered a knock on the door at home to find Leo's daughter Natalie smiling at me. She presented me with a beautiful bunch of flowers.

It was an action I'll always remember and cherish greatly.

I met the first aid attendant Ross many years later in 2015, ten years after I left the Foundry. He told me the experience was really life-changing for him.

CHAPTER 26
MY EXPERIENCES WITH ENERGY

I've mentioned my ability to beam energy and how it faded, and my beautiful energy shower experience at the Limburg Cathedral. During my life, many other experiences have occurred. Each time the feeling is so comforting it reinforces the fact that spirit is always with us whether we're conscious of it or not. It's a joyful experience.

Other strong energy flow experiences occurred while I was watching entertainers. Two instances were when Australian Aborigines were playing the didgeridoo. One occurrence was at the annual Floriade event in Canberra. I think it was in 2011. I was walking around admiring the beautiful and colourful display of tulips and other floral beds when I happened upon a marquee containing an Indigenous-themed display. My attention was drawn to an Aboriginal man inside starting to play the didgeridoo so I entered the marquee. He was obviously very skilled, as when he played a rush of energy engulfed me and continued to flow through me. It was a really beautiful feeling and lasted for about a minute. I believe it's 'spirit' entering the room. It's a sacred and very comforting feeling.

Another occurred in a travelling circus marquee in Toowoomba's Queen's Park, where Carole and I took our niece's two daughters one evening. The performance began. My attention was drawn to an Aboriginal artist sitting on a platform high in the tent mounted on the main mast pole and he started to play a didgeridoo. Within a minute of the unique earthy sound of the didgeridoo whirling around the audience, the same energy-flowing experience I had at Floriade occurred. I've come to believe this basic instrument can actually summon spiritual energy. Again, both were very positive and reassuring experiences.

Both were at the beginning of entertainment events, so I had the feeling those Indigenous musicians knew they were bringing a positive energy into the marquees to prepare the facility for the entertainment. Similar experiences, to a much lesser degree, have occurred when I've been watching theatre or concerts. The Neil Diamond concert was one I particularly remember, where Neil walked around the perimeter of the stage with great introductory music playing to build up the energy, which I could feel flowing in. At Cirque du Soleil in Brisbane during a drumming act when the entertainment commenced, I felt another energy shower.

Other very strong energy flows that I've had were explained to me by Maryann as past-life healings. These have occurred on my world travels. I spoke earlier of my first energy flow experience during the Truth Seminar, and a second one in the Limburg Cathedral in Germany.

When I was in Japan on business in late August 2008, I visited the Shogun's palace in Kyoto with my customer one weekend. We were chatting away as we entered the large entry gates, which were part of a large wall surrounding the palace, the gravel crunching under my feet. I stood in awe of the building's character. When I was just inside the grounds I stopped to admire this magnificent cultural building before me. Everything was in immaculate condition. I love Japanese architecture. Again I felt a beautiful rush of energy through me. It continually reinforces one's awareness, with the practicality, reality and knowledge of spirit.

While touring Berlin in 2010 I was near the Brandenburg Gate. Again, I had a powerful energy flow pass through me. In 2012 I revisited Japan with all my family. At Gion, the old part of Kyoto, at a bridge I felt an enormous energy flow through me. Shortly after at the Minami-za Kabuki Theatre entrance, a second flow occurred. I decided I lived in Japan in a past life. The exact experience reoccurred when the family and I visited the Shogun's palace. In St Petersburg in 2014 I was sitting in a restaurant for lunch when I was immersed in a comforting flow of energy. After this occurrence I came to believe what Maryann told me: these 'energy healings' were related to resolving past life events.

Another 'energy' experience happened after the Foundry successfully bid to supply a driveline component for Eaton Corporation, in Marshall, Michigan. Members of the sales and marketing team and I sat at the

Foundry at 2am participating in an internet auction for the supply of automotive differential components to the USA. I regarded these events as mercenary and necessary evils in a globalised world, where loyalty, long-standing business relationships, service and quality became subservient to the dollar.

I flew to Marshall in December 2000 and stayed in the Detroit area for about a week. I found I was unable to meditate during this time. I decided it must have been jetlag even though I felt I'd adjusted to the new time zone. I didn't like the feeling in the Detroit area, it seemed rundown, dying and 'unloved' – it was a feeling of depression. I was left with the impression everyone was too busy and 'down' to really care about anything. An old-school duty manager at the hotel, who very willingly and kindly assisted me with a flat battery in my hire car, really let off steam about the constant cost cutting and killing of customer service he had been exposed to over the years of his employ. The hotel was part of a well-known international brand. It was sad to see Detroit go into bankruptcy and disrepair in the next decade.

During the next trip with the business development manager to the Michigan area, I had the same feeling and inability to meditate. However, when we flew to our next destination in Ingersoll, Canada, the change in energy was total. I found by comparison that it was like meditating in a rainforest. Ingersoll was well kept. I felt this city was 'loved' and realised how different the energies of cities are. The obviously 'loved' and well-kept cities always feel much better. I feel this is important for the community's wellbeing.

As I've said, I now believe that many of the Indigenous people around the world, unimpeded by Western intellectual development and teachings, felt this energy on a daily basis. As a result they worshipped the spirit in most things – both living and inanimate – because they could actually *feel* the energy of it. It made me understand their sacred sites, because sacred is the most meaningful way I can describe these comforting energy flows. In my view, their spiritual beliefs were based on experiential, very real events. I feel this brought them closer to 'truth'. I associate a high level of integrity and personal respect with many early indigenous cultures. I believe we could learn much from a professional study of the many shaman in so-called 'primitive' tribes, and their relationship with the energies and spirits around them.

I was impressed greatly by the integrity displayed at an abattoir process on the outskirts of Kathmandu. During a visit to Nepal with Carole in mid-March 1990, we caught a tired old bus one Sunday morning, filled to the brim with passengers, to visit a local traditional public butchery at Dakshinkali. We all rocked back and forth as the bus swayed while the driver steered down a steep, rough gravel road. We drove into a heavily stoned valley, left the bus and walked to a bridge built from local stone where we could get an overview of the events unfolding.

Looking down on this gory scene we saw families sitting on large flat rock outcrops under tree canopies with their dismembered animals strewn about on the rocky surface. Parents and children were cutting and packing the various organs and portions in a sea of blood. Some children's hands were dripping in blood. It was a very sobering scene. Everyone in attendance knew exactly what was involved in providing meat for the family. The whole scene had an air of reverence.

A Hindu priest was carrying out the slaughter of the animals and village members were joining a queue with their animal to be slaughtered by him. The animals were only males and were visibly aware of the many deaths around them because they were all trembling while waiting their turn with the priest. A special area with red roofed buildings and a small temple was where the slaughter took place. When each animal reached the priest, he sought permission from the animal by placing his hand on their head. Most gave permission by immediately becoming calm. With this 'signal' the priest would quickly and efficiently slit their throat. Those that remained trembling were patted away because they were deemed not ready. I was greatly impressed by the integrity of the process taking place. I'm also aware of horse whisperers who can control horses through consciously using the energy from their gut rather than using verbal commands. At least this is what two horse whisperers, who certainly had an excellent rapport with horses, told me.

I now believe that, while humans are literally in essence a 'ball of energy', there is also an external universal energy flow that's always, indiscernibly, flowing gently through each person at any given time. I also believe that this flow is blocked when we don't verbally express what we truly feel. If this 'dishonest' behaviour persists, then the universal energy flow is restricted, and the resultant blockage manifests into either physical health issues, or illness. This is why one feels much better and lighter after clearing an issue with a person on an issue that's been stewing for a while.

The clearing interaction addresses the unsettling issue, emotion or behaviour, and hopefully it's done in a manner that leaves the dignity of the person intact. I came to this understanding while in the state of high awareness. Any small issue I left unexpressed was magnified to the extent that I felt a physical discomfort and my energy became 'heavy'. This rapidly disappeared as soon as the necessary communication took place. I often wish I could return to that heightened state, because having had the spiritual experience,

I still don't confront all issues in my life appropriately when they occur, often I'm simply not consciously aware of them. It's part of my human process, I guess.

I strongly believe modern medicine could greatly reduce hospitalisation and treatment costs significantly by taking the time to research and explore this energy area with an open mind. I'm still in awe when I think of the positive instantaneous changes I could initiate in my body by promptly addressing issues weighing me down during the revelational experience. Experiencing the healing I received in the rundown motel on the night after I assisted Jeanine left me in awe. Pirio's head massage and iron ladle- pourer Greg Paix's 'cooked meat' skull healing were other unusual events I experienced and described earlier. I remain astonished how spirit has the ability to instantly change our state of being (our energy level). It's miraculous! If we can only evolve ourselves spiritually to a point where it happens openly and regularly, medicine would move into an entirely new paradigm, in my view. This rapid change in energy state is the spiritual platform for miracles – they do happen.

I believe a serious mistake was made by Australia's health minister in 2018, when on the advice of the medical profession he had most energy healing practices removed from medical benefits. I know of two cases where the medical profession was unable to treat a serious ailment except by prescribing pain relief pills. Kinesiology fixed both overnight.

One case was a cynical lady who, after the treatment, went home saying, 'It was a complete waste of time and money. He hardly touched me!'

After many months of pain that was threatening her teaching career, she woke the morning after one kinesiology treatment pain-free, and the issue has never returned. I had an infected toe healed in one half-hour session with a kinesiologist.

This understanding of clearing one's energy is why I currently travel, and have travelled for nearly two hours each way every week since 1987, to receive a half-hour spiritual healing. I can feel the clearing of my energy each time. Sometimes, when discussing a blocked feeling I had during the week, the healer helps me identify an issue that caused the heavy feeling and it instantly clears.

I also believe the energy of trees and nature is vitally important to the well-being of the human race, and I'm dismayed at the constant and widespread clearing of trees in a so-called 'enlightened' society. One only has to stop and consciously feel the difference in energy between the centre of a busy concreted city and a rainforest, to practically understand there are huge differences in energy important for our well-being. The destruction of rainforests in the Amazonian, Indonesian, and equatorial regions, and in all nations generally, needs to be stopped. I believe we need to globally ban the destruction of any tree over forty years old, unless at least ten are planted in its place. I regard old trees as energy sentinels. They are also our oxygen and rain factories.

Urban planners are increasingly appreciative of the importance of trees in the development of communities in cities. The City of Salford, within the greater borough of Manchester, home of Manchester United, my son Sheldon's favourite football team, promotes itself as the 'City of Trees' and identifies nine reasons on its website for why trees increase the health and well-being of residents. Dr Kathleen Wolf of the University of Washington supports this in her paper.[28] 'The Science of Trees and Human Health & Well-Being'.

While running an R&D project at the Foundry on a world-patented new innovative crawler track link design, we worked closely with a local farmer, Bob, who had raised the idea with us. (The project 'died' under the new ownership).

One day Bob said to me, 'I often bulldoze dams for farmers as a second income stream, and all the dams I've built fill rapidly after rain – that's all except two. I was at a loss to understand why, as were the two farmers involved.

'A year or so later one farmer rang me one night all excited to tell me his dam filled during a recent storm. He believed the reason was that when I built the dam, a thick stand of gum trees was located in the upstream run off area, and when these were cleared to plant crops the dam filled after the first rain. He then reasoned the trees absorbed all the runoff water and were like tanks storing water and transpiring water to the atmosphere to form clouds, while shading the surrounding soil and keeping it moist.'

'That makes sense,' I responded.

Bob continued, 'I now believe tree removal is causing localised drought and saline water table rises in lowland areas.'

'It sounds very logical, I've never considered it, we've sure taken out a lot of trees in Australia, maybe that's why we're having so many dry periods.'

---

[28] Dr K Wolf, *The Science of Trees and Human Health & Well-Being; Washington University; 2009*

'It always rains over rainforests,' he quipped with a smile.

I have a neighbour who immigrated from Zimbabwe to escape violence. He is an electrician and was involved in a project to plant Australian gum trees in wetlands to provide tall and straight electricity poles. Many great poles were harvested but the wetlands were drying up. Research identified each tree was 'drinking' one hundred litres of water per day. The project was disbanded.

This view was also reinforced to me during a six-week cruise Carole and I undertook that circumnavigated the Pacific Ocean in 2008. The ship arrived at Glacier Bay, Alaska to allow passengers to view the glaciers. It sat stationary so we could see them carve. Unbeknown to me, a cherry farmer from Washington state was standing beside me at the ship's handrail as we watched large sheets of ice groan and drop spectacularly when they calved into the icy waters of the bay. A local ranger was giving an overview on a PA system as he described what was happening and the history of the area. He was taking questions from passengers.

'Is there any evidence of climate change in the bay?' a passenger asked.

'No, none at all,' was the ranger's prompt reply.

The man standing beside me erupted.

'Bullshit! What a load of absolute bullshit!' he exclaimed loudly with no concern about who was listening.

I turned to him and said calmly, 'Why do you say that?'

'I'm from Seattle. I come up here every five years. Five years ago there were close to a dozen glaciers carving into this bay and now there are only four. Don't tell me there's nothing changing!'

'Why would he lie?' I asked.

'So he doesn't scare off the tourists I suppose.'

He quickly changed the subject after hearing my accent. 'You're an Aussie aren't you?'

'Yes, I'm from Toowoomba in Queensland, though you've probably never heard of it.'

He continued, 'You Aussies almost sent me broke. I grow stone fruit and used to grow peaches, apricots, pears and cherries. Your farmers' produce was so good and cheap all the farmers in Washington state stopped all stone fruit production except for cherries. I'm now just a cherry grower.'

'I'm sorry to hear that,' I responded as he continued to speak, ignoring my remark.

'The trouble was that when the farms were originally set up, all the farmers had historically done widespread land clearing and had levelled all the trees. The end result was there weren't any windbreaks.

We ended up with such a wind-chafing problem on the fruit that it damaged around thirty percent of our crop. We were also experiencing poor rainfall.'

'That's a huge crop loss,' I offered.

'All the farmers got together and decided to plant avenues of tree windbreaks around all the fields to reduce the chafing issue. It took quite a while for the trees to mature, but when they did the chafing issue was fixed. Surprisingly, regular rains returned. I'm now an advocate of planting trees to bring rain,' he continued.

I told him of my experience in Australia and he just nodded his head in agreement. I knew trees had quite high moisture content in them from the days when I was doing architectural plans at night. I often discussed the effects of moisture on various feature timbers with wood suppliers. 'Doctor' Google searches yielded the information that some trees have up to forty percent moisture, and the water weight in the tree can in some cases be twice as heavy as the timber in the tree. It seems to me to just be common sense. I just can't understand the massive ongoing destruction of the Earth's forests. Forests are the Earth's lungs and water storage 'tanks'. Our exploitative use of its resources must surely be giving our planet emphysema. We need trees for rain and oxygen. We also need their soothing energy for our well-being.

I remember hippies always speaking about people with good or bad vibes, and prior to my spiritual experience I used to arrogantly dismiss it as 'hippy talk'. I believe that because everything is energy, the universal and absolute energy in every living and inanimate thing is the same and is God, as mentioned previously. The differences occur at a particle or molecular level when the energy vibrates at different frequencies and these different vibrational frequencies decide the life form or the inanimate form – the frequency may be low for inanimate objects and ultra-high for human beings.

We have much to learn and understand about energy.

CHAPTER 27
THE PRESENT MOMENT AND
UNDERSTANDING GUIDANCE

I've learnt that being in the present moment, something that's often difficult, is beneficial. In our fast-paced and busy society, full of head noise, it's critical to develop a feel for the energies around us. I'm now mindful that I can be feeling fine yet, upon walking into a room of people, I can suddenly feel quite low. If I'm not conscious of this energy change, my mood can be sullied for the rest of the day. Eckhart Tolle in *A New Earth* places huge emphasis on the importance of being in the present moment in order to grow spiritually.

It's a case of unconsciously picking up the energy of one or multiple persons in the room who are not in a good place at the time. If one is aware of it, one can simply make a conscious decision to not let it impact. I imagine myself in a gold cage and imagine any 'bad vibes' just bouncing off, and it ensures my energy isn't affected.

People who are 'feelers' (as I am) are more likely to be more sensitive to a change in energy. It all depends on how spirit communicates to us.

While I've noted the language of spirit is feeling, people can receive guidance in other ways. I now believe there are four ways we receive guidance from spirit. I came to this view many years ago. A female representative of the global Inner Peace movement, from Canada, presented at a motel function room in Toowoomba to explain the four gifts that people use to keep in touch with their intuitive self. I've seen these gifts actively working in the people I've worked with over the years and I can relate to each of them.

The first of them is the prophetic gift, when people have the ability to clearly see future events.

I remember speaking with the Foundry's maintenance manager after my experience. He was a religious person but had an open mind. He often questioned me about my beliefs and we had a very open relationship.

'Doug, I've told no one about this, but not long after I started at the Foundry I saw the future twice,' he said one day.

'What do you mean?' I asked with curiosity.

'Well, you might think it silly but one day not long after starting at the Foundry as a young boy, I walked into the boiler house when suddenly a boiler steam pipe exploded and steam burst out everywhere. I jumped back in shock but when I looked back again everything was normal.'

'Wow, that's amazing,' I noted with surprise.

'I went up to the engine driver, as we called them in those days, and told him a boiler tube was in need of urgent repair. He just told me to piss off.'

'What happened?' I enquired.

'A week or so later I was walking near the boiler house again when he called me over and said, "How did you know that pipe was going to explode?" I was so embarrassed I just shrugged my shoulders and walked off.'

'That's a precious gift. You're privileged to have experienced it.'

'It happened a second time,' he quickly volunteered.

'Really?' I asked.

'You know the small entry man door you have to bend over to get through in the non-ferrous foundry?'

'Yes, I know it. I've entered the shop through it many times.' The small door was fixed inside the large sliding door and was used to provide access and prevent strong winds blowing into the shop when metal was being poured. Aluminium and brass castings were made in this shop, which was separate from the large iron foundry. It was to avoid damaging contamination by these metals if they accidentally found their way into the molten iron.

'Well, I was just entering the shop through the door when a mould exploded violently, sending molten metal flying everywhere. I almost fell backwards through the door because it was such a shock. Yet again when I looked back everything was normal. I gathered myself and went over to Dumpy and said, "Dumpy, I think you need to check that mould".'

Dumpy, as he was affectionately called, was a very short stocky Chinaman with a very pleasant, happy and willing personality. Everyone loved Dumpy. He always wore a navy blue singlet and shorts with large black boots and black socks. He was always smiling and joking.

'Dumpy said to me, "Sure David." He walked over to remove the cope half [the top half] of the sand mould. Lifting the cope half off, he turned to me and said, "It's full of water. Thanks Dave, it would have been a nasty accident if we poured that one." He never questioned me as to how I knew.'

'That's a beautiful gift you have. You need to cultivate it because it will be a really helpful guide in diagnosing maintenance needs,' I said excitedly. I remembered the book I read while on a cruise around Hawaii, it was about a Mr X who used the same gift to streamline maintenance practices on a freighter ship.

'I was told it was the work of the devil so I stopped doing it. It doesn't work anymore,' he said.

'I'd encourage you to ask spirit for it to return. It's really a wonderful gift from spirit.'

He was never able to reactivate it. I feel he also found it frightening. Some religious teachings are so misguided.

The inner-voice gift is a second vehicle for communicating with spirit. It's where people listen to the guidance a positive voice provides. I've met many people who use this gift daily. It requires trust in spirit and the ability to discern and work with the gentle and encouraging voice – not the destructive voice of the ego.

The intuitive gift is the third communication vehicle where people 'just know' what's required. Many people can be thrust into areas of new responsibility and perform well, even without formal qualifications because they follow their intuition. I worked with a great engineer at the Foundry who regularly displayed this gift. I sometimes found it frustrating as short, one-word answers would often be provided when a more detailed answer, that accurately explained the proposed course of action, was sought. I learnt to trust what the person was saying, and many successful projects reinforced this trust. I often thought that these decisions were also aided unconsciously by what felt right, and that feelings were part of this intuitive gift.

I like the definition in *Conversations with God – Book 3*: 'Intuition is the ear of the soul.'[29]

In my view, prodigies have this gift, but I also believe they're bringing skills with them from a previous incarnation. A great example of this, in my view, is a beautiful young seven-year-old girl, Anwen Deng from Perth, Australia. She plays complex classical music pieces effortlessly like a true master. At the time of writing she was studying at the prestigious Juilliard School of Music in New York. She's a joy to watch. The final gift is the gift of feeling, something I mostly use. I've reflected on my times when as a young lad faced with an issue, I'd often think to myself, if I wasn't educated and ignored what people around me said, what would I do naturally? I feel this approach as a young boy was another factor that led me to my spiritual experience, as mentioned earlier.

During my period as inaugural CEO of the Australian Green Infrastructure Council (AGIC), I met with a female scientist who had been doing volunteer work to assist me in getting the infrastructure rating scheme up and running. We were having lunch where she was employed. During the lunch she looked at me and said, 'You know, you're the most natural person I've ever met.'

I was quite chuffed to hear her spontaneous comment as it was something I'd aspired to.

I'd regularly do what felt right for me; however at the time I wasn't consciously aware that I was seeking a feeling on an issue. I can remember two specific occasions when I was general manager. One cost the Foundry dearly (when I ignored my feeling) and another when following a feeling proved a great asset. Prior to becoming GM in the late 1980s when the Foundry was in serious financial difficulty, a finance director committed the company to a casting supply contract with the customer Malco mentioned earlier. The day before the contract was due to be signed I went to his upstairs office.

'We need to put a condition in the contract that the metal addition we use to get the correct metallurgical properties will be the one specified and not their expensive copper-based addition that Malco used. If we have to use copper it will cost us close to an extra $100,000 each year.' I said.

'No way, we won't be putting any technical conditions in the contract and that's final.'

In spite of my persistent requests the finance director wouldn't entertain my needed inclusion in the supply agreement. The prior dealings I had with the company's GM led me to distrust anything he said. The brake-drum product required the metallurgical addition of an appropriate element to promote the

---

29   ND Walsch, *Conversations with God – Book 3*, Hodder and Stoughton, London, UK, 1998, p. 115.

correct pearlite microstructure to ensure the desired tensile strength and hardness properties. The product was a range of safety-critical truck and semi-trailer brake-drums we were producing.

While verbal assurances were given by the Malco GM that we could produce brake-drums using our particular inoculant, once production commenced he insisted on the copper-based addition. Our engineering department was instructed to comply under protest. The company wore the impact of the cost. After becoming GM I led a team that acquired Malco, as described earlier. We were free to change the specification. The metallurgist had researched an idea of using an antimony-based addition, by which we could achieve the desired properties while reducing costs to a level below our pre- copper production.

A research paper confirmed it as a suitable addition and tabled the range of percentages that could be used. Prototype product was manufactured for testing. The metallurgist specified it to be used at the upper limit. It was a safety-critical product and at the time every truck and trailer on Australian highways used brake-drums rather than disc brakes on their braking systems. After a million kilometres of actual road testing no failures occurred so our engineering team deemed the addition approved for production. This occurred circa 1996 at a time when our profit had dropped. I was under pressure to authorise its release to achieve a major cost saving. I sat on the decision for many months, much to the dismay of the plant metallurgist and manufacturing and engineering managers, because it didn't feel right to me. Out of frustration the manufacturing manager Daisy stormed into my office one day.

'You're not bloody serious about saving costs, otherwise you wouldn't be stuffing around for months delaying a decision on the change to antimony. We can make a huge cost saving immediately. You've been constantly at me to find areas of savings.'

We had a very open and trusting relationship so I turned to him and said, 'You're probably right; I just can't seem to make the decision. Okay, let's do it.'

I reluctantly accepted his berating. I still felt uncomfortable with the decision but I gave the go-ahead after reviewing the research papers and test results with the metallurgist and engineering manager one more time.

One million miles of testing, surely that's sufficient evidence, and the research paper says it's okay.

I told the leadership team it was a go.

Production commenced immediately using antimony as an addition and product was being despatched all over Australia. Within a fortnight, on a Friday afternoon I received a customer's field complaint about a brand new and loaded B-Double truck leaving Melbourne for Perth that had all its brake-drums explode on the first heavy application of the brakes, sending cast iron bits all over the highway and damaging brake lines on the trailer. Many more reports of other incidents rapidly followed. It was obvious the company had an extremely serious product liability in the market. During my twelve-year term as GM between 1993 and 2005, eight people were killed in Australia by large fragments of truck or trailer brake-drums being broken from heavy vehicles that smashed through passenger car windscreens.

I learnt that most were imported Asian drums because I'd ring the police once we heard of such an accident to ask them what markings were on the drum segment concerned. I dreaded the possibility that one of our drums could be responsible for a death. I immediately called the leadership team together the next day, a Saturday.

Everyone was on the phone to truck and trailer manufacturers and distributers. The quality and sales records allowed easy traceability and identification of the product concerned. The issue was promptly addressed and all stock of the product with the relevant date code was immediately quarantined and returned to the factory, and trucks were recalled as they were identified. The Department of Federal Transport was also notified on Monday. Over the weekend the leadership team had accurately identified where the vast majority of product was located, the exception being trucks on the road. The federal department deemed a national public recall program wasn't necessary when they realised we'd identified the offending stock so accurately and had the situation quickly under control. We stayed in close communication with the department.

Needless to say, I was highly concerned about the potential consequences and started making many requests to spirit for the incident to end without injury. Thankfully, all trucks were eventually tracked down and customers recompensed for secondary damage to trucks. In all, the recall and repair work cost just over $300,000. The immediate response, after an early failure, certainly helped to contain this cost. I was so relieved and thankful no injuries occurred. At the time we were just starting production of brake-drums for export to a Japanese customer. Coincidentally a small group from our Japanese customer was visiting the Foundry. I spoke to the Japanese quality engineer.

'We have had serious brake-drum failures in the market. I feel it's a mistake to go ahead with antimony that you specified as an addition in your product,' I said

'There is no problem with antimony, we've been using it for decades. What percentage are you using?' he asked.

When I told him he looked me in the eye. Without speaking, he raised his hand and pretended to slit his throat.

'At our percentages it's fine, at the levels you used, tensile strength can be halved and impact resistance reduced by seventy percent.'

Shit, was my first reaction. *The research papers our metallurgist used made no mention of this. Why did the test drums last over one million miles?* Then I stopped. *This visit is very timely. Another bit of synchronicity?*

We had no problems with the product exported to Japan using the antimony addition at the correct levels. It was deemed the best quality they had received. Our metallurgist had specified the addition at the top limit of the specification in the research paper and this had been an honest mistake. At the time I thought he could have researched it more thoroughly rather than relying on one technical paper. The reduction needed was a very minor percentage, about 0.2 percent, highlighting the critical nature of metallurgy.

When I reviewed the lessons learned it became clear that all our prototype testing was performed by one older and extremely careful driver who was gentle on the brakes.

There was another incident, a more positive example, where trusting my feelings helped a desperate situation. It occurred when the high voltage switchgear on the old second-hand electrical induction furnace – which I'd argued about with Doug Curlewis – shorted out, vaporising large steel busbars that were forty millimetres, or one and a half inches square in size. The high voltage electrical short shook the whole thick chequer plate melt deck as it violently disintegrated, terrifying the melt deck crew. Repairs were done using old switch gear spares that came with the furnace. After about an hour of operation the massive short circuit happened again. Experts in high voltage were called in from our local energy provider and induction furnace supplier. Transformer experts were contracted also. The deck started up once more using the third set of spares; within an hour the melt deck trembled once more and the high voltage switch gear disintegrated again.

Frustrated and anxious, I immediately arranged a meeting with the engineering and maintenance managers, who said, 'We've run out of spare parts. The USA supplier had been contacted. The factory will be out for at least three to four months. They're an obsolete part. It will require a special build that will take time to source the necessary materials and parts.'

That's all we need, that bloody old furnace.

I wondered what we could do about the situation.

'If we paid a premium how quickly could we get it?' I asked.

'We've asked that. It won't make any difference because it's a material lead time issue. They're obsolete parts,' was the depressing response.

Needless to say, when told, head office in Melbourne urgently wanted a status and recovery report. I set about writing it. While writing I had a strong feeling to go into the factory. I remember talking to myself, *You don't have time to walk the factory, just get this bloody report written.*

Head office was breathing down my neck chasing the report. The feeling became so strong I decided to wander down to the shop floor and ended up in an old warehouse.

While I stood there, my head talk said, *What the hell am I doing here when the report is so urgently needed?*

I looked up and saw a pine box on top of tall pallet racking. It was an 'Aha' moment! I immediately, intuitively, knew there were spare switches in there so I called the engineering and maintenance managers on my mobile who had it opened. Another set of switches was in the box. The old furnace electrics had come in many small boxes and this one had been separated from the spares held in the maintenance stores. Neither the maintenance manager nor the engineering manager knew of it.

The new switches were fitted, much to my relief, late that night. At around midnight I received a call telling me they also had blown up. All the experts were stumped. At 1:30am we anxiously pondered our situation around an electrical fitter's bench. The young electricians reminded me we wouldn't be able to get the specialised spares from the USA for months, even if we paid a premium price to speed up the supply. The problem hadn't been identified by any of the experts we'd consulted. I was pondering how we could design and build new switchgear. While reviewing options with engineering and maintenance staff at that ungodly hour and feeling very despondent, an older electrician, Wyn, walked up and said, 'Leave it to me Doug, I've a theory that may work.

'I'm pretty certain that the vaporising of the solid steel bars had left an invisible, conductive film on the high voltage switch areas. I'm sure the insulation is being rendered ineffective, resulting in our repetitive electrical short circuits.'

'You could be right, it's logical. It's worth a try,' I said hopefully.

'What about getting new switchgear?' was the next question I raised, with concern in my voice.

'Aw, I've checked out all the blown switch sets. I reckon I can make up one good set with some improvisation,' was Wyn's much-welcomed response.

He began the painstaking process of thoroughly cleaning every element in the high voltage area over two long days. I appreciated that he went without sleep one night so I shouted him a restaurant dinner and gave him a day off. After going through all the damaged sets of switches, he managed to build a complete new set with some improvisation, as he predicted. A day later we restarted the melt deck. It worked reliably for years until it was replaced with the latest technology induction furnaces in 2005, the year I was fired. About six months after the incident a head office financial director from Melbourne visited the site. While I was showing him around, Wyn, who saved the day, walked past slowly because he had a slight shuffle, the result of an earlier stroke.

The financial director looked at me and said, 'Why don't you sack someone like him? He's much too slow. You need someone more energetic.'

I had to contain myself.

'That man has earned his salary for the next fifty years. I wish I had more like him. He was the only person who understood the cause of our furnace outage that would've crippled the Foundry. Experts in the industry were of no assistance.' While talking I was thinking, *Dickhead*!

The director looked embarrassed and quickly changed the subject. I had many head office finance people visit over the twelve years I was GM. I grew tired of defending my policy of paying bills on time within contracted terms, along with some who made instant and critical judgments on factory employees, particularly those standing and waiting for a short period on a process delay. I often reflected when these criticisms arose on how many times I saw the same directors engaged in chatting at the coffee table at head office for longer periods at a far greater cost.

I dislike double standards, one rule for some and another for others. I call it two sets of rules.

I used to spend time wondering how the broader population could become more in touch with their essence. I decided all the religious beliefs are patriarchy-driven. I feel it's time for a matriarchal approach. I like and agree with Eckhart Tolle's view in his book *A New Earth*:

> Although women have egos, of course, the ego can take root and grow more easily in the male form than in the female. This is because women are less mind-identified than men. They are more in touch with the inner body and the intelligence of the organism where the intuitive faculties originate.[30]

I believe moving to appreciate the inner journey based on one's feelings and actual life experiences, rather than pure intellectual belief, will bring more wisdom. I also believe that if we base our beliefs on what we observe, experience and feel rather than what we're told, then we're on a faster path of spiritual evolvement and maturity.

To achieve this we all need regular quiet time, something many city folk never experience. I find that often, but not always, I'm transported to another beautiful and peaceful place when I'm in a relaxed state of mind during my daily meditations. One can come to really enjoy the present moment without the need for earphones channelling music or podcasts; it's not always easy to do but it's a journey I recommend. The transition can take time but it's very rewarding.

Silence and the sounds of nature can be beautiful and healing.

---

[30] E Tolle, *A New Earth*, (10th Anniversary Edition), Penguin, London, UK, 2016, p. 155.

CHAPTER 28
THE SUNRISE WAY PROJECT

Now I need to go back in time to describe what was to become a major event in my life while working at the Foundry, and also after I left it.

In 2001, four years before my Foundry employment was terminated, I was sitting in my office when the phone rang. It was the city's mayor, Di Thorley.

'Hi Doug, it's Di. You've done a bloody good job turning the Foundry around. I need you to join a board I'm forming to address the drug issue in the city, it's out of control. We've got 13,600 needle exchanges a month happening at the Base Hospital and two to three young people a week are dying as a result of drugs. The board will be responsible for developing a community-led drug and alcohol rehab centre. We've got no money or a building so we're starting from scratch. Can I count on you?'

'For sure,' I responded.

The request came at a time after the Foundry had been profitable for eight years and as GM, I was looking for another community project for the company to be involved with as part of a Corporate Social Responsibility (CSR) contribution. I was proud of the fact that the Foundry employees, on their own time, had built a well-equipped retail shop in a disused factory area on the city's main street for a charity to use at no cost, to sell second-hand goods. Factory supervisors had also assisted local hospital patients with mental health issues and some disabled people to learn production skills. I joined the board.

At the first meeting in City Hall, Di turned to me and said, 'I want you as an engineer to take responsibility for the infrastructure. We've got no money or facility yet, but I'm working on it. When I find a suitable building, we don't want a rundown place, I want the best. Nothing is too good for these people, we need to show we care. They need to know that they're important.'

We should be able to get something running within a few years was my first, misguided, estimation.

I optimistically assumed that within three to five years we'd have a facility operational, never thinking that, after finding a facility and twelve years of consistent effort, the board would come within a day of losing it to the local hospital. At the start of the project, the local newspaper editor made an interesting observation.

'You're a brave man taking this on Doug, it's not a popular issue, I guess if someone can do it you can.' I didn't fully appreciate his meaning and cautionary tone at the time.

I found the death rate difficult to believe. I was sure the mayor had exaggerated. However, a month or so later I was presenting at an occupational health and safety seminar in the city attended by local emergency services personnel, ambos, police and even the local television cameraman who listened into emergency frequencies. All assured me that this number was certainly correct. It was rarely spoken of in the media, and as Toowoomba was a conservative city, it seemed it was kept 'under wraps' away from open and public discussion (as was significant child abuse). Even now, drug raids and arrests are regular inclusions in the local daily newspaper, but hospital and emergency services' statistics are never highlighted. I believe at a very minimum, each year the stats relating to this scourge (kept by the local and regional hospitals, the morgue, police and emergency services) need to be publically advertised and discussed, with strategies developed at all government levels. If you can't measure it, you can't manage it, or have accurate knowledge of trends.

The board was initially called the Greenfields Board and later, following my suggestion, it was called the Sunrise Way Board. We had no funds or a building, so we scratched around for twelve months, not really moving forward. The mayor was a very outgoing, no-nonsense, forceful woman. I remember at one meeting where I suggested the new organisational name and an intent summary Di turned to me and said, 'You know, I think you're a man with a woman's heart.'

In 2002 her efforts resulted in the Premier of Queensland and Health Minister visiting the city. He announced that an old heritage-listed, derelict health building, on a large area of real estate in Toowoomba at the top of our range escarpment, a premium city site, would be made available through a five-year, renewable, peppercorn lease. This announcement was a surprise to the board. It was a shock to surrounding residents. Within days, negative media items were common and the board received threatening legal letters, which were simply ignored and binned. Support among local residents improved over time but I'm sure many still resent its presence. Local people had the idea it would be a drop-in centre for drug-affected people, whereas it really is like a hospital, with residents mostly detoxed before entering the facility.

The 1906 building was on one and three quarter acres. While the site had many beautiful trees and shrubs, some almost one hundred years old, the building was derelict. The first time I toured the facility after work to assess the magnitude of the task, I was struck by the enormity of the extensive works needed. I walked through, developing a growing mental list of challenges in my mind while I observed the dereliction. I noted the challenges to overcome:

- 120 smashed panes of glass.
- Broken window frames.
- Over twenty doors ripped of their hinges.
- Holes punched in most walls.
- Rotten and sagging floorboards.
- Absolutely putrid and stinking toilets.
- All plumbing stuffed – many leaks.
- Some rewiring needed.
- No fire protection.
- Asbestos sheeting.
- Peeling paint
- Leaking walls and roof.
- White ants.
- Borers.
- Heavy mould everywhere.
- External computer and power cables screwed on walls everywhere.
- Heritage areas severely corrupted

It's bloody heritage-listed – shit, where does one start! In one central room I came across piles of papers and letters stashed under ply sheeting that was leaning against a timber wall. It looked like someone had been preparing for arson. I picked up a letter and was surprised to find a cheque from Toowoomba Foundry for meals in the next door restaurant. Many more mail items from the restaurant were found and returned to the grateful restaurant manager who soon changed his mailbox security. It solved the current complaint from the restaurant that the Foundry hadn't paid its bill! I learnt later that the building was painted with lead paint, presenting another major challenge.

Each night when I walked through the building, the hairs on the back of my neck would bristle. I often had this 'hair-raising' feeling when I toured the building after work, alone at night, working out what the tradesmen needed to work on next.

It's just your silly bloody fear generated by being alone in this big old building at night. But I was to learn differently.

The main house area, built in 1906, was originally the home of Sir Littleton Groom, the son of Toowoomba's first lord mayor and politician William Henry Groom. Littleton Groom took over his father's seat in a by-election and held it until his death in 1936. Three wings were added over the years because the building was used by a local hospital caring for mothers who had trouble breastfeeding their new-born babies. Other government offices with various administration functions followed, then it was abandoned and left derelict for about six years. When the Sunrise Way Board signed the peppercorn lease it was in gross disrepair. Little did I realise that my 'spiritual' education and my understanding of spirit were to move forward as a result of the Sunrise Way project.

Initially the Building and Infrastructure Committee (BIC) that I chaired started cleaning up the facility. We erected fencing and started small jobs with great enthusiasm. Funding was intermittent and coming in small lots, so progress was very slow, until a surprise visit by Buddhist Venerable Master Chin Kung, from China. He led a team from the local Pure Land Learning College, which was a newly formed Buddhist centre in Toowoomba, and met with the mayor, the Sunrise Way Board president and me.

He was dressed in light grey robes and walked very stately into the mayor's office with his female interpreter, followed by an entourage of orange-robed Buddhist monks and devotees. The Master listened to each of us communicate our plans and intent for the facility. Through his interpreter he said, 'I feel this is a very worthy initiative to support. I'm pleased to donate $20,000 to the project.'

The Master looked surprised at the interpreter's statement. He gently elbowed her while whispering something. He obviously understood English in relation to money because the interpreter blushed slightly, obviously embarrassed, and quickly quipped with a big smile, 'My misunderstanding, the Master wishes to donate $200,000.'

We almost fell off our chairs in surprise and delight at this generous gift.

The mayor thanked the Master profusely and we all left City Hall to tour the undeveloped facility with the Master and his many orange-robed followers.

A town planner, a responsible construction company and a site manager were appointed. The works began in earnest. I was the part-time project manager. When in town I visited the site each morning at 7am as well as during lunch break and after work each day to meet with Ron, the site manager, as I wanted to ensure daily tasks were defined and any pressing issues resolved promptly. This became my routine for the next two to three years.

Each Thursday night and most Saturdays for three years I'd lead a few dedicated volunteers to keep the site tidy and make improvements. Some nights a local business would have many of their employees assisting, making it a fun night. To save time, I initially often made remarks with a felt pen on walls and other areas instructing Ron and other tradesmen to demolish, patch, repair or change building features. Not long after works commenced I received a phone call advising me that a state government heritage officer was going to visit the site to see what we were doing. I left work at the appropriate time in readiness for the meeting. The female heritage officer introduced herself when she arrived. I sensed she wasn't pleased because the introduction was very formal and not affable. We hadn't walked very far and I observed her reading my scribbled instructions on a few walls. She stopped and turned to me.

'These works are totally unacceptable; I'm shutting down works immediately. Tell your tradesmen to stop work. No further work is to resume until our department has completed a full appraisal of the intended works,' she said in a very forthright manner.

'I'll tell Ron to cease work immediately. I'll tell him to explain to the other tradesmen that they must down tools.'

Crikey, how are we ever going to get this bloody refurb completed now?

She turned and left abruptly without saying anything else. The site was closed down. All work stopped. Once Ron and the tradesmen left I hopped in my car and headed to the mayor's office.

'We've been shut down by the bloody Heritage Department, I've just had a heritage officer on site. She wasn't happy,' I announced as I walked up to her desk.

'Bloody hell, I'll soon sort this out. Shit, this project's important, we can't afford long delays.' The mayor picked up her phone to call the relevant state minister. A meeting was soon scheduled.

About a week later the mayor and I travelled to Parliament House, Brisbane to meet with the State Minister for Heritage and the Environment. On arrival the mayor presented the minister with a bottle of chilli sauce she had made the previous night. She gave him a hug and after some discussion it was soon agreed work could resume with certain covenants. A detailed list of our plans was promptly made and these were written into the ministerial formal approval document for works to recommence. A three-week delay resulted. Work was intermittent because many tradespeople volunteered their time. As they were very busy at the time, I often had to wait many weeks for particular tasks to be performed. Works also stopped as funds ran out. Delays, resulting from these regular issues, dragged the timeframe out.

Maryann arrived one day to check out 'Harland's new community project'. I guided her around the place. After walking inside for about twenty minutes, she stopped.

'We need to go outside for a while,' she said.

We walked out into the front garden.

'This building can't be a place of healing at present. There were at least 100 spooks in the facility. I watched you pay no attention to them, you just brushed past them. I need to arrange to have the facility spiritually cleaned. I also noted that one room in particular had been the site of great cruelty to the mothers and babies. That room will need special treatment. The old laundry appendage off the male wing has to be demolished. It was a site of gross sexual abuse. It's just too "dirty" to clean.'

I'd no doubt that what Maryann was saying was true. It explained the weird feelings I was experiencing as I toured the facility late in the evening.

There is a lot of history in this old building. Who knows what went on in this place over the past century?

I came to call these spooks 'lost souls', similar to the one in the motel room I spoke of at the Gold

Coast when I was supporting Jeanine. I wasn't about to demolish anything on a heritage-listed property without advising the mayor, so I met with her to tell her what Maryann had identified and the actions needed. The mayor, an ex-nurse, surprised me.

'I'm well aware of what transpired in these old institutions,' she said. 'I witnessed such terrible behaviour during my nursing career in similar care facilities. Just get rid of the bloody laundry. I walked through the gents' wing and it felt like shit, the energy was crap. I never want to walk in there again. Do what you have to do.'

'Okay,' I replied.

This is all new to me and strange, but women seem to be more in touch and aware of the stuff. I've got a lot to learn about the goings-on of spirit.

'During my nursing days I witnessed old nursing staff scrubbing young lads with coloured skin with a strong bristle brush trying to remove their colour. I'm well acquainted with the cruelty that went on in these places. A lot of them were run by old resentful spinsters,' she said.

I then told Ron, the site manager, what was about to happen and he said, 'It all sounds a bit weird to me.' He gave a smile and chuckled.

Ron was a true craftsman and saved the board tens of thousands of dollars with his unique and highly skilled approaches to potentially expensive repairs or construction problems. He generously donated much of his time. He also worked at a highly discounted hourly rate.

After Maryann had completed the spiritual cleanse, I called in after work the next day to discuss progress with Ron.

'I don't know what's been done Doug, but the place certainly feels different. It feels good. I was always glad to get off the site at the end of the day. Now it feels so good I'm in no hurry to leave. Whatever was done has made the place feel much better. More pleasant and peaceful.'

Even now, visitors to the site regularly comment on the peaceful feeling it exudes. During a fundraiser lunch held on-site by a local Rotarian chapter just prior to Maryann's cleanse, I offered a tour of the facility to the group, as I did at all similar events. A local accountant pulled me aside during the tour.

'I need to talk to you privately when everyone has left,' he said.

'No problem,' I replied.

He must have a family member or friend with an addiction issue.

The tour ended and he came to me. I was surprised when he said, 'I've the gift of feeling. That second room from the end in the ladies' wing mustn't be used for accommodation. Make it a store room. Too much cruelty took place in that room.'

Another female visitor to the site made the same comment. These people are very reticent to speak of their gifts because they fear condemnation when, in fact, it's something that needs recognition, nurturing and support. I'm certain hospitals need a regular spiritual 'clean' to rid them of the build-up of the energies of trauma and fear, as do many workplaces as well as prisons and police stations. I believe hospitals would be less prone to in-house infections such as golden staph if regular spiritual cleanses were performed. I also understand that many in the medical profession would be outraged by such a statement, but until one actually engages with spirit it's difficult to understand the energies playing out in our daily lives and their influence on our well-being.

I observed that many organisations helping disadvantaged people were often allocated old, rundown buildings. Unless the energy in those facilities was cleaned, and cleaned regularly, the site wasn't in its best condition to assist those in need. Master Kung, at our invitation, revisited the facility sometime later, with his followers, to inspect progress resulting from the generous donation. His eyes lit up as he walked into the foyer. He remarked through his interpreter, 'The energy feels so much better here now, the works are making a huge difference.'

'No, tell the Master we've had the facility spiritually cleaned. It's made a huge difference to the feeling of the place,' I informed the interpreter.

'Then we must perform a spiritual cleanse also,' was the Master's reply. He arranged for a cleaning ceremony a couple of days later. A few carloads of Buddhist monks and devotees in orange robes arrived on the appointed day with the Master and his interpreter.

'As the leader of the works you must lead the spiritual cleanse. I'll explain what you need to do,' the Master said.

'That's fine – just tell me what I need to do.'

This is going to be interesting, I wonder how this works?

I had to lead the group with the Master behind me. He'd be waving a lit incense urn sideways, followed by the many monks. I was to walk around the perimeter of each room in turn until all rooms and hallways had been covered. In the room where I told him Maryann recognised great cruelty had occurred, they left a battery-operated chanting recorder with us. It was to be left in the room for a couple of months. I had great fun explaining the chanting noise coming from the ladies' wing to the many 'tradies' visiting the site. Most were very interested to understand the background to where the chanting was coming from. Some were quite amused by it and cynical about its purpose. Others spoke of it as amazing. It seemed to reinforce their belief in spirituality devoid of religion.

'I can believe it, there is so much we just don't understand,' one young tradie said respectfully.

I shared my spiritual experiences and the unusual building issues openly with visitors and I found many then shared their experiences with me. One visitor to the facility with a spiritual gift told me that the term 'shoot up' in relation to drug use actually describes the person's first big drug 'hit'. Apparently when the body experiences its first strong drug hit, the soul shoots up out of the body very rapidly and a tremendous feeling of euphoria results. It was explained that on subsequent uses of a drug, the soul has anticipated it. The soul is already out of the body so the great euphoric feeling isn't repeated and the user has a vacant 'nobody at home' look in their eyes. In reality their essence 'isn't at home'. The person is left always looking for the same great 'hit' but never achieves it. The comment strongly reinforced my belief that the eyes are the window of our soul. Ross's incident when he witnessed Leo's passing was an example of this belief. The shock took Ross out of his body and he then viewed the world through the eyes of his spirit.

I soon found the part-time workload very demanding. Most weekends and each Thursday night, I was leading a small, dedicated and capable group of volunteers, performing routine site-maintenance functions, as well as taking on new improvement tasks. Without the solid support of a few volunteers I don't feel I could've sustained the eleven years of constant effort. I came to appreciate them greatly. Jim Pillar, my ex- Foundry production planner, and Barry Caple, a friend in my neighbourhood, were the two stalwarts who never missed a working bee. A friend, John Eastwell; vice president of Sunrise Way Robert Ketton; my cousin, Keith Bradshaw; and a donor, Lyle Dornbusch, made up the other intermittent regulars along with hundreds of others too numerous to mention. They were a very committed team.

During the week I'd spend nights organising contractors and paying bills because all building issues were my responsibility. I made sure all invoices were paid on time or earlier. In 2002, the inaugural president of the board of Sunrise Way, Pam resigned with a health issue. As no other board member volunteered for the responsibility of president, I somewhat reluctantly became the newly elected chair. This increased my workload further. This occurred three years before I was sacked as GM of the Foundry in 2005. The Foundry was performing well and growing at a fast rate each year yet, because head office had found itself with cash flow problems resulting from some poorly performing divisions, a decision was made to divest the Foundry to assist the corporate cash issue.

This period of managing the sale of the business; an ownership change; rapid growth; factory capacity issues; huge unprecedented raw material price increases as China rapidly developed; and developing export markets in Canada and the USA, was particularly demanding. Progress on Sunrise Way regularly suffered as a result.

In addition, production at the Foundry couldn't keep up with demand. Because the sale and ownership change resulted in capital investment on the Toowoomba site being put on hold, we undertook a foray into India to gain the additional manufacturing capacity required to meet Canadian demand. A machining facility was set up in Chennai and the whole project ultimately and unnecessarily became a disaster.

Once I accepted the role of Chair of Sunrise Way, I knew the board needed to function in a 'hands-on' style as the development of a drug rehab centre wasn't very popular with many of the community leaders. I realised I was shouldering most of the responsibilities and called a couple of board members to a meeting. I said words to the effect of, 'This isn't the normal way a board operates. Because of the nature of the facility a more hands-on role is needed to get this idea functioning. You're either committed or out.'

With that they both resigned.

Shit, that didn't work, I won't try that again.

As a result, over the many years I carried most of the responsibility to get the facility operational.

The rehab project dragged on. Many original board members resigned and new members were appointed, to the point that many in the city started to voice their view that the facility would never be completed. One local woman, the mother of a friend and grandmother to the famous Will Power who was the first Australian to win the Indianapolis 500 in 2018, did her walk-past each Saturday. She delighted in yelling out to me, 'It will never happen.'

It bloody well will, I'd say under my breath.

After my employment of forty years at the Foundry was terminated in 2005, Carole and I spent several months preparing my unfair dismissal case. This was finally settled out of court three years later, in my favour. All costs were recovered. During the few months of detailed preparation, Sunrise Way projects again suffered.

Once preparation was completed for our case, with the assistance of Carole and daughter Samantha, I set up a manufacturing consulting business. I soon had all the work I needed. Samantha helped me find a logo for my consultancy and set up the accounting system with knowledge she'd gained in her Master's in Business – which she completed after graduating her degree in engineering. During this period I mostly worked two to three days a week. The remainder of the week was spent organising, administrating and working with volunteers on refurbishment tasks for Sunrise Way. Good progress was being made.

I became a professional beggar!

It wasn't something I was entirely comfortable with when I approached many businesses, trades people and community members for support. I found locally-owned businesses quick to agree to any support requested, whereas multinationals rarely gave their support. In fact, one manager of a major national retail chain refused point-blank, saying, 'Unless there's something in it for us I'm not interested.'

They were only interested in a marketing campaign, not true giving, which is totally different and generates more positive energy. It's giving with hooks, as one lady told me.

In 2006 my lawyer had a serious health issue, delaying my unfair dismissal case twelve months. He took six months to recover. A further delay of six months was a result of the lawyer working on a less effective approach that we decided to rethink just before he took ill. The new approach was overlooked on his return.

This delay, combined with growing legal costs, created significant stress, because I needed to get the settlement behind me and get on with my life. But I was in a stress spiral.

I was also consulting for a company, and the management incompetence I witnessed actually started to make my stomach churn. I could see so many fundamental mistakes being made. Each time I raised an issue, it would be dismissed. In addition, I'd run out of funds for Sunrise Way, and many people were publicly writing the project off as a lost cause. All this, combined with a few personal issues, led to a stress-related heart malfunction. I was on a consulting job and suddenly felt unwell, and decided I'd head home so I picked up my briefcase to walk to the car. I was halfway there when I felt very weak and my briefcase seemed to weigh a ton. I knew I couldn't make it to my car. I just knew I was having a heart problem, so I rang one of my staff.

'Jason, I'm in the yard entry near the front gate. I think I'm having a heart attack. Would you come down and drive me to St Vincent's emergency department?'

'Sure, I'm on my way, do I need to call an ambulance?'

'No, I don't feel that's necessary, just hurry,' I replied. I was sitting on a crate.

Bloody hell. I hope I don't need a bypass like Graham had.

Jason brought his car around and drove me to the hospital emergency department.

I was admitted immediately. A doctor was by my side in an instant, performing tests. Carole had arrived and we waited for the results.

Preliminary tests showed nothing.

The doctor remarked, 'Your blood pressure's perfect. Pulse and heart rate are normal, your eyes are clear. I'll arrange a blood test to determine what's going on. I don't believe it's a heart issue.'

A blood sample was taken. I waited on the emergency bed with Carole for the results. I was feeling okay but weak. Within the hour the doctor returned.

'There's tissue damage and we're now able to confirm you've had a mild heart attack. You'll be placed in an intensive care ward until we can be sure of your condition.'

I nodded in agreement.

Bloody hell, that's all I need.

'I'll arrange a coronary angiography procedure with a local cardiologist after you're discharged.'

Three days later I was discharged and the procedure was completed some days after that, confirming a blockage at one arterial junction. The good news was that my heart had built another artery to provide blood to the blood-starved area.

'I've seen hearts build new arteries before. It happens rarely and you're fortunate. An operation will not be required. I agree, this was a stress-related event,' the cardiologist said.

My doctor then prescribed an aspirin a day to thin my blood, plus a Lipitor pill. My cholesterol was on the high side but within acceptable limits, but because of the incident, it was recommended I try to lower it. I started taking Lipitor and within a fortnight my ability to recall names and data instantly was severely impacted and I had dizzy spells. I immediately stopped taking Lipitor. Over time I tried a few other prescribed statin-based pills, and finally stopped taking any at all. I decided I'd rely on a healthy diet, my meditations and weekly healings to keep me healthy. The instant recall difficulty has continued to this day and is a huge frustration to me. I've met several people with similar recall loss experiences after being prescribed Lipitor. It reinforced my view that the medical profession needs to understand a human's energy state, through which I feel more causal factors will be found rather than treatment based only on the observance of symptoms. When will the medical profession accept that we have a soul and its 'our engine'.

The mayor decided not to stand for re-election again and moved away from the city. I visited her to say goodbye and she explained why she was leaving.

'I cannot stand the child abuse in this city, it's abhorrent. It upsets me greatly. I have to leave because I cannot take it any longer.'

Her words were coming out and I watched her mouth moving yet I had no feeling at all of the truth in what she was saying so I said nothing. I thought, *You've been treated abominably and cruelly over the innovative idea to recycle our sewerage water into drinking water by many in this city. I feel that's the real reason you're leaving.*

She then looked me in the eye, and directed a blast at me that stunned me.

'You should've finished Sunrise Way by now, you've done it too good. It should be running. I'm really disappointed.'

I said goodbye and left without saying anything else, feeling low.

Fuck you. Your original words to me were 'nothing is too good for these people' and now you're criticising me. She's never spoken to me since.

I arrived home. 'A thank you would have been nice after all your effort,' Carole said.

The responsibility then became a very lonely one because I didn't have the support of the next mayor, who visited the facility with another councillor for a tour.

'What are you going to do in five years' time when you still have no funding?' he and the councillor said repeatedly.

This was another low point on the protracted journey. I understood the loss of support from the city's mayor was resulting in negative comments about the centre. I was being told of these comments by board and some community members. A couple of city councillors were bagging the project as a waste of money and mayor Di's crazy idea.

Sometime earlier I was approached by a local women's art group. The artists wanted to have an exhibition of their works in the many rooms of the facility and donate monies from the sale of their work to Sunrise Way. Although meetings were held, the exhibition never eventuated, but an artist in the group named Kathy Pollitt volunteered to paint the decorative ceilings in the ladies' wing. Kathy became a good friend – and she wasn't just a friend, she also increased my spiritual knowledge and confirmed my belief in reincarnation.

Kathy spent many weeks planning the artistic layout of the ornate plaster-ceiling designs, working with colours selected by Maryann for their healing qualities. The colours were different for each room. She worked tirelessly over months spending much time alone on site at nights and weekends. The results were stunning. It was a labour of love. I was sure that love energy would benefit residents. All visitors were impressed by the effort and designs, some trimmed with gold leaf. After work when I visited the site Kathy would be working away.

'How's Sunrise Way's Michelangelo going tonight?' I'd ask. It was a title many of the volunteers had given her.

'I've got a very sore neck,' was her usual reply.

She tried many different positions and techniques to stop an aching neck, before settling on a backward stance on a ladder to apply her artistic skills. It was during my visits to see how her artworks were proceeding that she gave me a practical confirmation of reincarnation. Kathy and I were chatting often, and one night I confided in her my revelational experience. She then told me she also had a very unique experience.

'It was 1994,' she began. 'I was seriously ill with an extremely bad asthma attack, and was rushed to the emergency department at Toowoomba Base Hospital. After a week I was well enough for the doctor to allow me to return home. He told me the condition was still potentially serious and in the event I had even a minor attack my husband was to bring me straight back for admission.'

'What happened?' I asked.

'On the Sunday evening of the June holiday long weekend, the asthma I'd been battling with for twenty-four hours became far worse. I'd never had an attack like this before so I didn't recognise what was happening and tried to sleep. My husband placed me on a bed near the lounge room combustion heater to keep me warm before he fell asleep in the bedroom.

'The attack worsened with my breathing becoming very difficult and ineffectual. It became a struggle to draw breath and I was unable to speak. I began to realise that I may die. In my spirit there was a constant reassurance not to fear. I believed this to be the Holy Spirit. This calmed me and I prepared to let go of life. I breathed out my last breath and it felt as if my lungs were like torn bellows. I couldn't breathe in again. At that point a wind blew across my chest and I heard the words, "Do not fear, I will be your breath." I was then able to take the shallowest of breathes. Instead of dying, I remained in this altered state until early morning.'

'That's incredible, what happened next?'

'After struggling with fear and doubt for about twenty minutes and ignoring the pain in my chest, I calmed enough to sense a beautiful, angelic presence in the room with me. I realised that something very rare and precious was happening. I moved my right hand slightly to make sure I was alive, not dreaming or dead. Then on the wall in front of me I saw an image, like a video, of my husband's profile. I was startled at this and asked, in my spirit, "What's this, what's happening?"'

'Wow,' was my only response.

'The reply was, "Tonight you will be given an opportunity to make great headway in your spiritual life, but if you choose not to, it will not be held against you." I decided that as I had come this far, I wanted to proceed. I then saw, unfolding on the wall, several stories about a man and woman, who were in love but never able to be married for various reasons. The stories were like movies. They showed different clothes, countries and situations but the couple was kept apart by religion, race, wars, distance and family interference over many lives. I then recognised the couple as being myself and my husband.'

'In each life we died alone and unhappy. We met again in my current life and we 'knew' we'd be together. The stories continued to unfold on this night and I experienced chest and heart pains, which I believe now were the reliving of my deaths in those past lives.'

'Struggling and with great confusion, I asked for help and understanding. I heard a gentle voice to my right tell me that I must, "forgive the man for the heartache." I heard "the answer to everything is love and forgiveness." Much to my surprise, I found this forgiving very hard to do. I knew without a doubt that the woman I'd seen was me. The stories brought such raw grief and anger to me that I knew I was watching my own past lives. Eventually I forgave and let go of all the past anger and hurt. I did this, and the pain I was experiencing lifted from my body.'

'I then experienced great joy and lightness in my spirit. I was full of questions and asked why and what was happening. I lay on the mattress and I saw, near my right shoulder, the edge of a white gown and two feet. When the question of the identity of this person formed in my mind, I saw that the feet had wounds in them. With great awe I realised that this was Jesus, standing next to me. He said, "This is what I came to Earth to teach, but my teachings were changed. The answer to everything is love and forgiveness. When you die your spirit lives on and carries with it the emotional pains and joys of your past life."

'"You are born into the same family tree or group of friends in each life. This enables you to have the opportunity to repay spiritual debt or have it repaid to you. If a debt is not paid, there will be another lifetime, in the future, when you will have to confront the same situation again and make a better decision. When this is done your spirit is free from the burden of that debt and you can move on and grow spiritually as can the other person."

'"Every spirit or person is born into every situation, rich or poor, male or female, victor and vanquished, to allow you to experience every situation, every emotion. You are given the opportunity to deal with spiritual debt from past lives, so you can never say that you didn't have the chance to make things right."

'There were more visions that night, which helped to explain certain family relationships. Some insights were fleeting, some were very distinct. All involved forgiveness.'

I was speechless. I felt her sincerity.

'You're a very lucky lady to have experienced that, thank you for sharing it. It's such a privileged experience you've had,' I said finally.

I was constantly told in Sunday school and my religious instruction classes in school that the soul is eternal. Consequently, I had a theory that we probably come back around on planet Earth but had no understanding as to why, or if, it was really true. Many prophesied that karma would have you return as an insect or some animal, if you misbehaved in your current life, particularly those I met with a Buddhist belief system – a view I do not endorse.

My first real interest in reincarnation was triggered at a wedding function in 1996 where I sat beside a female Anglican minister. Naturally, our conversation turned to spiritual matters. She spoke of her frustration with people interpreting the Bible literally and commented that much of it is symbolic, as was the style of writing at the time. During the conversation the issue of reincarnation was raised. She told me many in theology have come to understand the Bible was censored in this regard because some of the original scrolls, apparently, confirmed that reincarnation happened.

After this discussion I often reflected how it made so much sense. I often wondered why the soul would return many times and what the actual purpose would be. Kathy's account and the book *Conversations with God* confirmed and explained that for me. I now believe that with each incarnation we're given the opportunity in each earthly life cycle to experience certain life experiences that assist us to come to know who we really are and grow spiritually. If we choose not to address them and ignore the needs of the soul, then one simply keeps coming around through many incarnations until one 'knows thyself' and the soul is nurtured. I believe the soul is trying in each incarnation to reach its ultimate real identity, that of pure love and the knowledge it itself is God.

I don't think my next reincarnation on planet Earth will find me on a peaceful and healthy planet. If one needs to believe in hell, then living on this planet is where it's at when compared to our 'spiritual home' in the other realm, where I'm convinced we reside in love and joy after we transition from our earthly body. I also feel there is a spiritual accountability that's part of a person's reincarnation cycle, as Kathy's experience revealed. However, I cannot intellectually explain what that means, although the saying, 'We reap what we sow,' is practically relevant somehow. I like a statement in the book *Conversations with God*: 'That which you condemn will condemn you, and that which you judge, you will one day become.'[31]

Patrick Francis, in his book *The Grand Design –1*, writes in his chapter on reincarnation:

---

[31] ND Walsch, *Conversations with God Book 1*, Hodder & Stoughton, London, UK, 1999, p. 38.

There is no more mystery about the fact of reincarnation than there is about rosebushes repeating the growth of roses.[32]

He ends the chapter with the comment: 'I can't offer proof of reincarnation I can only repeat that it is a fact.[33]

We need to understand our journey on planet Earth is a journey of the soul, as I stated earlier. The mind and body, important as they may be, are simply hitchhikers. I believe the soul is trying to move to an ultimate experience of its highest self, that being love. I believe the distractions of alcohol, drugs, sensation, control and power trips simply slow this journey down and ensure we're likely to recycle ourselves on planet Earth.

The rehab refurbishment was going well but the Buddhist's donation had been spent and we were relying on other funds to complete the project. It was at this time I attended the Buddhist dinner I described earlier and heard the story of the submariner and his fear of water.

It was also around this time I hit my first really low point on the Sunrise Way project, and more were to come. It was a Saturday morning. Plans were in place with a local Apex community organisation to assemble the heavy steelwork for a long, extensive and costly wheelchair ramp at the rear entrance of the building. Work was needed to get ready for the pouring of the concrete ramp the steelwork supported, the following week. The Saturday morning started early with an admonishment from Carole as I prepared to leave.

'You should be earning money instead of spending so much time on Sunrise Way!'

I was feeling somewhat bruised as I arrived on site at 7:30am to prepare for the 8am start. I'd told my regular volunteers that I had lots of help and if they had other plans they could have a day off. It had been a long journey negotiating and getting the steelwork on site because much of it was donated, as was the galvanizing of all the beams in Brisbane and the supply of the various nuts and bolts. The fabricator welder had also worked at a highly discounted rate. The 8am start time arrived. No-one! When the Apex club volunteers hadn't arrived by 9am I was becoming forlorn. I rang the organiser of the work crew.

---

32 P Francis, *The Grand Design – 1: Reflections of a Soul/Oversoul*, 8th Impression, Colour Books Ltd, Dublin Ireland, 2004, p. 21.

33 P Francis, The Grand Design – 1: Reflections of a Soul/Oversoul, 8th Impression, Colour Books Ltd, Dublin Ireland, 2004, p. 22.

'Where are you?' I asked.

'We all had a late night out on the grog and won't be coming.' His explanation shocked me.

I hung up quite disgusted without saying a word.

Thanks very much, bloody hell what's a man to do?

My legs weakened and I actually sagged to the ground feeling very low and close to tears. I was wondering how the large heavy structure would be assembled in time. I was about to ring the concreters to cancel them, when I heard a car pull up. My volunteer saviour, Jim, came around the corner smiling,

'Where's all the helpers?' Jim asked.

'The buggers were on the piss last night. I was just told they aren't coming. How's that for community spirit?'

'Well we better get started if we're going to have it ready for the concreters Monday,' was Jim's positive reply.

My spirits immediately rose. Shortly after this, Barry also arrived and then John for a short while, and we had it all assembled over two long days, rather than the one day planned, in readiness for the concreters. Each Sunday morning I'd spend one to two hours picking up branches, fallen seed pods and litter that had blown into the Sunrise Way grounds. I was determined it would always be kept pristine to avoid derogatory comments. One Sunday morning, after being told by numerous people about negative comments they had heard about Sunrise Way during the week, I walked back to the car feeling down.

Maybe you've bitten off more than you can chew Douglas. But I'm sure spirit is fully behind the project. If it is then it will prevail.

Trust, Douglas. Trust.

This became my self-talk

CHAPTER 29

I'M CEO OF THE START-UP ORGANISATION KNOWN AS AGIC

Early in August 2008 I was approached by the chairman of the board of a new national organisation called the Australian Green Infrastructure Council (AGIC). I was in Brisbane for my weekly healing and meditation at Maryann's Inner Energy Centre. I dropped in to touch base with my daughter Samantha to deliver a package. She was in the middle of a meeting with a group of engineering professionals discussing a joint consultancy.

Samantha was now a sole trader as a civil engineer with her own business. At the time she was the Queensland Chair of the Society for Sustainability and Environmental Engineering (SSEE). Not long afterwards, she became its national chair. The national chairman of the newly formed Australian Green infrastructure Council (AGIC) was at the meeting with Samantha and two others in her 'hobbit house' discussing aspects of the consultancy. A royal blue tablecloth was spread over her craftsman-made Tasmanian oak-legged table with a thick white glass table top, covered with papers and folders. Samantha introduced me.

'What sort of meeting is this? You're all sitting there drinking red wine. I'd bet not much work's being done,' I joked and everybody laughed. The chairman looked up at me.

'Samantha tells me you'd be a great candidate for a job.'

'What job?' I questioned.

'We're looking for a CEO to bring the newly formed, not-for-profit Australian Green Infrastructure Council, or AGIC as we call it, into a national working organisation. Samantha told me you'd be a good candidate. Are you interested?'

Samantha was smiling at me, acknowledging she had 'dobbed me in'. The chairman, who was also a professor, was surveying me with curiosity.

'No,' was my first response, 'I'm doing okay where I am. What's it all about anyway?' I said, dropping the package on Samantha's kitchen sink.

'It's a new initiative the AGIC Board has started. Its aim is to bring more sustainability practices to Australia's national civil infrastructure like roads, rail, airports, pipelines and dams.'

I walked back to the table listening, as I was curious. I found the concept interesting and a worthy pursuit. I agreed I'd look at it. It had been a sustainability strategy that partly resulted in the turnaround of the Foundry. The need for society to embrace more sustainable practices was something I saw as an urgent one. I decided I might be able to make a difference, albeit a small one. I was only moderately interested.

'It's an industry initiative, not government.'

This secondary comment triggered an increasing interest. The chairman gave me some brochures and documents to read.

'I have to go. I'll leave you to your meeting. Don't drink too much though. It was good to meet you all.'

'It will be a world's first also,' the chairman added as I turned to leave.

The prospect of being involved in such a significant undertaking started to appeal to me as I always enjoyed a challenge. So I replied, 'I'll think about it.'

My earlier spiritual revelation stopped my material 'want list' and my need 'to get'. It changed my motivation to a need 'to give', as mentioned earlier. It also increased my understanding of the precarious state of planet Earth and how we humans are actually raping her as we pursue a flawed economic strategy of continuous growth and increased population and consumption. After reading about AGIC's intent later and following the AGIC Board's review of my CV and their endorsement of it, in July 2008 I agreed to take up the position. I was sixty-one years old. I gave a commitment to the board that I'd do my best to have the organisation launched and running successfully in four years, when I would be sixty-five and a younger person could then take on the CEO role. I'd then retire.

I told the chairman I'd start as soon as Carole and I completed our scheduled holiday. Carole and I went on a great six-week cruise around the Pacific Ocean. I became the inaugural CEO of AGIC on October 7th 2009 after the cruise had ended.

During the appointment meeting the chairman said, 'We've only funds to pay your salary till March next year. You'll be our first and only full-time employee. You'll have to grow membership to pay for your salary and grow the organisation. The board has identified we'll need $1.3 million to fund authors to write each assessment category and to test the scheme on real pilot projects before it's ready for market.'

What a challenge!

The plan was to develop a national infrastructure sustainability rating scheme, similar to the Green Star rating scheme for commercial and industrial buildings.

AGIC was being supported financially by a few foundational industry corporations who seeded the start-up. Two companies, Thiess Constructions and GHD, were providing one industry professional each, on a part-time basis.

I started work on my laptop at home to consider how I'd build the national membership to a level that would sustain the organisation financially. Two challenges became clear. First, I had to develop the national membership and through membership fees achieve a stable financial platform for the short-term administration of AGIC.

Second, it was clear that the long-term viability of AGIC depended on finding funds of $1.3 million, as identified by the board, to have the infrastructure sustainability assessment criteria determined, authored, peer reviewed and tested on real projects. Only after scheme launch would registrations for a rating and training provide the revenue needed to sustain this national organisation long-term.

I met with a board director in Brisbane for a briefing.

'Three volunteer working groups, comprising industry professionals spread across Australia, have developed marketing material, governance policies and the initial criteria for assessment of infrastructure,' he said.

The volunteer working groups were to be my 'staff resources' until permanent staff could be afforded.

It was obvious an impressive and inspiring number of professional volunteer hours across Australia had been provided to get AGIC to this stage.

I based myself in Brisbane, living alternately with Sheldon or Samantha. I started to travel regularly while I visited potential member companies. Various coffee shops in the CBDs of capital cities became my office.

One day I was sitting at a table in a Brisbane CBD coffee shop. Out of the corner of my eye I watched a well-dressed professional woman start to enter the shop and quickly retreat when she saw a customer at the counter. As she stepped backward onto the footpath, the shop barista looked at her and mouthed something. The woman nodded. My curiosity was aroused.

The customer left and the barista mouthed, 'The usual?'

The woman mouthed, 'Yes'. She disappeared for a brief moment, returning with a large coffee container. Pretending not to look, I saw the barista pop a white tablet into the container and fill it with coffee. The woman left.

Wonder what work she'll do this afternoon, what a poor state we're in socially. There sure is a need for Sunrise Way.

Living in Brisbane and returning home each weekend meant I could only address Sunrise Way issues on the weekend. This, combined with funding shortages, resulted in the work slowing dramatically.

Two months later, the chairman, a professor at a Brisbane university, arranged an office for my use on campus. I relied heavily on volunteer support and was impressed by their enthusiasm and dedication. However, quite a few times major tasks with a fixed timeline were delegated to a volunteer, only for a baby to be born, a job changed, or an important work commitment suddenly appear to divert their focus.

I'd find myself stepping in and burning my weekends and lots of midnight oil to ensure an important task was completed. This also impacted the progress of Sunrise Way. I regularly worked until 11pm on AGIC business and I remember one night at Samantha's, my son Sheldon said, 'You're mad working all these hours for this mob.'

I felt the AGIC scheme was important and that it justified this commitment.

I had a real problem with one board member. In spite of my heavy workload he'd send an email each day with questions he wanted answered. He had an expectation of a prompt response. I responded for the first few months until the number of queries increased, with answers demanded. I decided he was a control freak and rang him.

'I'm too busy to answer your many questions. I will not be responding in future, I report to the board not you,' I said.

This received an immediate tirade and he said, 'I'll have the board conduct a disciplinary session with you, this is totally unacceptable.'

He hung up.

The next day I was called to a meeting of the chairman and two senior directors. I was unsure of what was to take place. The chairman explained the complaint made against me and a senior director then turned to me and said, 'You're doing a great job Doug, if he causes you any more problems we'll have him resign from the board. Keep up the good work.'

The problem director resigned a few months later. I actually felt sorry for him because his work commitment was total. He was very competent, but his need for control was obsessive.

The vast majority of companies I approached were keen to change to the more sustainable practices proposed by AGIC. There was a recognised industry need for a common national language and nationally recognised assessment criteria for sustainability in infrastructure that provided a great platform. It allowed me and other AGIC personnel to build membership to eighty-five organisations, employing 70,000 people, within four years. Many companies were seeking innovative ideas to improve their sustainability strategies. I regularly quoted a great saying I saw in the BMW museum in Munich: 'Today's innovation is tomorrow's tradition.'

I was able to convince many organisations that the rating scheme would be the stimulus to breed innovation and best practice which, over time, would become business as usual. Sustainability thinking was responsible for huge cost savings during my term with the Foundry.

In 2009 sufficient revenue was achieved to open an office owned by a foundational member, Arup, in a sustainability hub comprising several businesses in Adelaide Street in the heart of Brisbane, at reduced rent. An office manager, Liz, was then appointed. AGIC soon lifted its profile via regular newsletters, teleconferences, website updates, an annual conference, and regular presentations to industry. Liz and I were kept extremely busy meeting all the necessary responsibilities. Over $800,000 was raised from industry and government bodies to author the scheme. The board decided to start the authorship process and advertisements were placed. Author applications were reviewed, selected, appointed and contracted, along with pro bono peer reviewers for each criterion paper. A global review panel of very experienced infrastructure professionals to oversee the whole scheme was also identified and appointed to ensure the scheme's suitability, consistency and integrity.

The authorship process was being managed by two professionals sponsored by a member company, and they reported to a part-time AGIC director who was overseeing the whole process on a voluntary part-time basis. It soon became apparent the director was heavily overloaded. He expressed his desire to resign his job and become a full- time employee of AGIC. The organisation was still relying on membership fees to fund its operation and the cash position was tight, so to allow the addition of this much- needed resource in the year of launch I took a twenty percent pay cut. I moved my hours back to four days a week, although the fifth day was often spent on AGIC business. I felt the importance of the scheme justified this approach.

The scheme was finally authored and documented and national project trials run. The IS Rating Scheme was rebranded and officially launched at Parliament House, Canberra by the Federal Minister for Infrastructure and Transport, the Hon. Anthony Albanese, on February 29th 2012. I retired on March 31st 2012 at age sixty-five, three and one half years after my appointment. The AGIC name was soon changed to the Infrastructure Sustainability Council of Australia (ISCA). The scheme is the IS Rating Scheme and is now running very successfully. It had new registered projects and projects rated by the scheme valued at $220 billion in 2022. It can be found online at: www.isca.org.au

My constant reliance on my feelings often upset executives I reported to because I was able to remain calm in stressful situations; I had the reassurance of the feeling all would work out and some took it as a lack of a sense of urgency. One example was during my term as CEO of AGIC where at financial year end the money situation would always be extremely tight as we brought the organisation to life. It was the year of the launch in the period I was working a four-day week. Unless training in the IS Rating Scheme commenced and brought in additional revenue for ISCA, it was possible the organisation could have traded insolvent by a small amount before the financial year end. The amount was estimated to be less than $10,000. I'd costed the training package and priced it with an appropriate gross margin and presented it to the board for approval. Two months passed and concern was raised whether the pricing was too high or too low. No decision had been made. During a Brisbane visit the chairman berated me saying, 'You've got to stop saying we have a financial challenge and convey a much greater sense of urgency, the financial situation is critical.'

I was shocked to learn that one board member, a solicitor, had provided him with a recommendation to have the board declare insolvent trading. I was stunned by this revelation. The training commenced and the additional revenue ensured the organisation remained solvent. Member companies were prepared to renew memberships early to assist any shortfall until revenue streams were activated. However, the auditing accountants dismissed the offer as contravening accountancy practice. One director was even prepared to personally finance any small shortfall via a loan if the revenue stream wasn't realised. It was to me another example of fears almost being realised.

I believe that which we fear the most we bring about.

Leo and his wife, Doreen.

Leo's wife, Doreen, is pictured with her family while visiting the robotic area of the machine shop on the day of the barbeque to assist closure for the family and Foundry employees.

Leo's daughter, Leanne, addresses all employees at the barbeque.

Leo's memorial plaque – an olive tree donated by an employee was planted beside it.

Sheldon's immaculate rebuilt 1972 Big Block 660 HP Corvette Stingray being performance tested on a chassis dynamometer.

Dedicated night and weekend volunteers John Eastwell, Jim Pillar and Barry Caple renovating the western wing.

The front entrance to Sunrise Way, a community-funded drug and alcohol rehabilitation facility.

The rear main deck area. Over 200 companies donated money, trade works or materials to the value of $2 million.

The beautiful grounds of Sunrise Way. Over $5,000 of pine trees and shrubs were donated by a local nursery and planted by volunteers.

Dedicated volunteer, a cousin, Keith Bradshaw, in the north wing. The verandah is typical of the high-quality standard throughout Sunrise Way. The aim was to assist healing by providing a positive home-like ambience.

Governor General of Australia, His Excellency Major General Michael Jeffery AC CVO MC, with Doug, the Town Crier Ralph Cockle and Mayor Di Thorley at the premature opening ceremony of Sunrise Way, April 24th 2007.

Kathy Pollit photographed while busy at work one night painting one of the many ornate plaster ceilings. Maryann Madden selected the colours for their healing qualities.

Sheldon aged ten in the mustard-coloured sweater his nan knitted during our stay in Wales.

The launch of the first national Infrastructure Sustainability Rating Scheme at Parliament House Canberra on 29th February 2012. From left, The Hon Anthony Albanese, Minister for Infrastructure and Transport, ISCA Chair David Singleton and CEO Doug Harland.

The Vette about to start the drive-past by friend and driver, Lloyd, and me at Sheldon's funeral.

Samantha the environmental engineer on Brisbane's S1 Sewer tunnel boring machine

Sheldon, Samantha, Doug and brother Graham, at Doug's Order of Australia Medal (OAM) presentation event. 20th September 2016

The wider Harland family enjoying Christmas 2016 at the Gold Coast. Brother Graham on my left was just starting the intensive part of his leukaemia journey.

CHAPTER 30
SUNRISE WAY IS A SUCCESS

The grass at Sunrise Way was growing rapidly and needed weekly attention during one spring. Having decided I'd always have the facility looking its best, Jim Barry and I became the weekend gardeners. I arrived on site very tired one Saturday after a week of rain and a heavy week at AGIC. It was 2009. I had been doing the weekly ritual for eight years. I felt my energy draining while surveying the long grass after only a week from our last mow.

I don't think I can do this anymore, it's just too much.

The following week another piece of universal synchronicity materialised when I received a phone call from Steve Kite, the owner of The Green Gardener landscaping company in Toowoomba.

'Doug, I'm president of the local Rotary Club. I wondered if we could look after and develop the grounds at Sunrise Way for you as a community project.'

'You certainly can, it would be greatly appreciated.' I replied enthusiastically. My spirit soared. Jim and Barry were very pleased also to be relieved of this responsibility. Synchronicity blossomed again! It reinforced my belief that spirit was still well and truly supporting the project. It was a great confidence boost.

During this time I'd also been grappling with technical issues in the extensive fire management system we'd installed – it was my biggest challenge. Constant legislated changes were taking place and this resulted in several elements of the fire management system needing to be reworked and updated three times. I often struggled to canvas the funds for the upgrades. The project dragged on until we received final building certification in June 2012. Finalising the fire system had been another stressful low point in my journey. Achieving the building certification milestone was a huge relief for me. It was appreciated that the local private certifier provided his services on a pro bono basis. The certification boosted my energy, but I still felt constant pressure because I was trying to find funding to operate the facility and I knew the project was losing community support. Many businessmen withdrew their support. I decided they didn't want to be involved with anything that might be conceived as a failure.

The drug and alcohol addiction statistics in the city had risen significantly. In 2012 the local base hospital had five hundred people seeking treatment. Additionally, 26,500 clean needle exchanges were occurring every month.

This was representative of 12,000 users from the greater region of Toowoomba – a city of 120,000 people. Not all users sought the clean needle service. It was a social tragedy. I met with the third mayor appointed during the term of the project, Paul Antonio, and it was a great relief to me that he was totally supportive of Sunrise Way.

'This project must succeed; we have 400 homeless in the city at present. Many are teenagers couch-surfing between homes or living under bridges. Their home environment is often the reason they're homeless. The drug and alcohol addiction statistics are a major concern and need to be addressed,' he said.

While all the representatives from community support service organisations I spoke with were horrified by this situation, it received very little publicity and direct support. No death statistics were available. I'm saddened by the fact that statistics, which were once widely known in detail by many agencies when we started the project, are totally unknown by these agencies now. Many say the problem has developed to a stage where it's all just too hard. A senior police officer told me that police no longer have time to collect statistics. I also found many public organisations were very fearful of speaking out. One example was what happened when a letter of support for Sunrise Way was requested for a funding submission from the police and other government community agencies working in the social area. Each of them was fearful of providing a letter of support in case it upset the government, in spite of those community organisations' active and strongly stated support locally.

I'm dismayed by the lack of mature thinking and the real fear at all levels in the area of public office

– truth seems to be feared in the public service. The drug issue is a huge social and financial cost to the community. At the time of writing, the drug 'ice' is causing havoc in Australia. Local hospital staff told us four wards men were required to subdue a violent patient on ice. Nurses and doctors had been punched and abused and seriously injured while rendering medical help. It's a global issue and I believe it's a result of our spiritual vacuum resulting in a poor sense of self, and ignorance by the human race about our spiritual (not religious) essence. This is leading to the loss of the inner contentment and stability that such knowledge brings. I've come to understand our journey on planet Earth is a journey of the soul, as mentioned many times earlier, yet our predominant academic, social and business focus is on the mind and body. I feel we need to learn about the soul and its journey without religion.

In 2010 a memorandum of understanding (MOU) had been agreed with the Salvation Army. It was going to operate the Sunrise Way facility, after it became obvious the original strategy to have the community sponsor and operate it was gaining no support. I was able to canvas this support after a trip to Sydney to meet with senior directors. I was pleased they agreed to meet. I took along a DVD my nephew Mark made incorporating a tour of the completed and pristine facility. After playing the video, director David Pullen turned to me with a smile and said, 'This is fantastic, we've also identified the need for a facility on the Darling Downs. Here you have a great facility ready to go. We'll definitely be prepared to operate it.'

The director approached the national Salvation Army Board. A decision was made to sign the MOU. The board decided later new money had to be found to fund its operation. This was another disappointment.

An earlier approach was made to caring bodies of different religious faiths and care organisations in the region to come together at board level to make it happen. This approach resulted in each saying their doctrines would need to be followed, in spite of all of them acknowledging the urgent need. I disliked this isolationist or 'silo' mentality. I found it frustrating. Also, Mayor Di Thorley had been immersed in Queensland's most severe water shortage, the result of a prolonged drought. She had become unpopular through an innovative attempt to provide potable water to the city by treating sewerage water, as mentioned earlier. Community fear killed this innovative idea. I was cognisant that many people were dismissing the facility as the mayor's idea. I found this personality-based thinking, practiced by some prominent people in the city, really sad, immature and bloody frustrating.

It made me reflect on many conversations I had with people about my involvement.

'Do you have a family member on drugs?' was a frequent question.

'What's in it for you, are you paid?' was another angle put to me. People seemed to struggle that one can commit to a need without desire for a payback.

In early 2013, the vice president and I were told by the chair of the local hospital board that we'd had the facility for eleven years and not opened it. If the facility wasn't running by October 31st 2013, it would be reluctantly resumed by the hospital. The hospital board was under pressure from the state government to utilise its assets. It was considered Sunrise Way had been given sufficient time to have the facility operational and the asset was grossly underutilised.

A mental health officer from the local hospital on the board resigned and shocked me with strong criticism of my leadership.

Soon after, in September 2013, a doctor from the local hospital who was a board member of Sunrise Way resigned also. He handed me his resignation accompanied by a blast, 'You're totally unsuitable as chair. You've blocked community groups from developing the facility by "squatting" on the facility. You're wasting valuable community funds.'

This personal attack was difficult to accept. It impacted heavily. It was another low point. Our fixed expenses were $22,000 a year. Through negotiation and calling in favours I had it reduced to $13,000 which had to be found each year. In the last few years it was mostly left up to me to find the money. It was a difficult time for me. I was under constant pressure because the challenge weighed heavily on me as I called in many favours. Many in the community had written the project off as a failure and a waste of money.

The doctor continued, 'You've wasted thousands of dollars over the last few years when it could've been put toward drug services elsewhere.'

He was obviously not committed to Sunrise Way opening. He had contributed little as a board member.

This was in spite of my repeated requests at board meetings to appoint a new medically trained chairman, rather than myself, and a new board to get the facility operational now that my responsibility to upgrade the facility was complete. I made many approaches to community groups to operate it and had approached medical practitioners to take the role as chair and form a new board. None accepted. The

CEO of a care organisation, Oz Care was keen; however, again his board would only take it over with new external funding.

I'd made trips to Canberra to meet with senior executives of the Federal Department of Health who made the funding recommendations to the federal minister. They told me a recommendation to fund the Salvation Army to operate Sunrise Way was made to the Minister for Health and received a positive response. We were full of expectation when a federal election was called, and with a change of government the initiative was lost. It was another blow.

The Salvation Army was then optimistic that the Queensland state government funding was going to happen in early 2014. The hospital board generously granted an extension of time. This optimism about government funding soon proved unfounded. Not long after, I received a call asking me to meet with the chair of the hospital board and its CEO later in the week. I knew the meeting's purpose would be to take the facility from Sunrise Way.

I had a restless night. I decided I needed to consciously let the project go. I'd invested so much in trying to make it happen, I realised I was now trying to force it into being instead of allowing events to unfold; I'd been desperately chasing any option away from the original intent to have it run by the community. Through my various spiritual experiences I intuitively learnt that one blocks universal energies when one forces issues and harnesses them when one simply allows events to unfold, no matter how uncomfortable one is feeling.

I put it down to my fear of failure. A fear to be overcome.

It's been a bloody long and difficult twelve year journey. You've given it your best shot, let it go Douglas, it'll crush you otherwise. But spirit has to be behind it. This is obviously happening for some reason. I don't understand it, but I must accept it. I must trust.

I consciously let it go. I immediately felt a weight come off my shoulders.

At least that's one fewer responsibility in my life. I'm sure spirit is still behind it with so many synchronous and positive events along the journey. I don't understand what's happening. Trust Douglas, trust.

On March 18th 2012, the vice president Robert and I again met with the chair of the hospital board, and its CEO. It was decided the facility would return to the ownership of the hospital. We left the meeting on a downer. As we walked back to the car I said to Robert, 'What do we do now? We've all those donated goods and furnishings. Do we ring all the donors and have them returned or auction them off? What'll be the compensation for the extensive work done in upgrading the facility? How do we tell all the volunteers and donors?'

'That's all we can do. Let's call a board meeting to make the necessary decisions. It's really disheartening,' was Robert's sad reply.

I went home and turned my thinking to how I'd break the news to the board and how we might handle this distressing event. I'm sure providence intervened. Maybe it was the energy change that was needed. A change brought about by the loss of my personal investment in the outcome and leaving it open to spirit. On the very next day, March 19th 2012, I received a phone call from a local businessman who wished to remain anonymous. He introduced himself.

'I'm ringing you to let you know my wife and I will fund Sunrise Way for three years. We'll provide $500,000 a year and work to achieve a sustainable operation.'

I couldn't believe what I was hearing. I thanked him profusely.

Miracles really do happen! That's really going down to the wire after all those years.

I slept soundly that night. Another nice piece of synchronicity!

It was like a huge weight had been taken off my shoulders. It was a great feeling of relief. Sunrise Way commenced operation in July 2014. A local childcare centre also donated $40,000 a year for three years. The funding was only sufficient to operate the facility at just over half capacity. Further funding was needed to allow it to fill all the beds in the facility. Prior to this, over 200 companies, private citizens and other organisations had donated just over $1 million. The volunteer effort and donated works and materials had leveraged this value to $2 million, as assessed by the Department of Queensland Health in Brisbane. When this department assessment was complete, the assessing officer turned to me and said, 'I'm envious of the quality of the work. I wish we could work to that standard.'

'It wasn't easy,' was all I could say in response.

Everyone who visited the site all remarked how peaceful the building and site felt. When I told them the energy had been spiritually cleaned, most just changed the subject or looked back with a disbelieving eye.

One day I hope the reality of universal energy will become known and understood by the masses. What a difference it would make!

The old Sunrise Way Board disbanded and a new operational board was appointed. I resigned from the board in October 2015 having served a further twelve months after gaining full confidence in the new board's commitment to the facility. I remained on the building support team where miscellaneous maintenance tasks were addressed on a weekly basis by Barry and me. I was able to talk to the residents and hear their stories. Many have told me Sunrise Way has saved their life – it made all the effort feel worthwhile. Barry and I ceased voluntary work on January 10th 2019. I decided eighteen years of effort was enough.

I was greatly surprised when in June 2016 I was awarded the Order of Australia Medal by Australia's Governor General for my efforts. I later learnt that Carole had submitted the application in December 2014 when we were still together. I was humbled by this unexpected support. It helped heal some of the bruising experiences I'd met along the twelve-year journey.

In June 2017, when private funding was exhausted, Sunrise Way was running so successfully that the federal and state governments provided funding for two years, and explained if performance indicators are met, ongoing funding would be forthcoming. In August 2018 I was presented with a plaque recognising my service. A federal minister was present and noted Sunrise Way was getting the best rehab results in Australia with last year's residents recording an abstinence rate of 79 percent after twelve months. A clinical advisory team, appointed to develop the care model, was focusing on the cause of addiction rather than the addiction. They are passionate about continuously changing the care model as necessary to continually improve outcomes. I had turned around a failing business into a world-class one; started and run a successful consulting business; and as CEO of ISCA brought a new national organisation to life in three and one half years, but none of those achievements stressed me as much as bringing Sunrise Way to life. It was a tough journey.

The reader can donate to the Sunrise Way trust if so inclined. At the time of writing, the centre is getting excellent abstinence results, as previously mentioned. This is totally due to the leadership and vision of the new board, the Clinical Advisory Team, and very committed staff.

The website can be found at: www.sunriseway.com.au

I finally felt free and in the mood to finish my book.

CHAPTER 31

MY DIVORCE

I retired in March 2012 to face another difficult situation. I watched Carole's increasing need to control and criticise what I did. I still had some love for her after forty-nine years of marriage but I knew the marriage wasn't as strong as in the past. I was struggling to decide how I could approach her to discuss what I was feeling. But each time I tried to communicate how I felt it was taken as a put-down of her and led to great emotional outbursts, it was not my intent.

I ultimately decided there was no way I could bridge this situation. I felt I was continually walking on eggshells. I started questioning who I was. One morning when Carole was admonishing me, I felt a sudden change within myself. It was as though a switch suddenly turned off. In an instant I realised I no longer felt any love for Carole. I decided we needed to separate, but I didn't have the courage to do it after such a long time together. I tried remembering all the good times and all the many fine qualities Carole had. I also didn't know how Sheldon and Samantha would react and this concerned me also. I tried again several times to communicate my feelings to Carole but it just resulted in those emotional outbursts that often caused an equally emotional reaction from me. I didn't like the fact I was reacting emotionally because I knew it was based in fear. It told me I had unresolved issues in the marriage. One night I asked spirit for guidance about my marriage. I had a vivid dream that left me in no doubt what I needed to do.

A spiritual person in a full-length shroud appeared beside me and was looking down at my ring finger. I'd worn my gold wedding ring since the day of our marriage. When I looked down, the ring flew off my finger, landing on a nearby wooden table and it spun and rattled slowly to a stop. The next morning I decided this was a pretty clear message. I couldn't really face the decision at the time and had concerns that Carole could still trigger emotional outbursts from me. About a month later, Carole, Sheldon, Samantha and I took a break over a few days in a cottage called The Mouses House, in the middle of rainforest near Springbrook in the Gold Coast hinterland.

Samantha had booked a massage for her and me, it was my delayed birthday present. The lady masseur came and Samantha had her massage, and after I had mine my ring finger became sore from the oil she used. I initially paid no attention to it until the burning sensation became intolerable. When I pulled the ring off my finger it was blistered underneath.

Okay, I get it, but I'm not sure I'm up to it. The ring was worn thin from years of manual work. When I took it to the jeweller to have it re-rounded and polished he told me the ring was too worn and couldn't be suitably repaired. I never wore it again.

I feel my personal and spiritual growth actually went backwards during this time. I felt myself shrinking rather than expanding. It was something I disliked immensely. My hand tremor increased also. I couldn't bring myself to face the daunting task of separation and pondered in my mind, *I think I'm addicted to comfort, or is it the fear of the unknown or fear of loss? Will I ever have the courage to face this?*

I was doing personal growth weekends, facilitated by Maryann, a couple of times a year to develop myself spiritually, so I signed up to another one to clearly identify my fears. I'd known from previous workshops that the fear of failure was a big part of my life and still lingered in me. I came to understand that the fear of loss and being inadequate made up the remainder of my fear portfolio. Following my retirement from ISCA on March 30th 2012 I received a personal invitation from a director at Findhorn in Moray in Scotland to attend a week on sustainability at Findhorn. I had met him when he presented on sustainability at an AGIC conference. I assumed the conference would be about addressing ways to mitigate and adapt to global warming.

I'd always wanted to visit Findhorn on Moray Firth, as I knew about the acclaimed achievements that Eileen Caddy and her followers brought to this desolate area in north-eastern Scotland. In the 1960s and 1970s large vegetables were grown in arid country often covered in snow. Eileen's spiritual faith allowed her to develop a lush, productive garden that still flourishes today. It was in an area deemed unsuitable for growing anything.

I anticipated it would be a week discussing world resources and climate change adaptation as previously mentioned. However, it was a week of personal growth focussing on one's self. My fear of being inadequate was again identified.

It reinforced my belief that if we want to change the world for the better, we need to change ourselves first. Knowing one's fear is the first step to mastering it. Over the next three years I worked on these fears through Maryann's weekends and by constantly reassuring myself. I'd learnt to identify often, but not always, when I was operating in fear.

In 2015 I found that no matter how much emotion Carole projected onto me, I didn't react emotively but responded quietly in my feelings. I realised I'd 'picked up all my rocks and turned them over'. This realisation, coupled with the huge reduction of my fear, provided the courage to face the most difficult decision of my life. One morning in September 2014 I sat down with Carole.

'I've come to the decision that we need to separate.'

This triggered a rapid and firm refusal.

I'd expected her agreement as she had said a year or so previously that she had considered separation. Stunned by her reply I went out and sat in the back garden, almost in tears.

What do I do now? I can't take Carole through a divisive legal process after all these years together.

I detest the divisive approach used by lawyers. It seemed to be not about fairness for both, but to get as much as you can for your client. Carole's rapid response at least confirmed my decision that there was no love between us; she didn't ask where we went off the rails and how it might be fixed. I was still mulling things out when Carole came to me, put her arm on my shoulder, and with a tenderness I hadn't felt in years said, 'Maybe we can work this out, let's think about it.'

That night I pondered about that moment. In the morning I said to Carole, 'I've thought about it all night. I know you want to move to Brisbane so let's move and see how it goes.'

'Are you sure?' was her quick reply.

I mistakenly decided a fresh start may be what we needed to bring us close again.

'Yes, let's start looking for a house and I'll tidy up a few things on this house to ready it for sale.'

I hadn't realised I was making an impulsive mistake, most likely based on fear, that proved traumatic and expensive. Over the next few weeks we made several visits to Brisbane without finding a suitable house. I drove to Brisbane each Monday to my meditation and would drive around during the day looking at potential houses. Finally I found one and was confident enough that I put a deposit on it. Carole agreed it was the right house and we purchased the property in May 2015 and started making plans and working on upgrades. However, our Toowoomba home wasn't selling. One night at meditation my healer asked, 'How's your week been?'

'For some reason our Toowoomba house isn't selling,' I replied.

'Have you thought maybe it's not meant to be sold?' His comment struck an instant chord with me.

I remembered the first time I took some household items to the new house. I reversed the Mitsubishi into the garage to unload the boxes when I suddenly felt sick in my stomach. I had a bad feeling about what I was doing.

Shit, what have I done? I dismissed this thinking.

During the second and third visit after that I had a recurring thought.

I'm coming here to die.

I found the decision to stay with Carole and relocate weighing very heavily on my mind. It was sapping my energy. I was starting to realise the mistake I'd made. Nonetheless I kept at it. Carole wanted a kitchen, ensuite and laundry upgrade, which I readily agreed to. Plans and quotes were sought for the renovation.

I'd planned to build a workshop and make some decorative timber screening to bring the warmth of timber into the house. I love being around the energy of timber, it promotes well-being. This was dismissed by Carole as unnecessary. This, coupled with some heated exchanges over finishing work I was doing on our Toowoomba home, placed me in an immobilised state. I felt quite paralysed and deeply regretted the decision I'd made. I could see our strained relationship wasn't going to change. I felt trapped. I also felt stupid about my impetuous decision. When I told Carole what my healer said, she said, 'Let's get the opinion of a higher authority. Maryann is speaking in Brisbane next Monday night so let's see what she feels.'

I agreed and a booking was made. Maryann's presentations involved a talk on personal growth, the theme for the night. It was followed by a break before the second session where the audience asked questions.

We decided to attend, and planned to ask Maryann about the possible house sale blockage during the question session. During the break I was downstairs checking out the library. Carole was upstairs having a cup of tea. Samantha came down the stairs and said, 'Mary wants to see you.'

I went up the stairs and met Maryann at the top.

'I need to speak to you somewhere private.'

There was no room available so we went into the lecture room where a small number of people remained and were still sitting and talking. All eyes were soon on us as we entered.

'I almost cancelled tonight's talk because I wasn't feeling well,' Maryann said. 'But something made me feel it was important to come. When I saw you in the audience I knew why. Doug, I've known you for a very long time. You're a very dear friend. It's not my nature to speak this way, but I'm making an exception here as I feel it's extremely important. If you move to Brisbane it will kill your spirit. I cannot say it any clearer than that.' Her words were quiet but firm.

'That's just what I've been feeling. I've been feeling I'm going there to die. It's been really troubling me.'

'I suggest you and Carole wait twelve months before you decide what to do. You could rent the Brisbane house for that period.'

'Thanks Mary.' It was all I could say as a feeling of relief came over me with the confirmation of my thinking.

We stood up and a number of heads and eyes quickly turned away. I became aware people had been intently listening to our conversation. I went downstairs to be met by Carole who was obviously displeased she wasn't included. Not much was said for the remainder of the night. We were in separate cars because I'd come from my meditation and Carole came with Samantha where she was stopping; I was driving to stay with Sheldon. Samantha lived in the 'hobbit house' and it only had one spare room. The next morning Sheldon came with me to Samantha's unit and Carole and I talked about a twelve-month delay in moving to Brisbane and renting the Brisbane house. I went downstairs to unload something from the car when Carole appeared in the driveway. I was stunned by a full-on furious attack over the events of the previous night.

My mind raced.

Douglas, you've really stuffed up. You've got a very difficult decision to make.

The sooner the better. I can't live like this any longer.

Christmas 2015 was looming. The Brisbane house had been tenanted and rented on September 30th 2015. I then made it very clear to Carole that I planned to separate. We had our last Christmas together as a family. Carole moved out of Sardon Street to Samantha's unit in Brisbane on February 25th 2016, before moving into her new luxury unit, also in Brisbane. Our luxury holiday unit at Caloundra was sold at a fire-sale price and the money used to finance Carole's unit and make a major contribution toward a new car.

Immediately after our separation, I had my monthly superannuation payment halved and arranged for the other half of the payment to go to Carole. I didn't want her to suffer financially, but I was soon to learn she didn't reciprocate the sentiment. I thought naively that after forty-nine years together, a fifty-fifty split would be fair and agreed to. Carole had been dependant on my income throughout our marriage, and in fact she managed the money while I focussed on my professional responsibilities. I never questioned Carole's spending during our marriage. I willingly gave her the freedom to spend our money as she chose.

During her move, I'd allowed Carole to take whatever she needed from the house to furnish her new unit and Sheldon and I loaded a hire truck and assisted her to relocate. Once Carole had relocated, I set about transferring the ownership of the Toowoomba house and car into my name, because it was in joint names. I was told that without a court order I'd have to buy my half of the car and house and pay stamp duty on both transactions. I went to a lawyer to determine what was needed for a court order. Carole by that time had made it clear I had no legal right to her own relatively recent inheritance.

My first question to the family law solicitor was, 'Most of my personal wealth generated through my career was spent on many luxury cruises. Carole has a good inheritance following her mother's death three years ago in 2012. She claims I've no legal right to it. Is that correct? It seems very unfair if it is.'

'I'm afraid under the law a recent inheritance remains with the recipient and cannot be included in any settlement.'

Shit. I then asked what I needed to do to gain a court order for the separation. I sought a second opinion about the inheritance the next week and it confirmed I had no legal right to it. Carole's demeanour changed dramatically around this time as anger, hurt, fear and the reality sunk in. I was subjected to many abusive and critical tirades. I had a vivid dream which showed to me I was ready for the journey but Carole wasn't. Once the draft consent order was made, a copy was sent to a lawyer acting on behalf of Carole. A consent order is structured to have the distribution of funds and assets agreed by both parties before presenting it to the courts because it's then a simple 'rubber stamp' process for the Family Law Court. It's more efficient than having a separation processed entirely by the courts.

Her animosity toward me, and the prospect of me moving from a financial position in the top five percent of wealth in Australia, to being a part-pensioner, really shocked me. My monthly payment from my superannuation wasn't covering my expenses because I was buying household appliances and other miscellaneous household items I needed as I reset up the house.

My credit card became 'maxed out' and while the estate funds were in dispute, in a semi-panicked state I decided to apply for some menial jobs to top up my monthly finances. I applied for three positions unsuccessfully. I then made a drawdown of $10,000 from my super to tide me over during the finalisation of a court order until I became eligible for a pension. This resulted in an abusive call from Carole. I'd always had a plan to be financially independent, and while grateful for the Australian Government pension, I had to become resigned to my new and more frugal lifestyle.

Almost twelve months to the day after our physical separation, the consent order had been finalised and signed. It was February 2017. A court order was signed later in the month. I was able to keep the small balance from the sale of the unit and my superannuation was split 50/50. I was relieved to see this finally resolved. While disappointed and angry at the outcome, I simply decided to get on with my life.

I quickly adjusted to my new lifestyle in the much-reduced financial position of being a part-pensioner and once more I became relaxed and content. Life was good, but a lot more uncertain financially which often caused me unease. I started the process for divorce proceedings. After forty-nine years of marriage, we separated in September 2015. I divorced Carole in October 2017.

Little did I know that in July 2017, before the divorce was granted, my life would be shattered.

CHAPTER 32
THE DEATH OF MY SON

I developed a routine each week where I'd drive to Brisbane on Monday morning for my weekly healing and meditation, something I'd done since 1987. I'd do maintenance work for Samantha or Sheldon who both lived in Brisbane, often staying Monday night, and returning home Tuesday evening. Sheldon had been promoted progressively as he used his innovative skills to solve problems in the various milling sites where he worked. He was sent to Sydney to look at ongoing reliability problems in a plant at Homebush. By re-engineering areas in the first two months, a significant improvement in performance resulted so Carole and I felt certain he'd become permanently based in Sydney.

He was enjoying the Sydney lifestyle. An opportunity came up for the position of site manager at the Homebush plant and Sheldon was sure he'd be the successful applicant. He was greatly disappointed when he didn't get the job. He dressed casually when not in the flour milling whites and had a pony tail, which management wasn't keen on. He then heard the mill manager at the Brisbane Mill, who he had worked with over the years and respected greatly, was moving to head office so Sheldon rang him one night.

'What are the chances of me getting your job when you go to head office?' he asked

'You're well qualified for the position and could handle it easily, but you'd have to wear a suit to the interview and get rid of your pony tail.'

'Okay, I'll do it,' was his reply. Sheldon applied for the job with a short back and sides haircut and wearing a suit. He was offered the site manager position on the spot and he accepted, spending many happy years in his management role.

While he loved his job, constant harassment from a new head office boss led him to resign in November 2012 from his well-remunerated position as site manager. A new major expansion in a state-of-the-art mill was just completed. He often expressed to me his dissatisfaction with the head office people he reported to. He had been approached for a promotion to head office a year or so earlier but refused. He said to me, 'I couldn't work in that office, the energy feels like shit. It's not a happy place, no way could I work in that environment, it feels toxic.'

I understood a month or so later when Sheldon said.

'A director is reassuring major biscuit companies that they're receiving old season flour, when it's a lie,' he said. 'He had us reduce the stocks of old season flour, presumably to improve cash flow, and is sending freshly milled bags. Our customers are having quality problems as a result. I won't lie to customers, so if I'm asked I'll just refer the customer to head office. I don't like this dishonesty.' He was obviously very uncomfortable with the decisions coming from above.

A new executive who'd been appointed at head office under the MD soon made life hell for Sheldon. He removed Sheldon's control of all areas that were traditionally his responsibility but left him with full accountability for them. He belittled Sheldon for not having a degree and took no notice of his recommendations. In fact, Sheldon had a 'degree' in flour milling. He studied through Guildhall, London where he came second in the world in his final examination. During his professional training he spent time with farmers learning the various effects of drought, flood, harvesting techniques and silage on grain. He spent time in a bakery learning the important features of flour in the cooking process, and then in a laboratory to learn about nutrition, disease and various elements of the various grains' makeup and the importance of them. He also learned how to design and operate all the equipment used in flour mills. It was training of such quality that I used it as a personal benchmark when discussing training strategies with the Foundry's training manager.

He won the milling industry's Australian Young Achiever of the Year award in 1998 and was sent on a study tour around the world looking at modern and other milling plants. Despite all this, his new boss placed no importance on his experience. Sheldon managed by walking around the mill and guiding employees, a very powerful management technique. Sheldon and one other remained the only managers left with this critical training. He told me his boss openly told the various mill managers at monthly corporate meetings, 'You don't have to understand how the process plant works; you have to be a businessman.'

I asked him if he received financial information, a cash position and the operation's financial return information. He told me he wasn't privy to this information, which made this approach a joke. It made me think his days could be numbered. A decision was made by his manager to purchase a new packing machine for bagging the flour worth more than $3 million. He saw it working in the USA and decided to buy it without seeking advice from his mill managers. A fortnight after it arrived on site Sheldon, who had the responsibility to supervise the installation, said to me one night, 'Dad, this new packing machine we're installing packs by volume, yet all our customers' bags are by weight. What'll happen when the flour density varies? Because it often does.'

'You'll have a lot of reject bags, that's what you'll have. Someone has made a serious mistake.'

The first production run produced many reject bags, as predicted. His manager abused him and accused the operators of incompetence. Sheldon started receiving calls from his boss at 6am demanding to know what was happening at the mill. He had other calls at night. It became the last straw on one Saturday morning when he was called and heavily verbally abused. He resigned.

'I can't take his abuse and stupid management any longer, he's such a dickhead. I really feel for the good people at the plant because he keeps reducing numbers. They're hyper-stressed already.'

I concurred. 'The business will struggle eventually and the board will probably be told it's the result of stiff competition or other market forces.'

I'd witnessed this type of incompetence in my career and its misguided justification in board reports. I initially considered going to Sydney to discuss the issue with a board member, but decided I'd only be seen as a protective father. I'd seen companies damaged by big egos and disliked seeing a great company run by incompetence. The annual report spoke glowingly of the value of employees. I was pleased to hear from a mill employee that a major biscuit manufacturer and key customer had rang the Sydney office and said, 'The mill has gone to pot since Sheldon left.' I know Sheldon felt good to hear that piece of customer feedback.

He had sold his large house and was living in a rented warehouse in the city, a site where he had started to run events. I could see his confidence had been damaged by the abuse handed out by his manager.

'Would you put the Corvette in your garage for a couple of months until I can find somewhere to store it in Brisbane?' he asked me after he sold his house.

His total rebuild of the tired 1972 Corvette Stingray he imported from California was a credit to his creativity, innovation and self-taught technical skills. I ended up with the beast in my Toowoomba garage for the next few years, and naturally I had to give it a spin every month to keep the oil circulating, something I came to enjoy immensely.

Sheldon's confidence returned and he was holding many popular and well- attended events, covering all expenses but making little money. I'd arrive Monday mornings to help him clean up after weekend events and stay Monday night to assist with tasks on Tuesday. One Monday in July I arrived at the warehouse early and started to collect glasses and load the dishwasher. A winter ball had been the Saturday night event and about 240 people attended. I went to my meditation that evening. Sheldon made dinner and I slept in a spare room at the warehouse. The next morning I tidied up a few remaining tasks while Sheldon mopped the floors. We finished at about 11am.

'Do you want me to do your spreadsheets for your tax return after lunch?' I asked. Sheldon disliked book work.

'Nah Dad, it's been full on, let's have a chill-out day. I'll buy you lunch.'

The week before, he had his first visit to Toowoomba in many months as he and I did some maintenance on his work utility. We worked long hours and on the Sunday the week before the ball he took me for a drive in the Corvette to Scotty's Barn at Flagstone Creek at the foot of the mountain on which Toowoomba is located. It sits in a beautiful bush setting beside a creek. We had coffee and Sheldon toured Scotty's impressive auto museum and the art deco function centre he had developed over the years.

After coffee we went for a drive in the country in the Corvette, his first drive in a couple of years. The Vette, as it was called, took a backseat while he developed his business and he was even thinking of selling it. I could see he was enjoying his drive while winding through a back country road, giving the Vette a healthy burst every now and then.

'You're enjoying this aren't you,' I said.

'Yep, it's a great road for the old girl,' he said with a broad grin on his face.

I didn't know this would be Sheldon's last drive of his treasured car. I'm so pleased he had come to Toowoomba that weekend.

The warehouse jobs were complete and we caught the City Cat, a commuter ferry on the Brisbane River near to the warehouse. Sheldon picked the spot for the warehouse because it was in the centre of a popular eating area close to the river where he often used to walk to 'chill out'. He loved being near nature and often tried to bring greenery into the warehouse. That was his only criticism of living in the inner city building.

'I miss my lush garden and outdoor area at Oxley,' he'd say.

We usually went for a quick sandwich in a nearby coffee shop and paid separately, but today Sheldon set the agenda and took me to a Mexican restaurant in the popular West End suburb. We chatted over the meal and I felt there was something special about the day, particularly at the end of the meal when we sat just looking at each other. Normally we'd return to the warehouse but Sheldon had another idea.

'Let's go to the Three Monkeys, they have great chocolate biscuits. You can have a coffee and I'll have a tea.'

The Three Monkeys was a boutique restaurant with unusual décor and a great atmosphere. We ordered and went into a beautiful dense open garden area out the back that Sheldon obviously knew about. We chatted for about an hour and walked back to the warehouse.

We arranged for him to visit Toowoomba next week and fit extractors and do other work on his work ute.

I packed my things and got ready to leave, then he said, 'Before you go, I've got a roof leak over my bedroom. What would be the best way to fix it?'

The warehouse was a two-storey building and his bedroom was at the front on the second level.

'It's a new roof so something must have come loose or wasn't screwed down or sealed properly,' he said. Sheldon didn't like heights and walked me to a small fire exit balcony on the second floor.

'I'm goin' to put a ladder here and climb up on the roof to find and fix the issue. There's not much room but it should be safe. Maybe it's just a couple of screws needed or some sealant.'

I nodded in agreement and simply said, 'Be careful.'

We walked downstairs, I gave him a hug and said goodbye and he thanked me for the help. I headed home to Toowoomba around 3pm. On the drive home I couldn't stop thinking how special the day was and how I loved Sheldon. That Tuesday was the last time I'd be with him. I came to believe at a soul level he was saying goodbye to me. He had dinner with Samantha that night in the 'hobbit house'.

On the Wednesday I started having really bad feelings – similar to those I felt when Bill Hawes passed away. I hadn't heard from Samantha for over a week. She wasn't answering my calls so I started to feel concerned about her. On Wednesday I tried to ring Sheldon to get him to check up on her. This misguided focus on Samantha was prompted by a strange happening in September 1997. Carole, Samantha and I attended an ex-neighbour's wedding at Caloundra on the coast north of Brisbane. The ceremony concluded. As photos were being taken it started to rain quite heavily and Carole, Samantha and I sought shelter in the Church foyer. Samantha decided to check out the empty church interior and after studying the various church features she came walking down the centre aisle towards us.

'I'm going to die before you, Dad. But you'll die before me,' she said, looking at her mother.

An icy chill ran down my spine.

Where on Earth did that come from? Carole and I looked stunned.

'What prompted that?' We asked. Samantha shrugged her shoulders. The rain eased and we went to the reception. That remark has caused me a lot of disquiet over the years.

Is her spirit just preparing me for the future event? I don't want to think about it, I love her so much.

On Thursday, the feeling was so bad I contemplated driving to Brisbane to check on her. Sheldon wasn't answering his phone, which wasn't unusual because it would often be ringing on the kitchen table while he worked downstairs. He wasn't good at returning missed calls.

'If it's urgent they'll ring back,' was his standard explanation.

Thursday evening I was still trying to reassure myself that Samantha was okay. I tried to ring Sheldon once more. It was 8.12pm but he didn't answer. I was considering driving to Brisbane, but decided I was just being a bit paranoid, when at 8.43pm the phone rang. It was Samantha. I felt instant relief until I realised she was crying.

'I've got bad news,' she said. 'Sheldon's had a serious accident. We've lost him.'

I went from instant relief to instant shock.

'I'm coming straight away,' was all I could say as a huge shock impacted my very essence like a physical blow.

'I'm at the warehouse,' Samantha replied and I hung up saying, 'On my way.'

I was in shock and kept saying over and over the whole time while I was packing,

'Please God this can't be real, it can't be, it can't be true.' Tears flooded my eyes.

I threw some clothes in a bag, ran to the garage and backed the Merc down the driveway. I rang my brother Graham. I'd been trying to see him daily since he'd been diagnosed with terminal leukaemia. I wanted him to know I wouldn't be visiting for a while and said, 'Samantha rang me and said Sheldon has passed away.'

'Oh no, not Sheldon, it can't be,' Graham said, crying.

I interrupted. 'I'm on my way to Brisbane; please don't tell anyone because Carole doesn't know yet.'

I didn't know it but his phone was on speaker and his wife heard it and apparently rang her son who lived near the road heading from Toowoomba to Brisbane. She arranged for him to go with me so I didn't drive alone after getting the bad news. My mobile rang, it was Graham's wife.

'You can't drive to Brisbane after that news. Mark will meet you and go with you.'

I thanked spirit for a police-free run and hammered the Mercedes hard – I used the concentration on driving to focus me on getting to Brisbane as quickly as possible and keep my mind off this awful new reality. I didn't want the distraction of a passenger, no matter how well intentioned, nor the complication of dealing with accommodation issues and things like that. I drove past Mark's place and begrudgingly stopped to ring him to explain what I was doing. I was about fifteen minutes from the warehouse when the in-car phone rang, it was Samantha.

'You can't go to the warehouse, the police won't allow it. You've to go to the CIB headquarters in Mary Street,' she said, referring to the Criminal Investigation Branch.

This news put me in further shock.

Holy shit, surely he hasn't been murdered? Why are the police involved?

I'd convinced myself he had fallen off the roof. I ignored Samantha's advice. I went directly to the warehouse. There were several police cars pulled up outside and police standing at the doorway with police tape restricting entry. I parked the car and hurried to the tape fence. There was no activity up the passageway door near the fire- exit stairway.

I realised he hadn't fallen off the roof, so I headed towards the police out front.

'I'm his father, what happened? I want to see my son. I want to be with him. I want to touch him.'

'I'm sorry you can't do that, this is a potential crime scene.' A police officer behind the tape said to me. I started to press hard to see Sheldon when a well-dressed detective standing some distance away saw I was getting agitated. He walked over to me.

'I'm controlling this investigation. I know this is extremely difficult for you as his father, but we have procedures we must follow when a potential crime scene is declared. Please respect this. I need you to go to our headquarters at Mary Street and give a statement. We need to understand what's going on and you can help us with that.' He said it in a very calming voice.

He then told me Sheldon was found on the floor inside, and asked about him. I settled myself and spent about five minutes explaining what he did and that I couldn't think of anyone who would want to do him harm. Then I left the warehouse. I arrived at Mary Street CIB and was accompanied upstairs by a very caring female detective. She took me to Samantha who was obviously very upset, and sitting beside Sheldon's friend Rose. We hugged and cried together.

'I haven't called Mum, because I know she'll faint. I thought we'd tell her early in the morning,' Samantha said. It was about 11.30pm.

'Yes, you're right, that sounds good.'

Rose had been a long-term friend of Sheldon. He had convinced her to move from Sydney to Brisbane. She moved into his warehouse and rented the second bedroom while he helped her to find a suitable unit, which he did just days before his death. It was Rose who, returning from an after work medical appointment late on Thursday night, discovered Sheldon lying on the floor in the warehouse. She called triple zero and two young policemen driving nearby were first on the scene. Sheldon had passed away the night before and unfortunately Rose was away. Rose was told to leave the warehouse immediately because it was a possible crime scene.

He'd fallen face down and over a large bean bag so his feet were higher than his head. The lady detective told me later that because of this all his blood settled near his head and his face was badly discoloured after the long period before he was found. The young police mistook it as bruising. Rose, Samantha and I went with separate detectives to separate offices to give our statements. At around 2.30am on Friday morning all statements were taken and we drove to Samantha's unit for the night feeling totally drained and exhausted. We walked into the unit like zombies, got organised, hugged each other and went to bed. I made a makeshift bed on the floor of Samantha's unit, set the alarm and tried to sleep. I couldn't stop crying. I could hear Samantha sobbing every now and then and felt totally helpless.

During the sleepless night I decided to call him.

'Come to me Sheldon, I love you, come to me Sheldon,' I kept repeating. After a short time I felt energy envelop me and I immediately felt reassured and calmer. I just knew he was there with me and it comforted me a lot. Samantha shared the same experience. We woke early and Samantha and I drove to Carole's unit and arrived at 7am. We rang the security intercom, and Carole answered.

'It's Samantha and me, we need to talk to you,' I said.

'What about?' Carole asked.

'We'll tell you when we come up.' The entrance door opened and we took the elevator to Carole's level and found her waiting for us beside her open door in her pyjamas as we walked along the passageway to her unit. She knew something was terribly wrong as soon as she saw our faces.

I led her into her unit as she kept saying, 'What is it?'

'It's Sheldon,' was all we said. Carole cried, 'Oh no, it can't be.'

'We've lost him.' Carole collapsed on to the carpeted floor and I sat down beside her holding her and we were all crying.

We told her what we knew and sat on the floor gathering our wits and working out what to do next. After about twenty or thirty minutes we started to talk about who we should break this horrible news to first. We were still trying to come to grips with our grief. Just when we started to get up and think about who to ring, her phone rang. It was her nephew voicing his condolences. It was quickly followed by two calls from another nephew and a niece, one overseas.

'Shit, what's going on?' I exclaimed.

'How do these people know before me? I'm his mother!' Carole cried.

We grabbed our phones and started ringing people who needed to be told. We were all super stressed by this intrusion of our privacy; we had no time to grieve together.

Graham's wife hadn't told her son, Mark, not to tell anyone and the family grapevine was soon running hot. I was angered by this intrusion and being robbed of important time to grieve together as a family. I then regretted calling Graham. Carole was naturally and understandably very angry that she wasn't told first, as Sheldon's mother. I understood completely but couldn't change what happened. We were only acting in Carole's best interests. I felt terrible that I'd created a situation where Carole at a time of enormous grief was now very angry at both Samantha and me.

A few days passed before the police confirmed there was no foul play. They released the site and we could access the warehouse. His passing was eventually diagnosed as internal heart failure. Rose needed her handbag and clothes on the second day so we went and asked the policeman at the door, who refused entry. He wouldn't go and get items either. We were also concerned about Sheldon's much-loved cat, Husky. We gave the policeman cat food to put out for Husky as he wouldn't appear or come when called. He was a timid but beautiful cat and would have been hiding somewhere as strangers were wandering through his territory. Husky was his mate and would have been with him as he lay there for almost two days.

The next day we went to the warehouse again and called Husky. This time a senior detective was at the door and Rose explained her situation. He was very considerate and supportive of our circumstances.

'I can get your handbag, but no one else can enter,' he said.

Rose said, 'I need some clothes also, as I only have what I'm wearing.'

'What do you need?' he asked hesitantly.

Rose described blouses and coats. When she said she needed underwear he blushed.

'You don't want me to rummage through your underwear do you?' he said with a funny look on his face.

Rose assured him that was indeed the case. After instructions he set off and returned, handing the goods to Rose. We all laughed at his embarrassment. He took it in good humour. We then asked if we could enter the gravel area beside the warehouse outer wall and call Husky through a ground-floor window. We were relieved when the detective agreed. Rose and I rattled a cat food container, which normally brought him running, to no avail. I asked Rose to stand back because she was relatively new to Husky, and I gave him a call that I used many times when visiting Sheldon. I was on the point of giving up when he appeared.

He was constantly meowing, obviously agitated and frightened so I threw him some cat food stones which he gulped down in true Husky fashion. I called Rose and as soon as she appeared at the window he took off again. We rushed to the front of the building and placed the cage near the front door and asked the detective to find him. I told him about Husky's usual hiding spots and a few minutes later he appeared smiling, with Husky in his arms. I wasn't allowed to cross the doorway threshold as it was still a contained site. *Surely a bloke can at least step inside the bloody door.* I knew Husky would freak out when carried by a stranger outside the door. Sheldon used to carry Husky outside and Husky would struggle to get down because he liked to be in control the moment he was taken outside the building.

'You like to be in control out here, don't ya Husk?' Sheldon would laugh before putting him back on terra firma.

I had the cage ready just outside the door. As soon as the detective stepped outside to hand him over, Husky went feral from fear and we almost lost him. I managed with great difficulty to avoid his claws and push him in the cage. I smiled when I saw the detective's suit was covered in cat fur. He had scored a few scratches on his arms. Family friends took Husky in and he's now the much-loved pet of two young nurses.

It all felt so surreal. We were all 'numbed off'.

What to do next?

CHAPTER 33
AFTER SHELDON'S DEATH

I decided I'd stay at the warehouse and sleep in Sheldon's bed. Some found this difficult to understand. Why would I want to stay alone in the large empty building? I wanted to soak in his energy as long as I could because it made me feel close to him. I spent the days and nights sorting through his personal stuff. I worked late each night with a friend of Sheldon's who was a physicist and an IT expert. It took many nights before his computer and laptop passwords could be identified so the relevant contacts and authorities could be notified of his death. I was keeping busy to hide the pain.

We were relieved to be told Sheldon had just collapsed and his passing was quick and without suffering. I was eventually asked to make identification.

I was comforted by the spiritual experience I'd had thirty years before. It helped me realise my real Sheldon was in a much better place and this was simply his vehicle of choice.

I then thanked the chief detective later for the respect and dignity shown by all his staff toward the family and Sheldon's friends.

'We're not the traffic cops here,' he replied.

Carole started making funeral arrangements and Samantha was putting a slideshow together of Sheldon's life. The funeral was arranged, two days before what would have been his fiftieth birthday. Sheldon told me he didn't want to turn fifty but he couldn't change it so he was going to celebrate 'big time'. He had planned to fly to Sydney on the Friday night where friends had arranged a party. He then planned to fly back to Brisbane on Saturday to attend a large party his friends had arranged for Saturday night.

While it all felt surreal to me, it was a beautiful funeral. The Vette was on display. Carole, Samantha and I presented the eulogy. His best friend and confidant, Lloyd, tried to speak about his best mate but was too overcome with grief. His love for Sheldon was obvious; they talked each week on the phone and were together regularly. Lloyd had applied the impressive purple paint job on the Vette. Lloyd took me for a lap of honour in the Vette after the service and all attending formed a guard of honour. Lloyd had lovingly polished and prepared the car. It looked magnificent. He finished the drive-by with a big-block Chevy roar. It was great to meet his many friends over a lunch following the drive-by and hear the many experiences they shared with our son. It was heart-warming to hear the praise about his competence and abilities during his flour- milling life from workmates who attended, and in emails from past managers who couldn't. Another close friend of Sheldon's said to me, 'Sheldon told me after that drive in the Vette with you there was no way he could sell that car.'

The warehouse rent was quite expensive so Carole, Samantha and I decided to have all the warehouse items sold by the end of September. We spent days getting it marshalled and packed ready for display and sale. We gave a lot away to his friends and our family.

I'd planned to give Carole the divorce papers during the week Sheldon passed away, with a court date set in October. With his unexpected death I decided to wait until we'd had time to grieve, and kept the papers in a shopping bag in the warehouse, where I was still living. One day over lunch Carole and I were in the warehouse kitchen.

'Do you want me to sign the papers now?' she asked.

'What papers?' I asked curiously.

'The divorce papers in your bag.'

'How did you know?'

'I went through your bag.'

I was shocked. *Bloody hell, we've been separated for two years and nothing has changed!*

I agreed and the papers were signed. I cast my mind back to a week or two after I retired from ISCA and picked my mobile up off the kitchen bench at our Toowoomba home to find many of my contacts missing.

'What's happened to my contacts? There's a heap missing.'

'I deleted them, you won't need them anymore,' was Carole's reply. It stunned me and some heated words followed. Fortunately I had them backed up on my laptop and I soon retrieved them. It was an example of the extreme need for control Carole had developed.

About a week before we left the warehouse my bed and the kitchen fridge were sold so I moved back to Samantha's unit. I rang Graham that morning to see how he was and update him where we were at. I was saddened to hear he was in severe pain and in a terrible state, almost crying on the phone.

'My hips are cracking from the chemo and I'm in terrible pain. I can hardly walk and can't even bend over. I can't even lift up the bloody toilet seat. I just want it all to end. I'm going to end up just lying in a hospital bed. I'm sick of it.'

I just felt overwhelmed by his misery and so impotent about all the sad events suddenly pouring into my life. Samantha was suffering badly from Sheldon's passing. I felt helpless watching her in her distressed state. I was really tired and bedded down in the hobbit house. I crashed and was awoken when I heard Samantha talking to someone. *It's bloody morning already, Carole must be here.* I heard the unit door close as someone left. The unit went quiet and I immediately went back to sleep. It didn't seem long before my mobile rang beside the bed; it was an extremely traumatised Samantha. 'Mitzy got run over, I'm at the vet, they need to put her down.'

'I'm on my way.'

I was overcome and cried for Samantha.

Mitzy was Samantha's much-loved cat. Samantha had a routine of getting up in the middle of the night to let Mitzy in when she scratched on the door. That night Mitzy didn't come so Samantha went looking for her and found her lying badly injured in a garden under the unit stairs.

I ran to her and we hugged when I arrived. Both of us just sobbed and sobbed. 'How much more do we have to bear?' I said. 'Uncle Graham is in horrible pain and now Mitzy, what's going on?'

We held each other for some time until we both settled down. I rang Carole, who came over. It was 1.30am. Mitzy was still alive but in a bad state. She purred and after Samantha had sufficient time with her, she nodded at me and I called in the vet who administered the needle. The next morning I buried her in a garden at the unit. I rang Graham who was still suffering badly and told him about Mitzy.

'You can put the bloody cat out of its misery, but you can't bloody well put me down,' he shouted. We both burst into tears.

I hope there is nothing else in store for us. I don't think I can handle any more.

The next day I was explaining to another resident in Samantha's block about the loss of Sheldon and Mitzy when a large bright blue butterfly flew down between us and hovered about four inches from my face. It hovered for over a minute before I waved it away as I couldn't see the face of Samantha's neighbour. We were both trying to work out why it did that when it returned and hovered in front of my eyes again. I was quite captivated and didn't try to chase it. After about a minute it flew away. *Was that you Sheldon?* I hoped.

It was a difficult time pulling down his carefully planned décor, furnishing items and the lavish winter ball decorations. We left the warehouse a few days before the end of September, still full of grief and really struggling to make sense of what had transpired.

I returned to Toowoomba and found my normal enthusiasm had waned. Everything seemed to require effort. I'd always found Maryann's personal growth weekends beneficial so I decided to book another.

I attended Saturday's session and after it finished late in the evening I drove to a restaurant for a meal, then headed to the motel I'd booked. With my finances stretched after the marriage separation, I booked into a cheap one. When I arrived I was shocked to see a crew of Pacific Islander construction workers sitting outside near my room with music playing and drinking beer. A few were sitting outside my bedroom window and as I was unloading the car I almost decided to cancel and relocate. I found the men's banter friendly and they greeted me politely and respectfully.

It's Saturday night. They're obviously a work crew letting their hair down so I'll give them till 10pm. If they don't quiet down I'll speak to them. It reached 10pm and it was obvious they were having a good time because there was repeated good-natured laughter and all conversation, though often loud, was respectful.

Shit, they're having a good time, probably the only time during the week they get to relax. Don't be a wowser, Douglas. Give them till midnight. It's bloody frustrating but that's just the way it is. It's Saturday night.

Midnight came and all went quiet. I heard them saying goodnight to each other. *Sleep at last.* Suddenly, music started playing softly again but there was no conversation. After about five minutes I decided I was going to ask for it to be turned off. I went outside in my summer pyjamas and barefoot. It was a surprisingly cold night for Brisbane, with a clear cloudless sky full of stars. A lone figure, obviously very drunk, was sitting on a chair drinking a stubbie of beer. The music was coming from a small recorder on the ground beside him. He had a grey hoodie on and his head was downcast. I walked up to him and said, 'Hey Matey, would you mind turning the music down? I've just lost my son. I'm still grieving. I need to get some sleep.'

He sat up aggressively. He started to stand, I saw he was a solidly built man and a Pacific Islander. 'What'd you bloody well know about grief? You think you know everything, you know nothing.'

He sagged back in his chair, much to my relief. Then he said with a slurred voice that I couldn't understand clearly, 'My beautiful daughter, Mariasusana, was killed, what would ya know about grief?'

I couldn't understand his slurring voice but realised he had someone die recently. I suspected it was his daughter. I was standing over him so I put my hand on his shoulder.

'I'm sorry, what happened?'

He aggressively pushed my arm away as he started to stand up.

I realised I was hovering over him. He was again getting angry so I quickly squatted down beside his knee. From this position I was looking up at him. He then told me his beautiful young daughter Mariasusana was on a bus from school. He said she loved going to school. The bus stopped at the bus stop, she alighted, and excitedly ran around in front of it to cross the road to be with her mother waiting on the other side. A speeding truck driver, under the influence, mowed her down. I was cold and my knees were aching as he poured his heart out to me.

'What do I do now? My life is over, I'm finished. My wife should've been at the bus stop, I blame her. She's back in Samoa with me other daughter. I've also a daughter here in Brisbane staying with her aunty. My family's split apart. God's punishing me.'

I could see he was in deep grief and remorse, I hadn't seen anyone so crushed before. I told him about my spiritual revelation I'd had years ago and how my son and his daughter were in a beautiful place. There was no need to be sad for them, only us. I told him he's not being punished, that God only loves us and doesn't punish, and that misguided belief is bullshit. I said no one was to blame except the drugged or drunken driver. He eventually settled down and as we talked he asked me, 'Would you like to see a picture of my daughter?'

'Yes.'

'It's in the work ute, I'll get it.'

I was now shivering from the cold but I wanted to be there for him. He returned and gave me a badge with his daughter's photo on it.

'Let's go into my room where there is light so I can see it clearly,' I said.

I struggled to stand because my knees were aching and stiff. *This is what happens when you're bloody seventy*, I mused as I hobbled to my doorway.

It was a purple badge about seventy millimetres in diameter with a photo of Mariasusana's face on it. She was dressed in her yellow school uniform. She was beautiful and small plastic butterflies were attached to each side of the purple badge. I told him my son's favourite colour was also purple and it was the colour of his Corvette. I said he also loved butterflies and had three mounted on his dressing table mirror. I now have them on my bedroom mirror because it reminds me of his soft side.

It was the reason I was so much in awe about the blue butterfly flapping in front of my face.

We sat on the end of my bed and talked until four-thirty in the morning.

I was able to convince him his wife wasn't responsible and that blaming her would inflict a terrible extra burden on her at her time of extreme grief. I talked about how she carried her for nine months and how that makes it extra hard for a mother to lose a child. I also told him repeatedly that God wasn't punishing him, which he kept insisting on. I feel he started to accept what I was saying. The idea of a punishing God is misguided and very damaging – there is only love. All that happens here on planet Earth is the result of our free will.

He told me his wife and daughter went back to Samoa to grieve with her family. In the rush they didn't apply for a visa for her daughter and she wouldn't be allowed back into Australia. He wanted to be with his family here in Australia, and didn't want to return to live in Samoa because he had been promoted to supervisor on the fibre optic National Broadband Network (NBN). It's a national project and he was proud of it. He told me the job made it possible for him to buy a home and car. He said if he returned to Samoa to live, so he could be with his other daughter, he'd have nothing.

I offered to write to the federal minister for immigration and plead a special case so his daughter could return with his wife to Australia and the family be reunited so he could continue his NBN work. He was pleased that I may have been able to help and thanked me profusely.

'I need to go to bed,' he said finally, as he stood up. He was quite unsteady.

'We both do. Don't put off speaking with your wife.'

'Thank you, you're a true friend, this is the first time I've spoken about Mariasusana and her death. I feel so much better. May God bless you.'

I hugged him and he left. It was 4.30am.

In the morning I went to his unit. He hugged me again while thanking me profusely. Then we said goodbye.

We communicated by email a number of times. He wanted to catch up over coffee when I was next in Brisbane as he regarded me as a new friend. I felt a connection to him and was happy to oblige. I viewed our meeting as another piece of synchronicity.

Anyway, Maryann's weekend helped me but also brought the realisation it would be a long journey before I could experience the joy I had before Sheldon's passing.

I decided to keep Sheldon's great-looking, lowered, red Holden Commodore V8 work ute. I filled it up with petrol one morning and decided to check the tyre pressures. I was pumping up the front tyre and was parked beside an elevated walkway. A young boy, about ten years old, wearing a safety helmet, pulled his scooter up beside me.

'That sure is a cool-looking ute, who did the badges like that?' he asked.

I looked up at him. He was bright-eyed with blond hair poking out of his helmet.

He reminded me of Sheldon when he was young.

'My son painted the inside black.'

'It's really looks cool, how did he do it?'

I explained.

'Is that an SS interior?'

I wasn't sure and said, 'Yes, I think so.'

'Cool, I love the wheels, they're great.'

'Unfortunately my son passed away in July and . . .'

'Oh, that's so sad, I'm so sorry.' His very warm, heartfelt reply touched me.

'Yes, it was horrible. My son has another cool car, a Corvette he rebuilt. It's purple and chrome and has 660HP.'

'Is it an old C1 or is it a C2?'

This lad certainly knows his cars; I've no idea what he's talking about.

'No it's a 1972 Corvette Stingray.'

'A Stingray! That's super cool.' He said it with great enthusiasm.

'Yes it's beautiful, it took him three years working at nights and weekends to rebuild it. We're going to sell it to his best friend Lloyd, who painted it.'

'Don't sell the Vette, sell the ute, don't sell the Stingray,' he pleaded.

I opened the door to hop in while he looked down at me.

'It's too much responsibility for me now and . . .'

'That's not a standard dashboard, did he do that? It's really cool.'

'Yes, he was very creative, but he's not here anymore.'

The boy quickly responded, with great authority and sincerity, 'Please don't say that, every time you hop in and drive the ute he'll be sitting there beside you.'

I choked up and could barely say goodbye to him.

What a beautiful young boy, he's definitely an evolved soul.

The next weekend I took the Vette to the petrol station hoping to see him again, but I've never seen him again on my many weekly refills at my local servo.

These interactions somehow helped me along my journey of grief and made me appreciate daily life once more. I'm still attempting to get a sense of normality back into my life. I know my life will never be the same again. I still miss him terribly but take comfort in knowing he's in a great place; I'm only sad for me, not him.

I know in my heart that when the soul decides it has completed its earthly journey it leaves without concern for those left behind. I can relate to the words in *Conversations with God – Book 1*:

When the soul makes this decision, nothing the body does can change it. Nothing the mind thinks can alter it. It is at the moment of death that we learn who, in the body-mind-soul triumvirate, is running things.[34]

I wasn't able to return to my book for eleven months. The final two chapters were difficult to write, filled as they were with painful emotions and memories. But writing it helped me, and I've been compensated by some good feelings. It will be a long journey back. My life will never be the same.

I know in my heart Sheldon is just a thought and feeling away.

But some days it's difficult to believe.

Thirty months after Sheldon's passing, my brother Graham succumbed to leukaemia, suffering badly at the end. He passed away at 12.12pm on the 12th day of the 12th month in 2019 surrounded by many of his family. He was a best friend as well as a brother and I loved him dearly and miss him. A month earlier my cousin and pretend grandfather Keith Bradshaw also passed away. It was a tough period.

---

[34]   ND Walsch, *Conversations with God – Book 1*, Hodder & Stoughton, London, UK, 1999, p. 81.

CHAPTER 34

CONCLUSION

It's my view that humanity is moving away from a natural balance, is in an unknowing state and somewhat lost. As a result, planet Earth and its people are suffering. I now know inside myself that we exist on this planet with a higher purpose than to make money or feed materialism driven by ego, addictions and the need for sensation, power and control.

I believe the human race is still primitive, in spite of its enormous and amazing technological and intellectual achievements. My experience clearly demonstrated that to me. We're a race of people still killing each other while also killing our life support system – planet Earth – while many still egotistically and mistakenly imagine us as being a developed and highly evolved society. Eckhart Tolle in his book *A New Earth* writes:

> What looks like weakness to the ego is in fact the only true strength. This spiritual truth is diametrically opposed to the values of our contemporary culture and the way it conditions people to behave.[35]

I've arrived at the knowledge that our life is a journey of the soul, not the mind and body. Yet virtually all our institutions of learning and media, and our social norms, have a major focus on physical existence.

---

35   E Tolle, *A New Earth*, 10th Anniversary Edition, Penguin, London, UK, 2016, p. 216

The sole (soul) purpose of our stay on planet Earth, in my view, is to come to know who we really are and realise the full potential of the soul. 'Know thyself' is a profound statement. We need to learn to nurture the soul, rather than the body, to develop spiritually. Through such a process we'll begin to see each other and all life as intrinsically connected and not separate from each other, as we do now. We'll come to the realisation that might is not right.

I've also come to know God is really practical!

I hope my story shows that a practical, working life can be combined with a spiritual way of seeing things, and that it can help others do the same. I've been a family man, a mechanical engineer, a successful business manager and a corporate advisor.

I make no apology for including so many engineering and manufacturing stories in this book, because millions of good hardworking, creative and innovative people around the world in those industries could relate to what I've written. I hope I help spread a belief that one day every person can practically experience firsthand the kind of love I was exposed to – because they're worthy and loved by this wonderful entity.

It would make this book worthwhile.

I now understand that to find the inner peace and contentment that knowledge or belief in a higher power brings, it is not necessary to be a saint, religious person or spiritual leader. It only requires a real commitment to truth, honesty and integrity, and a willingness to treat others with respect and dignity. To achieve this state of contentment one must learn to trust one's feelings. A pure or open heart is a good start. Wealth and fame aren't necessary, because the road to true success in life is finding, knowing and loving ourselves from the inside out, instead of trying to maintain an external persona. Eckhart Tolle in *A New Earth* describes success as follows:

> What the world doesn't tell you – because it doesn't know – is that you cannot *become* successful. You can only *be* successful. Don't let a mad world tell you that success is anything other than a successful present moment.[36]

All that's needed is a real cry from the soul to bring about change.

---

[36]   E Tolle, *A New Earth*, (19th Anniversary Edition), Penguin, London, UK, 2016, p. 270

Little did I know as a nervous teenager that placing a Rotary sticker on my physics book at Harristown High School would start me on a journey of truth. The words on that sticker ultimately led me to a euphoric, life-changing spiritual experience and many other unimaginable happenings along the way. I feel enormously privileged and humbled to have had these in my life. The experience has grounded me and freed me of a big ego, but unfortunately at this time, not all of it. It freed me of so much fear.

It introduced me to the 'invisible' and elusive, qualitative world beyond the plethora of rules that my education and business life focussed on. Finally, humans may once again develop wisdom, and not be overwhelmed by intellectualism.

The qualitative issues in our life and in business are just as important (if not more important in some cases) to address than quantitative ones. Working qualitatively is often less comfortable because it regularly involves working outside of accepted structures and working with uncertainties. I've calmed my addiction to various aspects of my life, such as the need for status, other people's approval, money, security, fear, power, sensation and entertainment, to name a few. But at the time of writing I'm still working on my need for an 'image'.

I now believe I attract everything that happens to me, the good and the unpleasant. I've learnt to take personal responsibility for everything that happens to me, and not blame others.

I've learnt much from my experience, yet in many ways it's alienated me from many of the things that society embraces. I regularly feel at odds to the social norms I witness around me daily. I've no interest in organised religion but respect those who live their religion through their hearts.

The Dalai Lama said, 'I encourage people to embrace a path of higher consciousness, rather than one of religious teachings. This is a path of truth, in my view.'

I was in full agreement.

How right he is, pity all religious leaders didn't promote this more practical and meaningful approach.

He then went on to say, 'Break as many rules as possible.'[37] This was while giving his trademark smile and joyous chuckle. Many religious people think it irresponsible, not understanding that true integrity needs no rules.

Some people find it confronting when I share my experiences with them. I've had people assume I

---

[37]   Dalai Lama, Australian television interview, date unknown.

was seriously ill. Many quickly change the subject. Some are obviously confronted by the possibility that such an experience could happen. I spoke of one old acquaintance, an atheist, who became very angry and virtually accused me of lying, while a highly educated work associate indicated it's simply tricks of the mind, as previously mentioned. I often wonder why some people are so close-minded and threatened by the reality of the existence of a soul and a higher power that they're not open to discussion about it. Why do many rave about the release of a new iPhone and accept without thinking the miracle of a grand 100-year-old giant tree that started its life from a tiny seed pod? How moisture in the ground can travel to the top-most leaves on a forty-metre-high tree? It was Buddha who became enlightened after studying the miracle of a flower. We take nature for granted, and as I write it's being destroyed at an unprecedented and unsustainable rate, yet our very livelihood and existence depends on it. We must come to learn it is sacred.

I guess many now regard me as a boring person and a few of the following examples may help the reader understand why.

Since 1987 I've travelled to Brisbane weekly to spend half an hour receiving a spiritual healing and meditating at Maryann Madden's Inner Energy Centre. My first healing at the centre started this long commitment because I was, and remain, impressed by the simplicity and authenticity of the process, free of teachings and dogma. I feel it is a natural process whereas I came to view religion as a man-made process. All I know is that my energy feels clearer after a healing. On exhausting days during my working life when I didn't feel like my drive to Brisbane, I always enjoyed my drive home. I also know it's greatly assisted me to grow as a person.

I rarely drink alcohol, just the odd beer and a glass of wine on social outings. Prior to the experience I'd often drink a number of beers, along with a bottle or two of red wine on a night out. Now I don't like the clogging impact alcohol has on my energy and meditations because I'm far more conscious of it and don't like that feeling. Alcohol does impact negatively on one's energy. In the book *Conversations With God*, God notes bluntly that the human body was not designed to accept alcohol.[38]

I mostly prefer silence around me to the constant background noise of the radio or television. I've an increased enjoyment of the sounds of nature. I've much less fear, a lesser need for sensation and I'm far less emotional. Money is only important to meet my living needs. I no longer have a must-have list of material

---

38   ND Walsch, *Conversations with God – Book 1*, Hodder & Stoughton, London, UK, 2000, pp. 191, 192.

items. I lost my need to get, and found a desire to give. This, in turn, has simplified my life. I socialise much less. I like to be near nature because it has a healing quality about it. One just needs to take notice and experience the energy in a rainforest, compared to that of a bustling city, to feel the great difference. I really enjoy the energy of my garden.

I now believe all life, no matter how lowly, is interconnected in a strong way, which scientists have yet to identify intellectually. I also feel, as a result of my time as CEO of AGIC, renamed the Infrastructure Sustainability Council, that there is a growing awareness and understanding of the importance and significance of this interdependence through increasing study of this in scientific circles.

I meditate twice daily and enjoy both the quieting of the mind and sometimes the feeling of energy, especially when I'm very relaxed and free of stress. I find I can usually remove stress through my meditation – but not always. My body was often highly stressed by the various responsibilities I carried, and it reacted accordingly, but the deep inner contentment from the experience I had, and the knowledge of a higher power, are reassuring anchors each day. These things assist me to ease tension through my daily meditations.

I'm constantly saddened by the greed, self-interest, self-promotion, externalisation of identity, and ego-based power and control trips I see around me. Many business practices are just dishonest, lacking in integrity and increasingly greed-based, and these practices leave me cold. I've been exposed to many of these practices first-hand. The constant focus on the ultra-wealthy, sporting heroes and pop and movie stars, along with branded fashion clothing that generates huge profit on exploited employees, are areas where real change is needed. This focus has been a major influence on young people now seeking their identity externally, instead of finding themselves internally. Many young people have not learnt to love themselves, but instead have become 'full of themselves'.

I don't enjoy many violent movies because I find the energy quite dark. I firmly believe the energy of violent films and video games can desensitise people to violence because they continually 'soak' in this dark energy.

Everything is energy and every human being feels it either consciously or unconsciously. Individuals react differently to its exposure.

I aim to only give advice if asked to do so. I believe some of the lowest-paid people in our society, who've kept their self-esteem, can be some of the most spiritually advanced and wise people. This is because they have dealt with the issues of ego, control and so on through the hardship of their existence. I've lost my fear of death but still hope at the time of passing it's a quick transition. I see death as a very natural and inevitable event, the timing of it determined by the soul when one's spiritual journey this time around needs completion. This belief helped me with my grief when Sheldon passed away. Time has allowed me to move from feelings of deep sadness when thinking of him, to more comforting feelings of warmth about his memory, with a touch of sadness. I loved him so much.

I often feel dismayed as I watch the environmental degradation of planet Earth and the unchecked dominance of large multinational corporations. As an engineer who has been solving real problems all my life, and experienced the turbulence of the corporate world, I often pondered how people of all nations could operate in a different manner to bring peace, understanding and more equality. Why didn't we learn from the violence of Hitler? I'm sure civilisations are making progress as a world community when I reflect on long-past history. I can see we're evolving and becoming more 'enlightened' in many areas of human interaction. Progress is so very slow! Currently I feel we are going backwards, driven by fear-mongering.

Religion has historically been the vehicle that brought honesty and integrity into the activities of the human race – along with respect, dignity, kindness and all the qualities that emanate from love and arise from the heart (soul). Religion has been good for the human race's evolution, because it assisted many people to learn to live life with real integrity. It's seen the establishment of many charitable institutions providing excellent support to those in need.

Although the Chief Universal Designer made us perfect in her eyes, many still propound the notion of everyone as unworthy and that we must fear God. We've all been given the gift of free will.

I find it difficult to accept that people still venerate and take as truth religious doctrines written almost 2000 years ago, 120 years after Jesus lived, when the human race was poorly evolved and ruled by power-hungry patriarchs.

Feeling is aligned with a person's truth. I've the view that some proclaimed 'atheists', who regularly and unconsciously work in their feelings, could actually be more spiritually evolved than highly religious folk.

I noted earlier that I came to a personal realisation that God is both male and female, yet God is neither, if that makes any sense. I came to believe from the experience that God is all genders yet is also beyond gender – the dichotomy of God. At a soul level we have no gender because I believe we can decide to reincarnate in male or female form.

Prior to the experiences I mentioned, I had the realisation there is no right or wrong – there just is. When I speak of this to associates it often invokes a strong reaction. But understanding this concept at a feeling level automatically puts an integrity platform on one's thinking, and removes black and white attitudes.

I love the quote by Camus, 'Integrity needs no rules.'[39]

It's our differences that divide us, and fear is the platform for this thinking. What if we all looked through the prism of love? Acceptance of the many human differences must surely then result. I believe there is a spark of God in all things, be it animal, vegetable or mineral. Human beings also have this spark. It's simply our choice as to whether we fan the flame into something greater, or let it slowly die out. It's our choice whether we embrace the light or the dark.

We need to move away from a 'me, me, me' focus to a 'we, we, we' approach to life's experiences. Community well-being must become a genuine priority over corporations and shareholder returns.

As a result of my experience, I now feel as a global community we need to lessen our emphasis on religion and embrace simple and practical spiritual values.

The division of powers between church and state was a wise decision, taking religion out of governance. However, its downside was the loss of basic spiritual values of true integrity and transparency as a guiding principle in the governance of nations. Truth has become a stranger in politics.

History has seen the predominance of patriarchal leadership. When one views current and past world events it cannot be rated as a very successful model. Maybe the time is ripe for a matriarchal leadership approach to lead us to a more equitable and peaceful world. I don't profess to be a great economics scholar, but my first lecture at Melbourne University was provided by an eminent and well-respected Australian economist who started the lecture by saying, 'Economics is only a theory and it doesn't work, it's never predicted the future with any accuracy.'

I've since been told the same message by other economists.

---

39 A Camus, *The Myth of Sisyphus and Other Essays*, Penguin, London, UK, 2000, p. 66.

I believe it's time for a new set of world governance guidelines based on authenticity, not speculation. The rules of the economic game were designed by wealthy men, merchant bankers and industrialists for their benefit. We're now witnessing an increasing number of countries sagging in debt, and social inequity reaching extreme proportions. I feel it's time for world leaders to rewrite the economic rule book and take control and power back from multinational corporations.

The concept of unlimited growth on a finite planet is the first obvious flaw of current economic theory. I remember a question put to my son by his young female cousin in primary school.

'Sheldon, if every government wants more growth, won't we run out of things on Earth eventually?'

Why are world leaders desensitised to the wisdom of a primary school student?

How can we move our global emphasis to the community and not the corporation? Can we rewrite our economic governance rules?

We need to transition from fear-based societies to those based on love. I quote from *Conversations with God – Book 1*:

> Fear is the energy which contracts, closes down, draws in, runs, hides, hoards, harms. Love
> is the energy which expands, opens up, sends out, stays, reveals, shares, heals.[40]

A new way will only come if we have a 'spiritual revolution' or a change in consciousness where sufficient people come to understand their true purpose on planet Earth. Failure to arrive at this destination will simply mean a lot more reincarnations on Earth until people come to understand their divine purpose.

With global warming increasing and a dearth in values around the world, I'm not sure this will be a great place to be born into again unless we change our ways. I'm actually not sure planet Earth will survive as we move ever closer to the steep curve of exponential change in population growth, global warming impacts, deforestation and record extinction rates.

The soul wants to be free and joyous, and modern society is placing more and more restraint and control on people. This in my view causes increased pressure and anxiety in people. Our governance systems are bringing drudgery and hardship to the masses, whereas spiritually our journey is meant to bring joy. Just

---

40   ND Walsch, *Conversations with God Book 1*, Hodder & Stoughton, London, UK, 2000, p. 19.

maybe, if every person on the planet screamed from their essence, 'There must be a better way,' and really meant it, then we might just find it.

It worked for me so just maybe it could work en masse! I have come to believe we need less religion and atheism and more practical spiritual understanding regarding the purpose of our journey on planet earth. It would change the world for the better.

Finally, keep smiling; I hope the book at the very least gives you food for thought, as innovation comes from a divine given idea. Learn to trust your feelings!

In truth, our spiritual development is 'the only game in town'.

John Lennon had it right – all we need is love.

The human race needs it desperately.

Become a truth seeker.

APPENDIX: LEO'S EULOGY

Friday the 14th September was to be a day of celebration for Toowoomba Foundry; instead it became a day of great sadness, as we lost a cherished workmate on Thursday.

Leo was taken from us while operating our Computerised Robotics Machining Line, a technology this fifty-eight-year-and-nine-month-old readily mastered, and it was a job he loved.

I arrived at the hospital soon after Leo's admission, and was humbled by how the family embraced me and made it clear they wanted me to be with them to share Leo's final moments, something that touched me greatly.

I believe death isn't a terrible event. It's a natural process, and the timing, the vehicle and manner isn't of our choosing. There is purpose in it, and it's something our modern society needs to understand.

I now turn my address to Leo.

Leo was a very ordinary human being and this was his great strength. It's through our ordinary-ness that our extraordinary qualities blossom.

Leo may not have been as educated as some, but Leo had great wisdom, something that's becoming lost in our over-intellectualised society, and why I personally sought his counsel regularly at work.

I hunger for the day when our leaders strive for a wise nation, and not a knowledgeable or smart one, for then real values we need to take us forward as a human society will emerge. We've become too smart for our own good.

Wisdom isn't taught by our educational institutions. It rarely wears academic robes, and does not need to reside in big houses, or wear a three-pointed star or a blue and white spinning propeller on the car bonnet, or reside beside or in edifices, or need titles. It's rarely found in law.

Instead, wisdom is found in the clothing of simple human beings that have lived a real life, such as an experienced nurse, a housewife who has reared a family, a crises counsellor.

It's sometimes found in a doctor or a teacher, or in clergy who live religion through their hearts. It's also found in some factory employees, as was the case with Leo, he was wise.

It's a great shame to me that our 'sophisticated society' places little importance on these great role models, and prefers models set by gladiatorial sport, reality TV and ego-centred stars.

Leo was different, and while ordinary, his extraordinary human traits were many.

Leo was a man who knew who he was.

He wasn't sophisticated, which simply means he wasn't trying to be someone he was not, a very honest trait.

Leo epitomised simplicity, a key platform for truth.

Leo was a giver, not a taker – and in our society this is extremely extraordinary.

Leo exhibited no airs of superiority and importantly, he presented no display of inferiority, just equality.

Leo was renowned for his dry humour.

Leo had no ego to protect.

Leo never complained. Again, in our society, this is extraordinary.

Leo had no prejudices.

Leo was non-judgmental.

It was extremely rare for Leo to have a day off work (except back in 1997, when he had a week).

In summary, Leo had a simple, free, generous, forgiving and caring spirit, and these are the vehicles of real honest love – the key ingredient missing from the world today. If everyone on this planet behaved like Leo, how different the world would be.

His demonstration of commitment, integrity and family values was a clear statement that his life fully encompassed the traits of one very honest, tall man.

In conclusion, I found I personally had a significant realisation on Friday, and that was that I loved and deeply respected this man, Leo O'Leary, and I and many others will miss him a lot and all that he stood for.

I feel I have lost a member of my family.

www.ingramcontent.com/pod-product-compliance
Lightning Source LLC
Chambersburg PA
CBHW051626140626
46547CB00033B/2651

* 9 7 9 8 8 9 1 9 4 0 1 1 6 *